SUPERVISING POLICE PERSONNEL

The Fifteen Responsibilities

Fifth Edition

Paul M. Whisenand, Ph.D.

Department of Criminal Justice
California State University, Long Beach

PEARSON
Prentice
Hall

Upper Saddle River, New Jersey 07458

Library of Congress Cataloging-in-Publication Data

Whisenand, Paul M.
   Supervising police personnel : the fifteen responsibilities / Paul M. Whisenand. -- 5th ed.
      p. cm.
   Includes bibliographical references and index.
   ISBN 0-13-112316-5
   1. Police -- Supervision of. 2. Police -- Supervision of -- United States. I. Title.

HV7936.S8W48 2004
363.2'068'3 -- dc21

2003048243

Editor-in-Chief: Stephen Helba
Director of Production and
   Manufacturing: Bruce Johnson
Executive Editor: Frank Mortimer, Jr.
Assistant Editor: Korrine Dorsey
Editorial Assistant: Barbara Rosenberg
Marketing Manager: Tim Peyton
Managing Editor—Production: Mary Carnis
Manufacturing Buyer: Cathleen Petersen

Production Liaison: Denise Brown
Full Service Production: Naomi Sysak
Composition Management and Page
   Makeup: Integra Software Services
Design Director: Cheryl Asherman
Design Coordinator: Miguel Ortiz
Cover Printer: Phoenix Color
Printer/Binder: RR Donnelley & Sons

Pearson Education LTD.
Pearson Education Singapore, Pte. Ltd
Pearson Education, Canada, Ltd
Pearson Education–Japan
Pearson Education Australia PTY, Limited
Pearson Education North Asia Ltd
Pearson Educaçion de Mexico, S.A. de C.V.
Pearson Education Malaysia, Pte. Ltd

10 9 8 7 6 5 4 3 2 1
ISBN 0-13-112316-5

CONTENTS

DEDICATION

For my best friend, prized and deeply loved brother, John C. Whisenand, and in memory of an admired, longtime, trusted friend and co-worker, Robert R. Beans, Sergeant (Retired), Los Angeles Police Department.

My life has been profoundly influenced, enriched, and made fun due to these two guys.

Paul M. Whisenand, Ph.D.
San Clemente, California

PREFACE

A couple of years ago, the acclaimed secular ethicist Michael Josephson wrote:

"I just attended a moving graduation ceremony marking the transition of 40 men and women from police academy cadets to sworn officers in the Long Beach Police Department (California).

"At the beginning, the officers were fully uniformed, but they had no badges, and without the badges their uniforms were undistinguished. Yet once their shields were affixed, the uniforms and the people in them were transformed.

"So I began to think about the badge not only as an official symbol of authority and responsibility, but also as a symbol of honor—a symbol we should look up to and they must live up to. Although the badges were highly polished, experience teaches us that it will take vigilance and integrity to keep them untarnished.

"Looking at the very serious faces of Class #77, one could see both determination and pride as they officially accepted the huge responsibilities of a hugely important job captured in the Code of Ethics printed on their program.

" 'My fundamental duty', the Code begins, 'is to serve mankind, to safeguard lives and property; to protect the innocent against deception, the weak against oppression or intimidation, and the peaceful against violence and disorder; and to respect the Constitutional Rights of all men to liberty, equality and justice.' It concludes, 'I recognize the badge of my office is a symbol of public faith, and I accept it as a public trust'.

"Sure, most officers spend most of their time involved in important but unheroic activities like investigations, traffic regulation and crowd control, but they stand at the ready to put themselves in danger at a moment's notice and after the experience of September 11, I fear we don't appreciate them enough."

This book is committed to helping those individuals who are responsible for making this "code" a reality, as opposed to lofty, politically correct but shallow verbiage.

The responsible person I'm referring to is the **police supervisor.** You will find that to fulfill this vital role, one's **character** not merely counts, but **counts big-time.** You'll be asking yourself, "What do I, or should I, stand for as a supervisor—as a leader?" You'll also find that you are responsible for assuring that **15 RESPONSIBILITIES** are being pursued by you and those who work for you.

Being responsible (the "R" word) means exercising self-discipline and self-restraint. It means doing your very best and being self-reliant and **accountable for the consequences of your decisions.**

Team Fundamentals provides the infrastructure for contemporary police work—community-oriented policing. These chapters deal with character and integrity of purpose—*values, ethics,* and *vision*—and with the allocation of the requisite **time** to **communicate** all three. (The chapters on ethics and vision contain a lot of new material.)

Team Development starts with a supervisor's responsibility for serving as a *team leader*. This naturally encompasses *motivating, empowering,* and *training* one's staff, while ensuring that everyone is mentally and physically *well.*

Teamwork includes *organizing for action, measuring performance of that action, resolving conflicts,* and making certain that *community-oriented policing* works. I am convinced that it takes teamwork to make it work. Finally, the supervisor-as-leader is challenged to *anticipate* incoming demands or needs for change.

Being a police supervisor is much more than having more pay, more authority, more influence, more status, and the like. It is much more. It is a set of core responsibilities that you will soon encounter and consider in the chapters that follow.

My warmest thanks to Kim Davies, Senior Editor, Prentice Hall, who coached and inspired me during the writing of this edition; and especially Pat David and Rosie O'Shea, who expertly manicured and critically edited the manuscript.

Paul Whisenand, Ph.D.
San Clemente, California

AN OVERVIEW

The responsibility of a police supervisor is to lead other people in the performance of their jobs. Easily stated but not easily accomplished. Leading others—getting their followership—is a complex and challenging process. Why? You'll see.

"Leading" is an active verb. A true leader is a catalyst for action, and the proper measurement of leadership is change.

"Leading" and "supervising" are not the same. You can be a police supervisor and also a leader or not a leader. Police supervisors use authority (based on the right conferred upon them by their agency) to secure compliance to orders and direction. Police supervisors evolve into leaders when they display power (based on personal expertise and vision) to change or reinforce desired attitudes and behavior. We'll cover both, but definitely emphasize the latter.

> The test of leadership is: What is different now because of you?

IN FRONT

Think for a moment. What is the title of the boss of an orchestra? An orchestra "manager," orchestra "supervisor," or orchestra "leader?" "Leader" is the correct answer, but why is it correct? Because he or she is IN FRONT of (not on the side or behind) the players. You can actually see the leader in action. You're able to follow by visual example rather than a hard-copy memo, e-mail, or prior training. Being in front of the team also is a clear-cut demonstration of responsibility.

> The leader is responsible for leading by example. Being in front and being seen is the only way to do this.

Getting in front and staying there is difficult, and is becoming ever more so for police supervisors. It's a matter of **time.** Supervisors are frustrated by not having enough of it or more control of it. They realize that to lead, they have to be seen (and not just for 15 minutes at roll call). They have to be with and in front of their team. But tons of paperwork (e.g., personnel investigations), expanding technology (e.g., e-mail messages), and advancing administrative trivia (e.g., new rules, new regulations, new details) checkmate their quest to lead. They find themselves exclusively forced into the role of supervisor—giving commands, spot-checking to oversee if they're complied with, processing paper, and receiving and sending messages.

The effective supervisor, the one who wants to lead, is forging as their number one priority being in front and managing the allocation of time accordingly. Tough to do, at times risky, but worth it! The work team gets the leader it deserves, the police agency gets the quality of work it deserves, and the community is all the better for it. But there is no one best way . . .

No One Best Way

We have a lot in common as members of humankind. We have wants and needs, hopes and aspirations, likes and dislikes, successes and failures, and more. But we're also very different. My hopes may not be yours, we may not share the same problems, and our needs may be different. What motivates you may not motivate me. These differences are referred to as human diversity.

Dealing with human diversity is a significant challenge to a supervisor's success. Diversity guarantees that there is no one best way to handle every individual and every situation. Some employees respond best to a polite push, while others require a strong shove. Some want to be empowered; others want to be instructed. Some want to be listened to; others want to be mute. Some want a lot of challenge; others want routine.

> The leader is responsible for leading a team of diverse police employees. Diversity is treated as an asset and is celebrated.

Again, there is no "Supervisor's Golden Rule" or set of secret proven methods for supervising. That is probably bad news for you. Then again, if supervising the work of others were a simple and easy process, everyone would want the job.

There is good news, however. There are 15 job-related responsibilities that, if fulfilled, are likely to produce success. All 15 deal with the basic mission of a police supervisor: building teamwork. And . . .

THERE IS NO "I" IN "TEAMWORK"

We are born into this world totally dependent on others for meeting our survival and social needs. From our earliest beginnings we strive to kick aside our dependency and replace it with independence. We gradually gain dominance over our survival and social needs. We decide when and where we want to eat. When and where we want to sleep. What to buy and when to save. Whom to pal around with and whom to eschew.

Being independent is great. We prize it. But it causes problems when manifested in an organization, especially a police organization! Imagine for a moment a police agency consisting of sworn and civilian employees who think and, worse yet, act independently from one another. I wouldn't feel secure in that type of working atmosphere. Would you?

Police leaders are trained to think independently, but the work for which they are accountable takes place in teams.

All police personnel want to be recognized and accepted as individuals. Sometimes there are those who seem to the contrary (the group thinker, "Mr. Compliant"). "Being me" in a police agency is important. Simultaneously, "being me" in a team effort to provide much valued police services is more important.

> It is a police leader who is able to assure one's individuality (independence) AND develop one's teamwork (interdependence).

Team leadership depends on . . .

CHARACTER AND COMPETENCY

Character and competency are the primal pillars of leadership and supervision. The deeper, the larger, the stronger these twin pillars, the greater the leader and the better the supervisor.

Successful leaders and supervisors motivate us. They ignite our passions and inspire the best in us. When we seek to explain why they are so effective, we frequently mention strategy, vision or powerful ideas. The answer is actually much more fundamental. It is not as much what they are doing; rather, it is how they are doing it.

> Character is both what we stand for and how we stand for it.

> Competency is both what we perform and how we perform it.

Unfortunately, the "what we stand for" and the "what we perform" are often emphasized to the point where the "how" is ignored. You'll discover both the "what" and the "how" of your becoming a police supervisor and leader via our journey through this book. You'll learn HOW the supervisor uses authority to get results, HOW the leader uses teamwork to get quality results, and HOW the supervisor commands while the leader convinces.

Character focuses on the acquisition and projection of personal values and ethics. In the workplace it is devoted to acquiring and demonstrating professional values and a work ethic. Competency encompasses the requisite skills, knowledge, and abilities to perform the technical and technological aspects of the job of "overseeing" the work performance of line-level police employees. How supervisors accomplish the above work is not the same as why it is necessary to do it. Whatever leaders set out to do—whether it is creating strategy or mobilizing teams into action—their success depends on how they do it.

> Even if they get everything else right, if leaders fail in the primal task of driving character in the right direction, nothing will work as well as it could or should.

Is one more preeminent than the other? I agree with Teddy Roosevelt, Warren Buffett, and Michael Josephson that it's **character.** President Roosevelt wrote, "To educate a person in the mind but not the morals is to educate a menace to society." Mr. Buffett said, "When I select a manager, the first thing I look at is the person's character." And Mr. Josephson has spent most of his life pointing out that "Character Counts."

Character and responsibility are linked. The more you get of one, the more you get of the other. And vice versa. Everything is your **responsibility** when you're the leader—but much more so when there's a problem than when there's a victory. You share the credit and take the blame.

THE "R" WORD

There is a disturbing and unfortunate trend of people ducking responsibility while telling everyone else what to do. I'm not a part of this problem. It's all of those "other folks" who fail to stand and be accountable while simultaneously casting guilt on others. Kidding, of course. At times I am tempted to back off and seek protective cover and then point at the other guy as being responsible for the mess.

Have you noticed that those who shirk their responsibilities and refuse to be held accountable frequently attempt to lay blame for irresponsibility on someone or something else? It is sucking us into behavioral and political absurdities, which erodes our character. This phenomenon can be observed in both private and government organizations. We see it happening in police agencies.

> Our nation's legal language on rights is highly developed, but the language of responsibility is meager. This situation has hamstrung self-reliance, inner autonomy, and risk taking. No society, organization, or police agency can operate if everyone has rights and no one has responsibilities.

The blame game is perpetuated by a low tolerance for mistakes. This is especially prevalent in police work. Many police managers are quick to boast, "In our agency, we want our employees to take risks!" After a while, some believe that taking a calculated risk for all the right reasons will be supported. Then some poor person takes a risk and fails, and all hell breaks loose. Ridicule, sanctions, ostracism, tainted career, and more come down on the risk-taker. Is it any surprise that many police organizations have a culture of risk avoidance "Risk-taking—that's not my responsibility. Let some other fool try it."

An often overlooked obligation of ethical supervision is to establish an atmosphere where police employees are truly expected and willing to accept responsibility for improving the quality of programs and services—even if it means challenging existing policies or management decisions.

OK—let's sum up:

- Leadership and supervision are not the same. The former relies on personal-based power, while the latter depends on organization-based authority.
- Leadership occurs by example. Being with and in front of your staff is imperative.
- There is no one set of ideal supervisory methods. Human diversity is to be accepted and celebrated.
- The leader must blend a group of independent workers into a team of police personnel.
- Leaders and supervisors are judged first by their character and then by their competency.

Every police supervisor has the ultimate responsibility to assure that practices and procedures are efficient, effective, and consistent with organizational values and professional codes of conduct. This requires a full, hands-on, detailed knowledge of what the employees actually do, and an understanding of how things really work.

I have segmented the above-mentioned "ultimate responsibility" into 15 responsibilities. The first five deal with team fundamentals, the next five with team development, and the final five with teamwork. We'll now proceed with our first "R" . . . VALUES.

To be what we are, and to become what we are capable of becoming, is the only end of life.

—Robert Louis Stevenson

TEAM FUNDAMENTALS

RESPONSIBILITIES

VALUES

The police supervisor is responsible for developing consensus within the work group on its values and then ensuring that it behaves accordingly.

What lies behind us and what lies before us are tiny matters compared to what lies within us.

—Oliver Wendell Holmes

Values provide the character, courage, and consciousness for determining where the work unit is going and how it is going to get there.

Find a quiet place to read and think about the next few paragraphs. Make a conscious effort to project yourself into the following situation.

Picture yourself driving to a retirement dinner for a co-worker who is also a close friend. You park your car and walk inside the restaurant. You locate the assigned ballroom and enter. As you wander in, you notice the banners and flags. You spot the smiling faces of your co-workers and their spouses. You sense gaiety and happiness in the room.

As you approach them, you look up at the head table and see your name card on it. You also see the name cards of your spouse and three children. Overhead on a banner, printed in large letters, is your name and "Congratulations for Twenty-Five Years of Service." Below that banner is another that reads, "A Happy Retirement to You." This is your retirement! And all of these people have come to honor you, to express feelings of appreciation for your work.

You're escorted to the head table, where your spouse and children join you. You're handed a program. There are five speakers. The first is your spouse. The second is one of your children. The third speaker is your closest friend. The fourth speaker is an employee. The final speaker is your boss. All of these people know you very well, but in differing ways.

Now, think carefully. What would you expect each of these speakers to say about you and your life? What kind of spouse, parent, and friend would you like their words to reflect? What kind of supervisor? What kind of subordinate?

What values would you like them to have seen in you? What contributions, what achievements would you want them to remember? Look carefully at the people who have gathered to wish you well. What difference would you like to have made in their lives?

AN OVERVIEW OF WHAT FOLLOWS

Our values play a crucial role in our professional and personal lives. Basically, a value is something for which we have an enduring preference. As a police supervisor, one could be expected to value supervising and police work. Although associated with other concepts, such as needs and attitudes, values differ from them and are much more fundamental.

Values serve a variety of purposes; they act as filters, generation builders, individual distinctions, standards of behavior, conflict resolvers, signs of emotional states, stimuli for thinking, and forces that cause one to behave. Our values are primarily derived from the early, formative years. Values change over time, and we have a choice as to what we will value and its priority in our value system.

We are what we value, and thus we will supervise others and ourselves accordingly. Moreover, values become the beliefs that guide a police organization and the behavior of its employees. Responsibility One focuses on individual value systems. Later, in Responsibility Three, we'll look at organizational values, or a mission.

WHY VALUES?

Understanding human values—held individually and organizationally—serves three very critical purposes for police agencies, their employees, and especially police supervisors. Their three-fold purposes are:

- Acting as a **departmental compass**
- Developing a basis for **human communications and mutual trust**
- Inspiring **success as a police supervisor**

The Compass of Values

It is not enough to rely on supervisory authority to enforce moral or legal behavior. The compass of values has to be within a person and the department. Often one hears the contrary: that a police department should be an efficiency instrument, a bureaucratic machine that maximizes its output within rules set by the community; that departments that get distracted from this goal by community responsibilities end up ineffective. My own belief is that just the opposite is true.

For one thing, no community can control a police institution as well as the institution itself can, and if a department places outcomes above core values, then that organization is vulnerable to violating community standards, no matter how stringently laws and codes are written. And those violations will demoralize the work force, and produce ill will in the community, and perhaps lawsuits that will have a long-term negative impact on results anyway. On the other hand, the police agency that orients itself toward serving its community will reap long-term rewards in the form of loyal customers and positive community relations. The police supervisor must never lose sight of the purpose of the job, and the managers who run the agency should never compromise their values for the sake of expediency. Without purpose and values, both a police agency and the supervisors who work for it are in danger of losing their direction, given the continually changing landscape they must negotiate.

The modern individual is assailed from every angle by divergent and contradictory value claims. It is no longer possible, as it was in the not-too-distant historical past, to settle comfortably into the value system of one's forebears or one's community and live out one's life without ever examining the nature and the assumptions of that system.

—Carl R. Rogers

First Understanding! Then Comes Communications, and Then Comes Trust

The underpinning of effective communication within the workplace is the understanding of human values. I have to know myself first—my value system. Then, and only then, am I in a position to understand another's set of values. To understand and to be understood do not indicate agreement. We can understand someone else's values but not always concur with them. When we don't agree on our individually held values, at least—and most importantly—we understand why.

Once we understand one another's values, then we can really communicate. With this interaction arrives a basis for mutual trust. It is at this point the police supervisor has a perfect opportunity to gain the role of team leader.

We Are What We Value!

Human values are important to us because they are us. Simply stated, our past values have determined who we are and what we are pursuing in life, our present values are likewise shaping our life today, and our futures primarily will be shaped according to the values that we possess at each coming point in time.

It is vital for the police supervisor to know and appreciate human values because they serve as a destiny (an end or a goal) and a path (a means or guide) to reach that destiny. In summary, then, each of us should know his or her own values because they underpin his or her character, personality, and supervisory style and performance. This chapter will assist you in clarifying your own value system so that you can eventually apply it in a way that will support, rather than detract from, your responsibility to be an effective police supervisor.

> All that we value becomes a part of us. And thus we are what we value and . . . we supervise others and ourselves according to our value systems!

Please reread and give a lot of thought to the above conviction. It is an assertion that you and I—in our daily lives—are value-driven. Further, it states that you and I consciously and unconsciously transmit our values to others. We do this as a parent, a friend, a brother or sister, and especially as a supervisor. What follows will substantiate the centerplace of values in our lives.

Values: What Are They?

The term "value" has a variety of uses. For example, one may value one's family, value one's leisure time, value one's reputation, value one's position as a police manager, or value jogging. Each of these five values is different in several respects. One is a goal-oriented value: one's reputation. Another value, jogging, is a means to another desired state: one's physical and mental health. Yet another value, one's position as a police supervisor, is temporal; that is, it is a temporary position. We have a tendency to forget that what some persons may value highly, others may not. (For example, you may place a high value on the promise of a promotion, while someone else, satisfied with his or her present job, may not.) In fact, people are alike or different due to the commonality or the incongruence of their professional, personal, and societal values.

> A value is an enduring belief that a specific goal and means of attaining that goal are very important.

In this definition, note that for a person to hold a value, it must be: 1) an "enduring belief," not random or fleeting; 2) a "goal" or desired end state; and 3) a "means," or acted on. In summary, a value is:

- An enduring belief
- A goal
- A means for accomplishing the goal

For example, do you value your job? If so, you would value it consistently (enduring) and not in a casual or haphazard way. Further, you would strive to do good work (goal). Finally, each day you would perform your tasks to the best of your ability (means).

Because each of us possesses more than a single value, it is essential that we think in terms of a *value system*, which is an enduring organization of beliefs concerning preferable modes of conduct of end states of existence in a "hierarchical ranking" of relative importance. Hierarchical ranking means that some values supersede others. For example, which is the more important value for you: "family" or "job"; "spouse" or "friend"; health" or "compassion"?

There is not always a one-to-one connection between a means and a goal. One usually has approximately forty end-state values (goals) and seventy-plus modes-of-conduct values (means). For example, assume that one of your values is "success." Now, in your mind, how many ways or means are there for you to achieve success?

VALUES-LED POLICE SUPERVISION

Values-led supervision is based on the idea that the police supervisor has a responsibility to the staff and the community that makes such supervision necessary. Values-led supervision seeks to maximize its impact by integrating prized values into as many day-to-day activities as possible. In order to do that, values must lead and be included in a department's mission statement, strategy, and operating plan.

By incorporating an agency's concern for the community into its strategic and operating plans, values-led police supervisors can make everyday decisions that actualize the department's goals at the same time. Instead of choosing areas of activity based solely on the short term, the values-led supervisor recognizes that by addressing community problems along with efficiency concerns, a department can earn a respected place in the community and a special place in customers' hearts, too.

Which Values Lead?

For the purpose of this book, the values I'm talking about are progressive community values. I see values-led police work in general as promoting individual safety for the common good, advocating for the many people in our society whose rights are jeopardized, giving a voice to the people who are afraid, and helping to address the root causes of crime. Most citizens would prefer to be policed by a department that shares these values.

Being Open

Values-led police agencies need to be open about their mission and goals. How can people support an agency that is secretive about its programs and activities? A department that acts covertly locks the community out of the process. It deprives community members of the opportunity to use their power to support the police programs they believe in. The degree to which a police agency can be values-led depends on how completely the police employees have embraced, or bought into, the department's mission.

SOURCES OF OUR VALUES

The process of value creation may actually begin long before birth. Many experts suggest that some behavior patterns in our primitive ancestors might have been encoded in the DNA, which in turn now guides our behavior patterns. Whatever the degree of genetic input, for our purposes it is enough to assume that genetics shape broad patterns of human behavior. Our concern is with behavior patterns that are learned from the moment of birth forward.

Our value-programming periods can be categorized as imprinting, modeling, and socialization.

IMPRINTING. During the first six to seven years of age, in addition to physical behavior development, a tremendous amount of mental and values development takes place. The popular analogy "As the twig is bent, so the tree shall grow" is perhaps so obviously simple that we frequently fail to apply it to children. The early years of childhood may be compared to the foundation and frame of a building. The foundation determines the quality and strength of the structure that goes on top. The completed structure depends on its base, even if additions are built. The foundation of a person is the child, as values are programmed in his or her early years. The key figures here are Mom and Dad and a few others. Even though real "formal" learning does not start in the preschool period, there are many important stages that determine how, how much, how well, and what the child will learn as she or he develops. The question that we must answer and comprehend is, by whom and how were they value-imprinted in our formative years?

MODELING. From seven or eight to 13 or 14 years of age, the process of value identification—initially with the mother, then with the father and important "others" around the child—expands. The child shifts into intense modeling, relating to family, friends, and external "heroes" in the surrounding world. People the child would "like to be like" are carefully observed. As a result, our initial close models give way to more expanded contacts. Soon group membership begins to exert its influence. We identify not only with playgroups or gangs as a whole, but also with certain "important" individuals within them. New values and behavior patterns are combined with the ones we absorbed from our family. Once in school, the process of identifying extends to the heroes of history and fictional stories. Furthermore, our increasing involvement with media during this period will introduce characters from movies and television as additional heroes. We use these models to construct our internal value ideal, the person we would like to become.

The hero models in our lives are very critical people. They are the people we try to behave like, the people that we want to be like when we become adults. The modeling period is a critical period during which we absorb values from a diverse selection of models. Do you remember your own modeling activities? When you were ten years old, whom did you want to grow up to be like? Whom did you secretly look up to, try to imitate in the way you talked, the way you walked, the way you dressed, the way you wanted to be? What about your co-workers? Who were their value models at the age of ten or eleven?

SOCIALIZATION.   From 13 or 14 to around 20 years of age, our social life becomes structured primarily in terms of our friends. This intense socialization with one's peers results in people of common values grouping together for reinforcement. During the period of adolescence, we define and integrate the values, beliefs, and standards of our particular culture into our own personalities. It is during this period that we achieve full physical maturity and a dominant value system. This system determines our basic personality. During this period of socialization, we engage in experimentation, verification, and validation of our basic life plan. From about age 20 on, our value system programmed during childhood and adolescence locks in, and we then repeatedly "test" it against the reality of the world.

People of like interests, behavior, and developing value systems associate intensely with one another and reinforce each other in their development. Who were your friends? What was your "best friend" like? What did you talk about? What about sex? Were you a leader or follower, a joiner or loner? Did your friends have a nickname for you? What did you do together? How long have your friendships lasted? These same questions should be asked about your co-workers.

CHANGING OUR VALUES

Our values, while enduring, can be changed. This transition can occur in one of two ways. The first is a traumatic or significant emotional event (SEE). The second revolves around major dissatisfaction. Let us look at each condition more closely.

SIGNIFICANT EMOTIONAL EVENTS.   The common denominator of SEEs is a challenge and disruption to our present behavior patterns and values. In job situations or family relationships, such challenges might be artificially created (e.g., being fired or promoted), but, more likely, SEEs occur in an unplanned, undirected manner (e.g., being seriously injured or winning an athletic contest). We must be careful to distinguish between SEEs, which actually change our gut-level value system, and external events, which simply modify our behavior. For example, a departmental order imposed on us may demand that we pay attention to the needs of the employees. Our behavior may change accordingly, but our values remain the same. The closer SEEs occur to our early programming periods, the more likely it is that significant change will occur. The less dramatic the event is, the longer we hold our programmed values, and any change in values will occur more slowly, if at all. It is possible to "teach an old dog new tricks," but the learning is much more difficult than for the younger animal. SEEs are neither good nor bad. Their frequency, their type, and how we cope with them determine if they are positive or negative for us.

PROFOUND DISSATISFACTION. To be successful in this most difficult of transitions—psychological growth—requires a special combination of inner and, to a degree, outer circumstances.

A person must possess three attributes if he or she is to make a substantial psychological step forward:

1. The individual must be deeply dissatisfied. Otherwise, why change?
2. The individual must possess much psychological and physical energy. Few things are harder to break than old bonds, old views, old prejudices, old convictions, old loves.
3. The individual must have or acquire the psychological insight to know what will slake the driving dissatisfaction. Without this, the effort to change will be directionless, ceaseless, and pointless.

Only when all three of these factors are present simultaneously will a person have the motivation to change, the drive to act on the motivation, and the foresight to know where to go and when he or she has arrived. See Figure 1–1, which graphically describes this section.

VALUES: WHAT DO THEY DO FOR US?

In a general sense, values tell us much about who we are as individuals, as citizens, as consumers, as a nation, and as police supervisors. As you examine the remainder of this section, keep in mind the following:

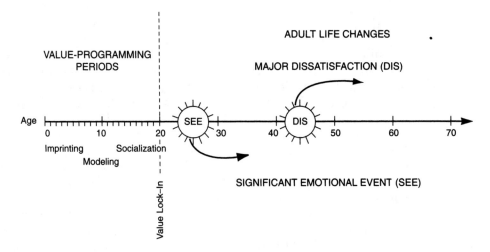

Figure 1–1 Value-Programming Periods and Change

- The total number of values that each person possesses is relatively small (30 to 60 is a flexible range).
- Everyone everywhere has the same values, but to different degrees.
- Values are organized into value systems.
- The origin of human values can be traced to one's formative years, culture, institutions, society, and—to some limited extent, perhaps—to one's unique genetic makeup.
- The consequences of one's values will be manifested in virtually all that one feels, thinks, and does.
- A large part of a police supervisor's effectiveness, or lack of it, is dependent on his or her value system.
- The success of a police supervisor is a direct result of knowing his or their values and the values of co-workers (bosses, other supervisors, and the line employees).

Our values determine our attitudes and behavior, creating:

- Filters
- Generation gaps
- Individual differences
- Standards
- Conflict resolvers
- Emotional triggers
- Thought provokers
- Motivators
- Attitudes
- Personality

Filters

Literally everything is sifted through the fundamental value systems operating in each of us. Values are our subjective reactions to the world around us. Although some items are purely functional and can be viewed rationally and objectively (chalkboards, picture books, light bulbs, rulers, etc.), most items involve the subjective reaction, especially when our feelings come into play. Gut-level value systems automatically filter the way we view most of the things around us. Your filters operate in degrees and shades of good/bad, right/wrong, normal/not normal, or acceptance/rejection.

Generation Gaps

In recent decades, the acceleration in the rate of change of technology, legal dimensions, social behavior, education, and economic systems has created vastly diverse programming experiences between generations. The differences in these experiences have created a spectrum of widely varying value systems within our society. The "generation gap" is a popular phrase—but it is much more. In volumes of material, people have attempted to reconcile differences between generations that, in reality, are irreconcilable—perhaps understandable, but non-negotiable. The fundamental value systems are, in fact, dramatically different between the generations that presently exist simultaneously in our society. Police organizations can have employees from four or more generations. Obviously, this can, and usually does, present a problem for the supervisor.

Individual Differences

Value programming is not simply a process of indoctrination. Nor is the behavior of people the result of a series of processes that simply overlay a particular culture on the biological core of individuals. Rather, society shapes a person's inherited temperament, but it does not transform that person into a complete opposite of his or her own basic nature. Each of us emerges with somewhat distinctive ways of behaving, despite the influences in our generation's programming. A wide range of inputs influences our basic physical and mental abilities. In broad categories, the major sources of programming experiences for all of us were 1) family, 2) educational experiences of a formal nature, 3) religious inputs, 4) the media, 5) our friends, 6) where we grew up geographically, and 7) the amount of money that provided a base for these other factors.

Standards

A value system acts as a set of standards and thus guides our conduct. It causes us to take a position or to abandon one previously adopted, predisposes us to accept or reject certain ideas or activities, gives us a sense of being right or wrong, aids us in making comparisons, acts as a basis from which we attempt to influence others, and affords us an opportunity to justify or rationalize our actions. Thus, our value system is, in effect, our individual "code of conduct."

Conflict Resolvers

We frequently find ourselves in conflict with another person because of individual value system disparities. In an intrapersonal way, however, value systems more often than not support us in making choices. "I prefer blue over brown" and "I choose to allocate my police personnel in a crime-prevention program over a crime-specific program" are illustrations of this. Briefly, one's value system assists in making decisions. Nonetheless, when individuals possess different values, they are apt to conflict with one another.

Emotional Triggers

Most people give the value of "fairness" a high rank. As a consequence, when seeing or experiencing wrongful personnel practices, one's emotional threshold is normally breached, and one becomes angry, depressed, threatened, or a combination of all three. If one has been the perpetrator of the unjust act, then the emotion of guilt is probably triggered within oneself. The police supervisor who disciplines an errant employee with reasonable cause may feel some sadness because of his or her value for the family unit, feeling that the employee deserved being disciplined, but also feeling sorry for the employee's spouse and children.

Thought Provokers

If we value being an effective police supervisor, does it not make sense that this value should provoke us into thinking about what means (e.g., enhancing one's job knowledge) would best achieve the desired outcome (success)? Fortunately, there are techniques for recording and exploring one's thoughts in a meaningful way so that we can put these thoughts to use. The techniques range from keeping a diary to following planned exercises. I will cover a number of such techniques later; in the meantime, remember that values generate thoughts, as well as guide them.

Motivators

The terms "motivation" and "motive" denote desire or actual movement toward an identified end. A person's value system motivates him or her to choose one path (means) as compared to any others. Thus, one can feel or see one's motivations by inspection of or introspection on one's behavior. What moves a person to act, or to want to act, in a particular manner stems from his or her own value system. In essence, one's values underpin and generate one's motives. As a result, if you value supervision, it is reasonable for you to be motivated to become a police supervisor. This sense of being motivated further serves as a motivation for acquiring the skills, knowledge, and abilities necessary for supervising a group of police officers.

Attitudes

Our human values, in conjunction with the organizational setting and our personal lives, shape work-related attitudes for each of us. I would underscore the "personal side" because what we feel and think about our job is very much influenced by personal or private events, and vice versa. Even if we do not want this connection or spillover from one arena to another, it happens. This is simply a manifest reflection of our holistic nature. An understanding of attitudes, attitude formation, and attitude change is important for several reasons:

1. Attitudes can be found in every aspect of police work. We have attitudes about most things that happen to us, as well as about most people we meet. In view of this universal characteristic of attitudes, an understanding of their nature is essential for supervisors.
2. Attitudes influence behavior. Much of how we behave at work is governed by how we feel about things. Therefore, an awareness of attitudes can assist supervisors in understanding human behavior at work. Changes in police employee behavior can be expected to the extent that supervisors can change or control employee attitudes.

3. Bad attitudes on the job cause problems. Poor job attitudes can be reflected in subsequent poor performance, citizen complaints, equipment abuse, turnover, and absenteeism, all of which result in direct costs to the police agency.

4. When an employee is expressing negative, carping, malcontented opinions, the typical response is "Officer X has a bad attitude," when, in effect, the officer is voicing a *value issue*.

Personality

Individuality and personality are not synonymous. Individuality is a natural covering for the protection of the personality or personal life. Individuality is seen by our independence and self-assertiveness. Personality is a characteristic evidenced by one's willingness to be a team member, care for others, and self-discipline. Personality is you in relationship to others.

> Your value system determines how you relate to your family, what products you buy, and how you vote. It dictates your leisure-time activities, what information you absorb, and your religious convictions. Of significance here is that your values decide how well you perform your job as a police supervisor.

VALUE CLARIFICATION

What you are [value] speaks so loudly I cannot hear what you say.

—*Ralph Waldo Emerson*

Select any one of your values (e.g., your job), and if you can answer each of the following questions with a "yes," you have identified and confirmed one of your values.

In terms of a particular value, are you:

1. Choosing freely?
2. Choosing from options?
3. Choosing after thoughtful consideration of the consequences of each option?
4. Prizing being happy with the choice?
5. Willing to make a public affirmation of the choice?
6. Doing something with the choice: performance?
7. Using the choice in a pattern of life?

Choosing Freely

The values that are chosen freely are those that one will internalize, cherish, and allow to guide one's life. Society or one's physical environment may impose a value, but it does not necessarily become one's own.

Choosing from Options

It follows that, if there are no options, then there is no freedom of choice. One would be hard-pressed to convince someone that he or she valued employment with a specific police department when in fact it was the only one that would hire him or her.

Choosing after Thoughtful Consideration

A value must be freely chosen after a careful review of the consequences of each option. In other words, the consequences must be known to whatever extent possible. After all, if we do not realize the consequences of a particular alternative, we do not know what is likely to occur and therefore cannot have freely chosen that alternative.

Prizing

Briefly, a value is something that we cherish, respect, and show pride in.

Making a Public Affirmation

If one values a person, an object, or a concept, it seems only reasonable that one would profess it openly. Are you pleased and proud to tell others that you are a police supervisor or not?

Performing

What one does reflects one's values. The importance of a particular value (such as acquiring a college education) can be assessed in line with how much time is spent on it (such as taking three units a semester, rather than nine). There is an obvious difference between thinking about a value and acting on it. Thinking about a value (such as losing ten pounds) may be an early indication that one is forming a specific value, but it is in performing the value (actually losing weight) that one can attest to its being a full value.

Using the Choice in a Pattern of Life

Values, because one acts on them, become a dominating influence in one's life. They establish patterns in thought and deed. Consequently, they motivate us to attend church or not, to get married or not, to have children or not, and to supervise effectively or not. It is interesting that we frequently think that we possess a value that, in reality, we no longer hold. We assume that because we once held a particular value, we continue to hold it, and we may be shocked to find that it is no longer a value, or at least no longer an important one. There are two value-clarification exercises in this chapter to assist you in analyzing your value system.

Structured Exercise 1-1

Let us take the next few minutes and explore some of your individually held values. The following two exercises can be accomplished either alone or in a group setting.

To begin with, complete the Value Indicator List by quickly writing down the ten things that you enjoy (value) doing in your professional, social, or personal life. In other words, of all the things you do in your life, list the ten that you enjoy the most. (They can range from the tangible [e.g., money, car, and family] to the intangible [e.g., love, respect, and freedom]). We are value-driven, and consequently it is critical for us to know what values reside in our value system.

VALUE INDICATOR LIST

Rank	Value	Symbol
_____	1. _____	_____
_____	2. _____	_____
_____	3. _____	_____
_____	4. _____	_____
_____	5. _____	_____
_____	6. _____	_____
_____	7. _____	_____
_____	8. _____	_____
_____	9. _____	_____
_____	10. _____	_____

Now study your list, and rank your values on the left side of the list in order of priority. The number 1 indicates the most valued, 2 the next most valued, and so on. Next, where they apply, place the following symbols on the right side of the list.

1. Put a "$" by any item that costs forty dollars or more each time you perform it. (Be certain to look for hidden costs.)
2. Put a "10" by any item that you would not have done ten years ago.
3. Put an "X" by any item that you would like to let others know you do.
4. Put a "T" by any item that you spend at least four hours a week doing.
5. Put an "M" by any item that you have actually done in the last month.
6. Put an "E" by any item that you spend time reading about, thinking about, worrying about, or planning for.

7. Put a "C" by any item that you consciously choose over other possible activities.
8. Put a "G" by any item that you think helps you to grow as a police supervisor.
9. Put an "R" by any item that involves some risk. (The risk may be physical, intellectual, or emotional.)

In looking at your list, the more markings you have put next to an item, the more likely it is that the activity is a value for you. This list is not necessarily a compilation of your values; rather, it may be an indication of where your values lie. Count the number of marks next to each item—the activity with the most marks being first, and so on. Now, compare your first ranking (left side) with your second ranking (right side), and note the following:

1. Do your rankings match?
2. Is your highest value in the first ranking the one that has the most marks next to it?
3. Can you see any patterns in your list?
4. Have you discovered anything new about yourself as a result of this activity?
5. Is there anything you would like to change about your preferences as a result of this exercise?

If you are studying as a group, you may want to divide into subgroups of four or five members each and share what you have learned about your values. This was an awareness exercise and not a test. Hence, your judgment—and not some outside criteria—measures its accuracy. Basically, if there are more symbols next to the values that you ranked the highest, then you've achieved "confirmation." Conversely, if the highest-ranked values have few symbols, then you're looking at "discovery." Finally, if the pattern is erratic, you're probably seeing both some confirmation and some discovery.

The main thing is, you have identified ten core values.

———◆◆◆◆———

Failing to Act on Our Values

We fail to act on our values when we:

1. Concentrate on short-term objectives that do not relate to our long-term goals.
2. Relive past failures.
3. Succumb to the "we can't change" syndrome.
4. Substitute egocentrism for altruism.

5. Allow conformity to overpower courage.

6. Ignore our purpose in life and, in so doing, place the ladder of success against the wrong wall.

Structured Exercise 1–2

Let us take another approach that is more supervisor-oriented. Complete the following statements by assigning 1 to the highest priority and then, in descending rank order, 2, 3, and 4.

As with the first exercise, if possible, form groups of four to five members each for the purpose of discussing individual rankings. The groups can create a single group response by consensus. Look for commonalities, trends, and surprises.

1. I think that the best police supervisor is one who:
_____ tells you what should be done.
_____ consults with you on important issues.
_____ persuades you to live up to your ideals.
_____ facilitates a consensus on important issues.
_____ other: _____

2. For recreation, I prefer:
_____ conversation in a small group.
_____ doing something together in a group.
_____ watching TV.
_____ reading the newspaper.
_____ other: _____

3. In my role as a police supervisor, I like to:
_____ work by myself.
_____ work with others.
_____ delegate responsibility to others.
_____ other: _____

4. I like to use my free time to:
_____ be by myself.
_____ visit my friends.
_____ catch up on work.
_____ other: _____

5. In my retirement, I would want to:
_____ work on my hobbies.
_____ travel.
_____ take a part-time job.
_____ other: _____

6. For my professional future, I should:

_____ stay just as I am.

_____ take on new interests.

_____ renew present interests.

_____ drop some of my present interests.

_____ other: _____

7. With police supervisor colleagues, it is best to:

_____ keep quiet about yourself and your work.

_____ ask for help, advice, or consultation when you need it.

_____ be friendly, but not talk about personal or important business matters.

_____ tell them about yourself and your work.

_____ other: _____

8. Does this list leave out any important areas? If so, add other areas, including possible approaches to that area, and then rank them as above.

BASICALLY . . .

Basically, the vast majority of us have the same values—so why do we differ? After all, how many of us would state that one of our values is not "integrity," or not "family," or not "justice?" The reason we do differ, yet hold common values, is because our values are screened by our *paradigms*. For example, my paradigm of "integrity" (if I do something wrong, and no one knows about it, I'm still wrong) may disagree from your paradigm of what the value "integrity" means.

The subject of paradigms is covered at the start of Chapter Three. Our life is filled with values, and every one of them is shaped, modified, or confirmed by your paradigms.

Structured Exercise 1–3

Please return to the scenario that opened this chapter. Now, commit the necessary time to answer in writing each one of the questions that are posed. When finished, a final question—What did you learn about yourself?

The real meaning of our lives is likely to be defined by how we are remembered. So, if you want to know how to live (value) your life, just think about what you want people (family, friends, coworkers, and others) to say about you after you die and then live backwards.

FROM VALUES TO ETHICS

The capacity to care is the thing, which gives life its deepest significance.

—Pablo Casals
Spanish cellist, composer, conductor

Let us move from values to a more profound concern, ethics. In review:

- A value is something for which we have an enduring preference.
- An enduring preference means that a value is both a goal and a means for its pursuit.
- We supervise others and ourselves according to our value system.

As a preview to Responsibility Two:

- Our values serve as the birthplace of our ethics.
- Some values are ethical in quality. Hence, all ethics are values.
- Our ethics become a part of us.
- We supervise ourselves and we supervise others according to our ethics.

KEY POINTS

The three main reasons for understanding human values are they:

- Act as a departmental compass.
- Connect communications and mutual trust.
- Increase the chance of being a successful police supervisor.

We supervise others and ourselves according to our value system.

- A value is an enduring belief that a means or a goal is vitally important.
- Values-led police supervision attempts to fuse higher-ordered values into the police department.
- Our values stem from three periods in our life: imprinting, modeling, and socialization.
- Although enduring, our values can be modified by a significant emotional event and/or profound dissatisfaction.
- Our values play ten significant functions in our personal and professional lives: 1) acting as filters; 2) creating generation gaps; 3) producing individual differences; 4) establishing standards; 5) acting as conflict resolvers; 6) serving as emotional triggers; 7) being thought provokers; 8) motivators; 9) attitudes; and 10) personality.
- Our values can be clarified, and it is important that we do so.
- Paradigms measurably change our way of defining and displaying our values.
- Certain values are ethical in quality, but not all values are laden with ethicalness.

DISCUSSION

1. How does the phrase "we are what we value" pertain to the police supervisor?
2. Indicate what was the most significant input to your value system during each of the three value-programming periods.
3. Has anyone had a SEE lately? What did it do to your value system?
4. Identify a value (e.g., "personal safety"). Discuss how this value acts as a filter, reflects generation gaps, produces individual differences, creates standards, resolves conflicts, triggers emotions, provokes thoughts, and motivates us.
5. What produces worker attitudes, and defines our personality?
6. What did you learn from Structured Exercise 1–3?

ETHICS

The responsibility of a police supervisor is to ensure that the employees understand and adhere to a professional code of ethics.

The time is right to do what is right.

—Martin Luther King, Jr.

Earlier you were informed that we supervise ourselves and others according to our value system (Responsibility One). Likewise, we also supervise ourselves and others according to our ethical standards (Responsibility Two). In the next chapter, we will see how important it is for the supervisor to constantly communicate and consistently reinforce both (Responsibility Three).

While most of us have a high self-image when it comes to ethics, **being a good person and doing the right thing are easier said than done**. For one thing, it's not always easy knowing what's right. Second, having the moral willpower to put ethical principles above self-interest and always do the right thing takes a lot of character, especially when no one else seems to be living up to such high standards.

The fact is that for most of us, trying to live a good life engages us in an ongoing conflict between what we desire to do and what our duties tell us to do. The best of police supervisors may fib occasionally, cut corners a little, and rationalize about responsibilities. It's human nature; none of us is perfect. However, it is also human nature to seek perfection and to care about our character. Basically, **while we may have some faults, the majority of us want to improve our character.**

ETHICS AND ETHOS

Certain types of values are ethical values. Values and ethical values are a branch of philosophy. Ethics is concerned with moral duties and how we should behave regarding both ends and means. Police work is an intrinsically practical service enterprise that judges its employees and acts only in terms of the effective use of power and the achievement of results.

Ethos is the distinguishing character, moral nature, or guiding beliefs of a person, group, or institution. What are your guiding beliefs, those of your work group, those of your department? Does the ethos support or conflict with the ethics? For example, the following are ethical values:

- Honesty
- Fairness
- Trustworthiness
- Integrity

- Respect for others
- Thoughtfulness
- Compassion
- Honor

- Law abidingness
- Loyalty
- Accountability

Let us assume that you possess the preceding values. Now, does your ethos or guiding beliefs agree? Further, do your acts reflect them? There are three vital steps to ethics:

1. Knowing what is right.
2. Being totally committed to it.
3. Doing it.

Here are some useful definitions that will assist us as we progress with this responsibility:

- Ethics   = Body of moral principles or values
- Morals   = Right conduct
- Honesty = Intending to act morally and thus subscribing to ethical principles
- Integrity = Behaving in a moral way and thus manifesting ethical principles
- Integral = Wholeness

Structured Exercise 2–1

Imagine that you are a police officer and you're at roll call training. Your newly assigned sergeant starts the training by introducing himself and then adds, "If you have any doubts about how I want you to treat our citizens, treat them exactly the way I treat you!"

Now imagine that you're a police sergeant and you've just introduced yourself to your newly assigned shift officers. One officer raises her hand and asks, "How do you expect us to treat the citizens?" What is your reply? On a sheet of paper or in the margin of this page, write down your response. Share this information with others in your group.

There Is No Such Thing as Police Ethics

There are some people who would argue that there is a distinction between ethics and a legal obligation. Further, they would allege that police ethics and business ethics are different. I believe that a legal obligation is an ethical one—not a simple business decision. A legal obligation is also an ethical duty; it's a part of being trustworthy—having character. I also believe that there isn't any difference between police ethics and business ethics, or any other type of ethics (medical, sports, spiritual, etc.). Ethics is ethics!

The theory of "police ethics" flourishes because some police employees compartmentalize their lives into personal and police domains, assuming each is governed by different standards of ethics. In police work, the argument goes, ethical principles like trustworthiness, respect, responsibility, fairness, caring, and good citizenship are simply factors to be taken into account. As a result, fundamentally good people who would never lie, cheat, or break a promise in their personal lives delude themselves into thinking that they can properly do so in police work. This rationale is fatally flawed.

Ethics is not concerned with descriptions of the way things are but pre-scriptions for the way they ought to be. Though we may face different sorts of ethical challenges at work, the standards do not change when we enter the workplace. There is no such thing as "police ethics." There is only ethics.

What is most puzzling about most instances of police wrongdoing is that they clearly contradict both the values that are held by most of us as individuals and the collective standards that we have established for appropriate professional behavior.

I'd like to conduct a brief quiz. Do you:

- Consider yourself to be an ethical person?
- Believe that it's important for police agencies to function in an ethical manner?
- Believe that you know an ethical dilemma when you see it?
- Believe there are clear answers to ethical problems?
- Believe that you always know an ethical dilemma when it arises and always know how to resolve it?

Clearly, all of us feel strongly about ethics in the abstract. But at the same time, each of us is keenly aware of the struggle we face as ethical dilemmas arise.

It is a common struggle between our own desire to be ethical and the competing pressures of police performance. Police supervisors struggle every day with how to create an organizational culture that promotes ethical behavior.

RISKY BEHAVIOR

When examining the ethics programs of police departments, it is useful to bear in mind the three very different approaches to dealing with ethical dilemmas. These are:

- Neglect—or the absence of any formal ethical programs
- Compliance-based programs
- Values-oriented programs

Neglect

It is hard to imagine that any police agency could rationally ignore the importance of ethics or fail to develop management policies and programs, given the effect ethical breaches can have on performance, reputation, and community support. But some departments clearly don't get the message.

The departments that ignore ethics do so on the basis of assumptions that are false and never challenged. They seem to view ethics either as unimportant or as a costly and inconvenient luxury. They are wrong on both accounts.

Compliance-Based Programs

Compliance-based programs are most often designed by legal counsel. They are based on rules and regulations with the goal of preventing, detecting, and punishing legal violations. The centerpiece is a comprehensive collection of regulations that spells out a universal code of police ethics. The code lays out rules for hiring practices, travel expenses, compliance with local laws, improper payments, gifts, and potential conflicts of interest. It is a long and weighty list of do's and don'ts for people to follow.

This approach doesn't work well. First, rules beget rules; regulations beget regulations. You become buried in paperwork, and anytime you face a unique ethical issue, another rule or regulation is born. Second, a compliance-based program sends a disturbing message to the employees: "We don't respect your intelligence or trust you!" Finally, one of the most compelling reasons for shedding this approach is that it doesn't keep police supervisors or employees from exercising poor judgment and making questionable decisions.

Values-Oriented Programs

The values-oriented approach relies on the identification of ethical principles. Each police agency is responsible for developing its own core ethical values. For now we will use the six advocated by The Josephson Institute. Together they are referred to as the Six Pillars of Character; they define for us our moral duties and virtues.

Trustworthiness. Ethical persons are worthy of trust. Trustworthiness is an especially important ethical value because it encompasses four separate ethical values: honesty, integrity, promise keeping, and loyalty.

Respect. The ethical value of respect is fundamental. It imposes a moral duty to treat all persons with respect. This means we recognize and honor each person's right to autonomy and self-determination, privacy, and dignity.

Responsibility. Ethical persons are responsible, an ethical concept that embodies three separate values: accountability, self-restraint, and pursuit of excellence.

Justice and Fairness. Another fundamental ethical value is fairness. The concept embodies the values of justice, equity, due process, openness, and consistency. Fairness is one of the most elusive ethical values, since, in most cases, stakeholders with conflicting interests sharply disagree on what is fair.

Caring. At the core of many ethical values is concern for the interests of others. Persons who are totally self-centered tend to treat others simply as instruments of their own ends, and rarely do they feel an obligation to be honest, loyal, fair, or respectful.

Civic Virtue and Citizenship. An ethical person acknowledges a civic duty that extends beyond his or her own self-interests, demonstrating social consciousness and recognizing an obligation to contribute to the overall public good. Responsible citizenship involves community service and doing one's share.

We examine ethical issues by first identifying which of the above six ethical principles applies to the particular ethical decision. Then we determine which internal and which external stakeholders' ethical concerns should influence the decision. This principle-based approach balances the ethical concerns of the community with the values of the police organization. It is a process that extends trust to an individual's knowledge of the situation. It examines the complexity of issues that must be considered in each decision, and it defines the role each person's judgment plays in carrying out his or her responsibilities in an ethical manner. This integrates ethics with departmental culture, which includes diversity, open communications, empowerment, recognition, teamwork, and honesty into every aspect of police work—from personnel practices to relationships with the community. This integration is the adhesive of a seamless organization.

COURAGEOUS CHOICES

Courage is what gives ethics vibrancy. So many people espouse ethics about integrity, trust, loyalty, and the like until the dilemma is theirs. Then, because of their particular circumstances, selfish needs, and uncomfortable feelings, the ethics become negotiable. Clearly, to resist the inner drive toward self-indulgence over character requires an ethical code that judges some behaviors as better than others—along with a specialty known as courage.

Moral Courage

Courage comes in different forms. Most often, we think of physical courage or bravery. That's the kind of courage demonstrated by those who risked their lives trying to help others during the terrorist attacks of September 11, 2001 and by others who fought against acts of terrorism. It's right and proper that we call these people heroes and acknowledge their valor.

But there's another form of courage that's just as important; it's called moral courage. It's the kind of courage C. S. Lewis referred to when he said, "Courage is not simply one of the virtues but the form of every virtue at the testing point." The testing point is the place where living according to moral principles may require us to put our comfort, possessions, relationships, and careers at risk.

For most of us, the need for physical courage is rare, but our moral courage is tested almost every day. Being honest at the risk of disapproval, lost income, or a maimed career; being accountable when owning up to a mistake that can get us in trouble; making tough decisions and demands with co-workers at the cost of their friendship; being fair when we have the power to be otherwise; and following the rules while others get away with whatever they can—these things take moral courage, the inner strength to do what's right even when it costs more than we want to pay.

The sad fact is that people with moral courage rarely get medals. Instead, they risk ridicule, rejection, and retaliation. Yet this sort of courage is the best marker of one's true character and a life that others who know you can be proud of.

A Public Office Is a Public Trust

Public office (e.g., police sergeant) is a public trust. This axiom, supported by the related idea that participatory democracy requires public confidence in the integrity of government, lays the very foundations for the ethical demands placed on police personnel and the laws establishing baseline standards of behavior. Laws and rules are especially useful when faced with choices on brutality, stealing, perjury, and bribe taking. Although the choice here is not always easy, it's clear and straightforward. Laws are needed to define minimum standards of conduct.

Referring to such laws and rules as "ethical laws" or "ethical standards" is misleading and actually counterproductive. It is misleading because the laws deal only with a narrow spectrum of ethical decisions facing police employees. It is counterproductive because it encourages us to accept only existing laws as ethics. We accept narrow technical rules as the only moral criteria of conduct. Hence, if it's legal, it's ethical. It would be like using the penal code as a substitute for the Bible, Talmud, or Koran.

Easier Said Than Done

One reason ethics is much easier said than done is that legal albeit **unethical** behavior has become so very ordinary, as we can see from these generic examples:

- Embellishing claims
- Scapegoating personal failures
- Shirking distasteful responsibilities
- Knowingly making unreasonable demands
- Stonewalling questions
- Acting insincerely
- Reneging on promises
- Covering up
- Making consequential decisions unilaterally
- Malingering
- Lying

None of these behaviors is scandalous. But each, nonetheless, violates a sense of what is the morally correct behavior (e.g., the behaviors of personal responsibility, honesty, and fairness), increases cynicism and distrust, undermines integrity, and can be a stepping stone to wrongful behavior.

Though laws can secure compliance within limited margins, they are far too narrow or minimal to act as a substitute for ethics. We expect too much from laws and demand too little from people.

Choices: Easy Versus Courageous

The easy choices typically involve clear-cut laws and rules. You take a bribe, the choice may result in the obvious—you're fired and go to jail. The hard choices deal with moral issues and ethical considerations such as an indiscretion, a rule infraction (e.g., sleeping on duty), deception in police investigations, the use of deadly force, the use of physical force, and off-duty behavior that may or may not be job related.

Ethical decisions—courageous choices—are much more difficult than we would like to think. It is not simply a matter of character or upbringing. Ethical decision-making requires an alert and informed conscience. It requires the ability to resist self-deception and rationalization. It requires courage and persistence to risk the disapproval of others and the loss of power and prestige. Finally, it requires the capacity to evaluate incomplete or confusing facts and anticipate likely consequences under all kinds of pressure.

> Some of us overestimate the costs of being ethical and underestimate the costs of compromise.
>
> —Michael Josephson

Structured Exercise 2–2

Ethics Survey: Take the Ethical Climate Survey

Ethical decision-making in government is essential to a community's health, vitality, and democracy. Ethical behavior and decisions maintain citizen trust and ensure effective and efficient use of resources. Yet an ethical environment does not happen overnight. Successful police supervisors, as well as setting the pace for ensuring an ethical police organization, provide the necessary tools and establish the climate.

The first steps toward building and maintaining an ethical organization are to assess the current environment and identify any changes that are needed. How do you know where to start? What actions are most critical? Do employees think the local government is ethical?

Circle the appropriate response below each question or statement, using the following categories:

SD = Strongly disagree   D = Disagree   A = Agree

SA = Strongly agree   DK = Don't know

1. Ordinarily, we don't deviate from standard policies and procedures in my department.

   SD   D   A   SA   DK

2. My supervisor encourages employees to act in an ethical manner.

   SD   D   A   SA   DK

3. I do not have to ask my supervisor before I do almost anything.

   SD   D   A   SA   DK

4. Around here, there is encouragement to improve individual and group performance continually.

   SD   D   A   SA   DK

5. The employees in my department demonstrate high standards of personal integrity.

   SD   D   A   SA   DK

6. My department has a defined standard of integrity.

   SD   D   A   SA   DK

7. Individuals in my department accept responsibility for decisions they make.

   SD   D   A   SA   DK

8. It is wrong to accept gifts from persons who do business with my jurisdiction, even if those gifts do not influence how I do my job.

SD   D   A   SA   DK

9. It is not usual for members of my department to accept small gifts for performing their duties.

SD   D   A   SA   DK

10. Members of my department do not use their positions for private gain.

SD   D   A   SA   DK

11. Members of my department have not misused their positions to influence the hiring of their friends and relatives in the government.

SD   D   A   SA   DK

12. I would blow the whistle if someone in my department accepted a large gift ($ _____ or more in value; this amount varies by local government) from a person who does business with the government.

SD   D   A   SA   DK

13. Promotions in my department are based on what you know or how you perform on the job, rather than on whom you know.

SD   D   A   SA   DK

14. I trust my supervisor.

SD   D   A   SA   DK

15. The jurisdiction has implemented a code of ethics.

SD   D   A   SA   DK

16. There are no serious ethical problems in my department.

SD   D   A   SA   DK

17. Co-workers in my department trust each other.

SD   D   A   SA   DK

18. My superiors set a good example of ethical behavior.

SD   D   A   SA   DK

19. I feel that I am a member of a well-functioning team.

SD   D   A   SA   DK

20. All employees have equal opportunities for advancement.

SD   D   A   SA   DK

21. Performance evaluations accurately reflect how employees have done their jobs.

SD   D   A   SA   DK

22. Performance evaluations address ethical requirements as well as other measures.

SD   D   A   SA   DK

23. Employees share negative information with supervisors without the worry of receiving a negative reaction from them.

SD   D   A   SA   DK

24. Supervisors are concerned with how employees achieve successful results, rather than just with the results themselves.

SD   D   A   SA   DK

25. When there is a disagreement between employees and supervisors on how best to solve a problem, the employees' ideas are listened to and considered.

SD   D   A   SA   DK

26. When employees feel that they are being asked to do something that is ethically wrong, supervisors work with them on alternative ways to do the task.

SD   D   A   SA   DK

27. In this organization, it is much better to report a problem or error than it is to cover it up.

SD   D   A   SA   DK

28. When something goes wrong, the primary goal is to fix the problem and prevent it from happening again, rather than to find someone to blame.

SD   D   A   SA   DK

29. The organization's decisions on how people are treated are clear and consistent.

SD   D   A   SA   DK

30. The organization's expectations concerning productivity, quality, and ethics are consistent.

SD   D   A   SA   DK

31. The same set of ethical standards is used in dealing with citizens, employees, and others.

SD   D   A   SA   DK

32. You can rely on the accuracy of the organization's information about what will or won't happen.

SD   D   A   SA   DK

33. The organization publicly recognizes and rewards ethical behavior by employees when it occurs.

SD   D   A   SA   DK

34. Doing what is right around here is more important than following the rules.
    SD   D   A   SA   DK

35. Ethical standards and practices are routinely discussed in employee meetings.
    SD   D   A   SA   DK

36. If there is suspicion that some employees may be violating ethical standards, the situation is dealt with openly and directly.
    SD   D   A   SA   DK

37. Employees are aware of where to obtain assistance when they need to resolve an ethical dilemma.
    SD   D   A   SA   DK

38. If one employee is doing something unethical, the other employees in the group will usually try to correct the situation before management gets involved.
    SD   D   A   SA   DK

39. Employees are encouraged to report their work results accurately even when the results are less than satisfactory.
    SD   D   A   SA   DK

40. Employees maintain the same ethical standards even when no one is observing their actions.
    SD   D   A   SA   DK

Use the scale below each statement to respond to the following items; circle the number that most closely represents your response.

41. My ethical standards are:
Very low   **Very high**
  1   2   3   4   5   6   7

42. The ethical standards in my department are:
Very low   **Very high**
  1   2   3   4   5   6   7

Circle the answer that best represents your response to this statement:

43. My behavior as a public employee is regulated by state law.
    Yes   No   Don't know

Ethical Framework

Your answers to the survey should begin to give you a framework that can help guide your next steps and actions. You also may find it helpful to give a survey like this to all members of your staff. This could provide you with more information and further guide your ethical actions.

Analysis of the Ethical Climate Survey

The first 40 questions of the ethical climate survey are organized in relation to seven important values that affect the nurturing and sustaining of an ethical work environment.

VALUES AND RELATED QUESTIONS

Accountability	Responsiveness/ Customer Service	Integrity/Honesty
1, 7, 12, 16, 22, 27, 38	4, 19, 28, 30, 34	5, 6, 8, 9, 10, 11, 40
Trust	**Fairness**	**Communication**
3, 14, 17, 32	13, 20, 21, 31	15, 29, 35, 36, 37

Leadership

2, 18, 23, 24, 25, 26, 33, 39

The questions are designed and evaluated based on an ideal and ethically healthy work environment, which would be reflected by "Strongly agree" answers. Therefore, a strong ethical work environment would be indicated by an average of the questions within each category with a result as close as possible to 4. An average of all the category averages also can indicate an overall perception by employees of the total work environment, based on the factors listed.

RATING VALUES OF SURVEY RESPONSES

1 = Strongly disagree   3 = Agree
2 = Disagree   4 = Strongly agree
                         0 = Don't know

Responses to this survey indicate a local government's ethical strengths and weaknesses. For example, if you gave high responses to the questions under the fairness category, your organization probably treats its citizens and staff in a fair manner. If your scores for the communication category were relatively low, however, it might be in the best interest of your local government to write and implement a code of ethics or routinely discuss ethical issues during departmental meetings.

This survey is only the beginning. It might indicate that some work needs to be done, such as including ethics in the performance evaluation system. And by taking the survey and analyzing the scores annually, it also might help you maintain an organization that already has high ethical standards.

An ethical work environment is reflected in ethical decision-making that results in important organizational values being addressed, such as productivity, responsiveness, accountability, and a sense of ownership in how the organization conducts its business. Ideally, the most effective organization has a high level of compatibility between the employees' ethical values and those of the organization. There also is a clear understanding of the manager's expectations of the organization and employee behavior and performance.

Reprinted with permission from the May and June 1999 issues of *Public Management* magazine (*PM*), published by the International City/County Management Association (ICMA), Washington, D.C.

WHAT KIND OF A PERSON DO YOU WANT TO BE?

Your response to this question—"What kind of a person do you want to be?"—dictates what kind of a supervisor you will be!

I have never heard of anyone who while at work is miserable, mean-spirited and deceitful, but is the complete opposite in his or her personal life. And, vice versa. Undoubtedly, who you are or want to be as a person translates into who you are or want to be as a police supervisor.

Keep in mind, only good people feel guilty. Guilty people rarely feel guilty because they deny, they justify, they rationalize, and they refuse to accept their share of responsibility. Only ethically aware people struggle with the distance between who they are and who they know they ought to be. Sometimes police employees (supervisors too) do wrong because doing what they know to be right is too hard for them, or because the advantage to be gained by taking a shortcut (ethics cut) is just too tempting. They may believe that circumventing what's right just gives them an even chance of winning. And this is O.K.

Sometimes employees who have done a misdeed are so remorseful about it that they follow up with another wrongful act to keep the first violation from being discovered.

Sometimes people behave badly out of anger. They may feel that life or society, or their department, or their supervisor is unfair, or dishonest, so why should they be fair or honest?

Sometimes employees feel compelled to support and defer to authority even when that authority orders them to perform an act that they find ethically troubling.

What Kind of People Are We?

Are we naturally good until external circumstances compromise our goodness? Or are we naturally bad, requiring outside authority to constrain us? The obvious answer is that we are both. All of us have right and wrong tendencies—sharing versus selfishness, truthful versus lying, helpful versus harmful, and fairness versus cheating. All of this is because we are human. And our humanness does not start or stop once we achieve the position of a police supervisor.

Yes, good employees do bad things. In fact I envision the good employee as one who keeps his bad notions within due bounds. An old axiom relates that the measure of a person's character is what that person would do if he were sure nobody could see him.

Structured Exercise 2–3

You are a police sergeant, and a business owner describes the following situation. He owns several coin-operated newspaper vending machines. Customers insert 50 cents, open the door, and take a paper. Now the problem—once the door is open some people are taking more than one newspaper. He has decided to place one of the three signs on the machine to discourage people from stealing. The owner asks you which of the following signs is likely to be the most successful:

1. This machine is under surveillance. If you take more than one newspaper, you will be subject to arrest. Stealing is against the law.
2. I depend on the income from this machine to support my family. Please don't steal from us.
3. Please don't take anything you haven't paid for. What kind of a person are you?

Which of these signs will be most effective for most people? And which of them would be most effective for you personally? (Turn to item six in the Discussion section of this chapter for what the majority of people chose as their answer to the above questions.)

Good People Will Do Good Things

Yes, good people will do good things—lots of them. Unfortunately, they will do bad things because they are human—violations of ethical standards and/or legal mandates. We make mistakes of the heart and mistakes of the mind. And frequently, we pay the price for these errors on our part. With fortitude and resilience, we will not be overwhelmed by guilt when egotistical impulse defeats our moral resolve. Conversely, we will understand that moral victory is temporary when we cast aside temptation. Granted, it is an ongoing struggle for all of us—daily, hourly, minute by minute.

The question remains . . . "What kind of person do you want to be?" The clarity and certainty of answer to this question provide a definitive and cogent answer to the question posed earlier in the Introduction . . . "What kind of supervisor do you want to be?"

ETHICAL DECISION-MAKING

Ethical decision-making is a skill that can be learned. The first step is to know what the ethics are. Figure 2–1 presents an ethical code—if you're a law enforcement officer (public or private), you should know it. Take a few minutes to read it now; you'll find it loaded with ethical values that are much broader than a set of criminal laws.

When faced with a decision that involves ethics, ask the following questions of yourself or your work unit:

1. Will the decision I make violate the rights or goodwill of others?
2. What is my personal motive and spirit behind my actions?
3. Will it add to or detract from my reputation?
4. If I were asked to explain my decision in public, would I do so with pride or shame?
5. Even if what I do is not illegal, is it done at someone else's personal expense?
6. Does what I do violate another's reputation?
7. If it were done to me, would I approve or would I take offense and react in pain?
8. What are the basic principles that govern my actions and decisions?
9. When I am in doubt, to whom will I go to check my decisions?
10. Will my decision give other people any reason to distrust me?
11. Will my decision build the credibility of my work or profession?

If you have time for only one thought, imagine that your decision is being made with your mother, father, and a newspaper reporter watching you. Most police personnel want to do the right thing. In fact, this desire is so compelling that some will unintentionally engage in rationalizations to justify ethically doubtful behavior. It is possible to increase the likelihood that police employees will act more ethically more often if they're trained. In fact, the better and more frequent the training, the higher the likelihood that an employee will opt for the courageous choice—acting ethically.

Structured Exercise 2–4

Read the Law Enforcement Code of Ethics that appears in Figure 2–1. Underline all the values that you discern in it. Next, highlight all the values that you deem to be ethics. Compare your findings with those of others in your class or study group.

Law Enforcement Code of Ethics

As a law enforcement officer, my fundamental duty is to serve the community; to safeguard lives and property; to protect the innocent against deception, the weak against oppression or intimidation and the peaceful against violence or disorder; and to respect the constitutional rights of all to liberty, equality and justice.

I will keep my private life unsullied as an example to all and will behave in a manner that does not bring discredit to me or to my agency. I will maintain courageous calm in the face of danger, scorn or ridicule; develop self-restraint; and be constantly mindful of the welfare of others. Honest in thought and deed both in my personal and official life, I will be exemplary in obeying the law and the regulations of my department. Whatever I see or hear of a confidential nature or that is confided to me in my official capacity will be kept ever secret unless revelation is necessary in the performance of my duty.

I will never act officiously or permit personal feelings, prejudices, political beliefs, aspirations, animosities or friendships to influence my decisions. With no compromise for crime and with relentless prosecution of criminals, I will enforce the law courteously and appropriately without fear or favor, malice or ill will, never employing unnecessary force or violence and never accepting gratuities.

I recognize the badge of my office as a symbol of public faith, and I accept it as a public trust to be held so long as I am true to the ethics of police service. I will never engage in acts of corruption or bribery, nor will I condone such acts by other police officers. I will cooperate with all legally authorized agencies and their representatives in the pursuit of justice.

I know that I alone am responsible for my own standard of professional performance and will take every reasonable opportunity to enhance and improve my level of knowledge and competence.

I will constantly strive to achieve these objectives and ideals, dedicating myself before God to my chosen profession . . . law enforcement.

Figure 2–1   Police Code of Conduct (Reprinted with permission of the International Association of Chiefs of Police.)

ETHICS TRAINING

All of us have been trained to read, write, and calculate numbers. We've been trained to operate a computer, a fax machine, and an automobile. We've learned how to protect ourselves from being victimized. We've learned many, many more things. How many of us have taken a course on ethical conduct? Have you? Ethics training for police employees has been nonexistent or superficial. This is changing. There is, fortunately, an accelerating trend to train employees in ethics.

It is possible for police agencies to create a positive ethical culture that nurtures and rewards moral behavior and discourages bad conduct. There are four ways to enhance ethics:

1. Inspiration
2. Collaboration
3. Education and training
4. Integration

Inspiration

Inspiration is fostered by the following:

LEADERSHIP BY EXAMPLE. We preach a better sermon with our life than with our lips. We've heard sergeants comment with detectable frustration, "The officers don't pay attention to me." Nonsense. They do pay careful attention to their supervisors and managers. For most officers, leadership either occurs or does not based on their relationship to their sergeant and, to a lesser extent, the middle manager. They rarely have direct contact with the administrators. Essentially, they see them on occasion and basically know them secondhand through what the sergeant may have to say about them. We're aware of some supervisors who imply that "management is the enemy." Little do they realize that the officer is likely to take such a warning one step further—"If they're my enemy, you're best not trusted either." Remember, your staff does give careful consideration to what you say and what you do!

VALUE ORIENTATION. Make sure that everyone, especially newcomers, knows and understands the laws, rules, and values that should guide their hearts and behavior. This establishes a culture of ethics. If your agency has a mission statement, a code of ethics, or a set of goals, periodically review it with your staff. Reinforce it with the decisions you make—live it minute-by-minute.

With all cultures, there are countercultures. Some countercultures may be good (e.g., a group of officers who refuse to accept bribes when others do so). Alternatively, we may see an agency striving very hard to provide high-quality services, whereas a counterculture of officers is advocating that the public (or most of it) is the enemy.

Culture-building is not a one-shot endeavor. It takes time and a lot of reinforcement. People want to know the rules, the laws, the goals, and the values that guide and measure their activity. Far too often we've been told by officers (sometimes by sergeants and higher-command personnel), "I do not know what our mission is here. I do not know if we have a set of goals. I really have a sense of aimlessness." The answer, if there isn't a mission statement or set of values or goals, is to create them for your staff.

LIMITATIONS OF LAWS AND RULES.   The technical compliance with laws is necessary, but not always enough! Laws cannot replace the need for a sensitive conscience, or free one of the moral duty to adhere to traditional ethical principles. To encourage good-faith acceptance of the moral obligation to abide by both the letter and the spirit of the law, every opportunity must be used to 1) clarify the reasons for the rules and 2) emphasize the importance of the "appearance of wrongdoing" test.

Supervisors expect and appreciate good ethics. The line personnel are no different—they expect and appreciate good ethics in their supervisors. Those supervisors who use the legal do's and don'ts, who impose the "should" and "should not" of rules, are missing their main power source— ethical values.

Collaboration

Collaboration can be achieved by the following:

UNIFYING THE GROUP.   Unify individuals behind the traditional ethical values. One way is to appeal to the common interest all personnel have in the ethical behavior of every individual. All should be informed that it is to everyone's advantage that police personnel (sworn and civilian) be—and be perceived to be—ethical. The goal here is shared esteem for duty and honor, and a workplace where it is obviously unacceptable for any member to place self-interest (e.g., taking extra rewards, such as free meals) above the public trust.

I've listened to a sheriff admonish his staff about not accepting gratuities. "Not one dime, not one cup of coffee," he asserted. Later he signed a permit to "carry a concealed weapon" for one of his key campaign donors. Something doesn't jibe here.

SPECIFYING GUIDELINES.   Specify guidelines and approaches for making hard choices. This task involves the development and pronouncement of minimum standards of behavior for various situations. It also involves guidelines for coping with totally unanticipated circumstances.

I recall a police sergeant that reprimanded one of his officers for poor performance with, "Maynard, you've only given the minimum here since I've been your supervisor!" Maynard snapped back, "Sergeant, if the minimum wasn't acceptable, it wouldn't be the minimum!" Either the "minimum" had not been conveyed, or it should be elevated. Hard choices require known guidelines.

Education and Training

Ongoing educational programs focusing on issue spotting, reasoning, and other decision-making skills are vital ingredients of an ethics program. I believe the following should be included in the program:

- **No sermonizing.** Moralizing about ethics is not very effective in sustaining or changing attitudes and behavior. Traditional lectures on ethics should be scrapped and replaced with group discussions. I'm confident that if police personnel were asked in the early 1980s, "Where might our major vulnerability for corruption be?" the answer would have been, in most cases, "Drug money and drug usage." The officers knew this, but, regretfully, few administrators asked them.

    (No one likes to be "should upon." I've attempted to avoid doing that here. If I fell prey to sermonizing, I apologize.)

    My intent here is to emphasize the following:

- Ethics is a subset of values.
- The general function of ethics is to serve as a moral compass.
- Ethical standards at times make for hard and courageous choices.
- Ethics can be taught.
- Supervisors often make decisions involving ethical matters.
- Individual acts of moral courage are never wasted—each instance of ethical fortitude provides a lasting example that teaches and inspires.

- **Practical problem-solving.** "Seeing ethics" is easier than "doing ethics." The first involves consciousness, and the second emphasizes commitment. We must learn how to better evaluate facts and make reasoned decisions on ethical conduct. There are some people who overestimate the "costs" of being ethical and underestimate the "costs" of compromising ethical values. Decisions that include deceit or coercion often cause secondary risks that are not seen or properly evaluated. If you wonder what I mean by this last statement, merely scan the front page or business section of a daily newspaper.

- **Recognition of ethical issues.** People should be educated and trained in early detection of ethical issues. They should be sensitized to the eight factors that tend to defeat ethical instincts:

    1. Self-interest
    2. Rationalization
    3. Self-protection
    4. Groupthink
    5. Self-deception
    6. Greed
    7. Self-righteousness
    8. Envy

Structured Exercise 2–5

Some of the following comments are signposts of ethical wrongdoing. Have you heard, or are you now hearing, them in your organization? Discuss this exercise as a group.

Denying or Trivializing Its Significance
- "Show me a victim."
- "It's not illegal."
- "You can't legislate morality."
- "It's just a technicality."

Invoking the Double Standard
- "Morality is a personal matter."
- "I don't mix business with my personal feelings."

Arguing Necessity
- "It's cutthroat out there."
- "If I don't do it, someone else will."
- "It's my job."
- "It will save some jobs."

Arguing Relativity
- "It's not illegal elsewhere."
- "In the United States, ideals are turned into laws."
- "No act is inherently illegal."
- "We are no worse or better than society at large."

Professing Ignorance
- "I wasn't told."
- "Ethics is a gray area."
- "The rules are inscrutable."

- **Anticipation of ethical problems.** Typically, those in the best position to anticipate ethical challenges are supervisors. After all, they've recently experienced identical or similar hard choices. Any ethics program must be custom-built by and for a particular agency. What may be an ethics problem for one agency may not be for another.

Members of an agency should be surveyed to discover ethical problems and issues. Once the critical concerns have been spotted, then training scenarios and simulations can be constructed.

- **Own reward.** An ethics course should acknowledge that integrity, trust, and honor may not give immediate rewards or gratification, and that they can be career-threatening (e.g., when informing the chief that a lieutenant is stealing). The absence of integrity, trust, and honor may go undetected and unpunished. In fact, great wealth and power may be gained. Therefore, being ethical must be its own reward.

- **Temptations.** Being ethical does not mean we're temptation-free. There are going to be exciting temptations toward which we will feel drawn. It is at that moment that we have the opportunity to make a choice for time-honored rules of conduct.

- **Motives.** Assessing motives is usually pointless and often harmful. It is pointless because motives are almost impossible to determine. We often don't know our own, let alone those of others. It is harmful because we almost always exaggerate the purity of our own motives and assign evil motives to others.

  The solution to this problem is this: we should judge actions—our own and those of others—not motives. An ethics course should emphasize that it is what we do, not what we intend, that counts!

- **Basically good.** The belief that employees are inherently good is one of the most widely held in society. Yet it is both untrue and destructive. As far as our proposition about "inherently good" is concerned, look around and you'll detect numerous infractions of rules and policies. The destructiveness occurs when people concentrate on the external forces (e.g., "My mom forgot to cut the crust off my sandwiches"), rather than the human will. Those who believe in innate human goodness view the battle for a better world primarily as a conflict between the individual and society. I think that, especially in a free society, the battle is between the individual and his or her character. A police department can survive a serious crime condition, but not its officers' lack of ethical conduct.

> A police department can survive a serious crime condition but not its officers' lack of ethical conduct.

Integration

Basically, this step involves combining inspiration, collaboration, education, and training into a comprehensive package that daily becomes a viable influence within our lives and our organizations. Unfortunately, exercising moral restraint does not ensure that others will do likewise. On occasion it places the ethical person at a disadvantage in competing with persons who are not constrained by ethical principles.

Do you agree or disagree that it is better to lose than to sacrifice integrity? One person quipped, "The trouble with the rat race is that even if you win, you're still a rat." We cannot turn moral commitment on and off as it suits us or the situation.

> An ethically based person cannot win by being dishonest, disloyal, or unfair any more than one can truly win a tennis match by cheating.

THE PARADIGM OF INTEGRITY

I have rarely met anyone who openly admitted that they did not have integrity. While we all possess it, our paradigm of integrity may differ—even conflict. What integrity means to one may mean something very contrary to you. For example, my paradigm of integrity is that if I behave wrongfully and do not get caught, I lack integrity. I know of others who have as their paradigm that if their wrongful act goes undetected, then there is no violation of one's integrity. Which of these paradigms do you agree with? Or perhaps you disagree with both of them and have one of your own.

Integrity means being whole, unbroken, individual. It describes the character of a person who has united the various facets of his or her personality so that there is no longer any quarrelling within about what is right—ethics. Having integrity means you are blessed with wholeness and peace. Having integrity means the courageous choices become the easy ones.

Structured Exercise 2-6

It's Not Easy

Let's be honest. Ethics is not for wimps. It's not easy being a good person.

It's not easy: to be honest when it might be costly. To keep inconvenient promises or to put principles above comfort.

It's not easy: to stand up for your beliefs and still respect differing viewpoints.

It's not easy: to be on time. To control anger. To be accountable for attitudes and actions. To refrain from gossip and hurtful words. To tackle unpleasant tasks. Or to sacrifice the now for later.

It's not easy: to bear criticism and learn from it without getting angry. To take advice. Or to admit error.

It's not easy: to really feel sorry and apologize sincerely. To accept an apology graciously. Or to forgive and let go.

It's not easy: to not complain. To stop feeling like a victim. To avoid disheartening cynicism. To make the best of every situation. Or to be cheerful for the sake of others.

It's not easy: to share. To be consistently kind. To think of others first. To judge generously. To give the benefit of the doubt. To give without concern for gratitude. Or to be grateful.

It's not easy: to fail and still keep trying. To learn from failure. To risk failing again. To start over. To lose with grace. Or to be glad for the success of another.

It's not easy: to avoid excuses. To resist temptations. Or to listen to our better angels.

No, being a person of character is not easy. That's why it's such a lofty goal and an admirable achievement.

Permission to use and reprint this passage is granted by The Josephson Institute of Ethics.

KEY POINTS

- Ethics focuses on moral duties and how we should behave.
- Ethos is the distinguishing quality, moral nature, or guiding beliefs we hold.
- Certain values serve as ethical values.
- There is no such thing as police ethics—ethics are ethics and must not be qualified.
- There are three very different approaches to handling ethical problems: neglect; compliance-based programs; and values-oriented programs.
- The six pillars of character are trustworthiness; respect; responsibility; justice and fairness; caring; and civic virtue and citizenship.
- Being a police supervisor is a public trust.
- Obeying the law is an easy choice as compared with an ethical decision, which can be a hard choice.
- Self-deception and rationalization will cause us difficulty with hard choices.
- Some of us overestimate the costs of being ethical and underestimate the costs of compromise.
- What kind of a person you want to be prescribes what kind of a police supervisor you will be.
- Ethical decision-making can be learned.
- Ethics training involves inspiration, collaboration, education, and integration.
- In education and training in ethics, it is best to
    - Avoid sermonizing
    - Promote practical problem-solving

- • Help in recognizing ethical issues
  - • Show how to anticipate problems
  - • Emphasize that ethics is its own reward
  - • Identify temptations
  - • Concentrate on actions, not motives
  - • Accept the fact that humankind is not basically good
- • Integrity means you are integrated, whole, and at peace with your inner world.

DISCUSSION

1. Develop a group setting. Identify and rank what you as a group believe to be the seven most important ethical values that a police supervisor should hold. Next, rate yourself against each value with a number of one (low) to seven (high). Discuss your highest and lowest ratings with your associates.

2. What does ethos mean to you? Cite a guiding belief that you believe represents your police agency.

3. Obeying the law is a relatively easy choice. Making ethical decisions is a hard choice. Why? Do you have examples?

4. Identify a recent motion picture that portrays "moral courage." Describe an act or activity. Why did you select it? What does it tell us?

5. What has this chapter not covered? Where did it push or sermonize? Where did it seem uncertain or lacking?

6. Over the past several years I have asked pre-service and in-service police personnel these two questions; the results were: 1) They nearly always rejected (A), arguing that the chance of being arrested for stealing a newspaper was too low to deter people; and 2) they chose (B) when it came to other people, but (C) when it centered on their own behavior.

VISION

The police supervisor is responsible for ensuring that his or her team shares in crafting a vision, setting goals, and building a strategy for providing high-quality police work.

An old story tells of three stonecutters who were asked what they were doing. The first replied, "I am making a living." The second kept on hammering while he said, "I am doing the best job of stonecutting in the entire country." The third one looked up with a visionary gleam in his eyes and said, "I am building a cathedral."

Responsibility Three draws from and builds upon Responsibilities One and Two. A vision is individual values (Responsibilities One and Two) put into action, for supervisors are responsible for leading people in the creation of a vision statement for their work unit. Through communications (Responsibility Four) and self-management (Responsibility Five), the vision becomes a reality.

Have you ever held a job, work position, or occupational role where you didn't have a clue about its purpose? You performed tasks, but couldn't see how they fit into a meaningful pattern. If so, what you—and probably the people you worked for—lacked was a vision.

Small but important choices that you make in your work life add up to one big choice to perform as a police supervisor in such a way that you make a difference. Unless you have a vision of where you want to lead others, you'll never be able to judge whether or not you have made a difference.

This chapter is about the supervisor's responsibility for:

- Creating a shared vision for his or her work team
- Developing shared goals in order to measure how much and how fast the vision is being realized
- Designing a shared strategy for helping the vision become a reality

You will learn that:

- Vision is the constancy of purpose.
- Goal-setting is the constancy of progress.
- Strategy is the constancy of change.

Further, you will learn how vitally important all three of the above processes will be.

Shared vision is the constancy of teamwork.

PARADIGMS

As a police supervisor you are in a position to shape a vision of where you want to go and where you want others to follow you. If you don't, someone else surely will. A vision starts with value clarification and a code of ethics. Values plus ethics are at the very core of any vision. Vision statements (also referred to as "mission" and "value" statements) are filled with values and ethics. Without values and ethics there is no vision!

Our values, ethics, and thus our visions are subject to mental rules and regulations that in effect act as physiological filters—we see and experience our world through them. Any data that exists in the real world that does not agree with your paradigm will have a difficult time getting through your filters.

What may be perfectly visible and perfectly obvious to persons with one paradigm may be, quite literally, invisible to persons with a different paradigm.

This is the paradigm effect.

In fact, you are quite literally unable to to perceive data right before your very eyes. Please pause and re-read the above sentence; anything wrong with it? Did you spot the second "to?" If not, your paradigm or rule for correctly reading a sentence overrode it. Let's see how your addition paradigm functions. Quickly add up the numbers below (no calculator allowed).

```
1000
  40
1000
  30
1000
  20
1000
  10
```

Your answer was: _____
What was your answer—5,000? Or . . . ?

A Learned Pattern

A paradigm is a learned set of rules and regulations that we apply to our values, ethics, visions, and indeed all facets of our lives. What we envision or fail to envision is determined by our paradigms. There isn't any vision that has not passed before the paradigm effect.

COMMON.   Our lives are bombarded by paradigms—some of our choosing, some injected by others. The police supervisor's job is a nest of paradigms—some complementary, other contradictory.

MORE THAN ONE RIGHT ANSWER.   More than one paradigm may be correct. Conversely, more than one paradigm may be wrong. They significantly expand the number of ways we solve problems. The supervisor's notion that "there is only one best way" is replaced with "there are several best ways."

SEEING AND BELIEVING.   Paradigms can reverse the old adage "I believe it when I see it" to "I'll see it when I believe it." Think about it. Aren't there some things that you strongly believe in (your paradigm) yet cannot actually see or touch?

PARADIGM PARALYSIS.   If held too strongly, one can develop the terminal illness of certainty—paradigm paralysis. "There's only one way, and that's my way."

SUBJECT TO CHANGE.   We can change our patterns. With concentrated effort you can change your paradigm. While comforting to know, the question becomes, "But which one is the correct paradigm for me and those who I am responsible for supervising?"

Some Visions (Paradigms)

Let's examine some visions ranging from distant to recent past. While absurd and amazing now, they were strongly held visions.

> "The phonograph . . . is not of any commercial value."—Thomas Edison, remarking on his own invention to his assistant, Sam Insul, 1880.
>
> "I hereby request that the U.S. Patent Office be closed because everything that can be invented has been invented!"—The Commissioner, 1889 (my favorite).
>
> "Sensible and responsible women do not want to vote."—Grover Cleveland, 1905.
>
> "I think there is a world market for about five computers."—Thomas J. Watson, Chairman of IBM, 1943.
>
> "A computer could avoid cable changes by storing instructions in its memory."—John von Neumann, 1945. (This paradigm gave birth to the modern transistor in 1947.)
>
> "There is no reason for any individual to have a computer in their home."—Ken Olsen, President of Digital Equipment Corporation, 1977. (In 1960, Olsen created the minicomputer. DEC grew in eight years to $6.7 billion. He could not see or react to the "personal computer" and was forced to resign).
>
> "640K (of memory) ought to be enough for anybody."—Bill Gates, CEO of Microsoft, 1981.
>
> "The cloning of mammals . . . is biologically impossible."—James McGrath and Davor Solter, writing in *Science*, December 14, 1984.

Some Police Service Visions (Paradigms)

I have collected these paradigms/visions from police personnel who I've met in training programs and consulting assignments. Many of those I've held at one time were eventually dislodged by another competing paradigm.

1950s

> Height of an officer must be at least 5'8".
> Women in law enforcement have clearly defined and curtailed roles.
> Sworn personnel die soon (three years) after they retire.
> Successful leaders must come from within.
> Police officers should not be too intelligent.
> Police officers are philanderers.
> More officers are the answer to the crime problem!

1960s

> Women in law enforcement will never successfully perform as patrol officers.
> All successful police officers must be able to climb a six-foot wall.

It is a good police management practice to hire civilians because their labor cost is low.

Police officers should not be too intelligent.

Higher salaries for police personnel is the answer to the crime problem!

1970s

Women in law enforcement will never succeed as police supervisors.

No pre-employment "hard" drug usage.

College education is necessary for success as a police officer.

Successful police leaders must come from other agencies.

The 4/40 work week will never work.

Police officers should not be too intelligent.

Affirmative action is the answer to the crime problem!

1980s

Women in law enforcement will never succeed as police managers.

Distress = disability disorders = medical retirement.

No "hard" drug usage in past several years.

Being bicultural or bilingual is necessary for success as a police officer.

The 3/12 work week will never work.

Police officers should not be too intelligent.

Computers are the answer to the crime problem!

1990s

Women in law enforcement cannot successfully perform as SWAT members.

No "hard" drug usage after employment.

"Life experience" is necessary for success as a police officer.

Must have a common interest with one's boss in order to advance in rank.

Police officers should not be too intelligent.

Telecommuting will never work.

Community-oriented policing is the answer to the crime problem!

Year 2000 and Beyond

Civilian employees will outnumber sworn police employees by 2010.

Computer literacy will be compensated as a second language by 2005.

By 2020 there will be as many contract police agencies as there are jurisdiction-based.

All administrative and support service units will be civilianized by 2010.

By 2010 the primary competitive edge in the recruitment of new employees will be benefits, and not compensation.

Outsourcing of line functions will be common by 2005.

All police supervisor will be trained as risk managers by 2010.

All police agencies will have a "Bureau of Volunteer Services" by 2010.

By 2005 the majority of police agencies will have civilian oversight boards.

Structured Exercise 3–1

Two battleships assigned to the training squadron had been at sea on maneuvers in heavy weather for several days. I was serving on the lead battleship and was on watch on the bridge as night fell. The visibility was poor, with patchy fog, so the captain remained on the bridge, keeping an eye on all activities.

Shortly after dark, the lookout on the wing of the bridge reported, "Light, bearing on the starboard bow."

"Is it steady or moving astern?" the captain called out.

The lookout replied, "Steady, captain," which meant we were on a dangerous collision course with that ship.

The captain then called to the signalman, "Signal that ship: We are on a collision course; advise you change course 20 degrees."

Back came a signal, "Advisable for you to change course 20 degrees."

The captain said, "Send: I'm a captain, change course 20 degrees."

"I'm a seaman second class," came the reply. "You had better change course 20 degrees."

By that time, the captain was furious. He spat out, "Send: I'm a battleship; Change course 20 degrees."

Back came the flashing light, "I'm a lighthouse."

We changed course.

Constancy

This chapter began with a challenge to strive for constancy of **purpose, progress, change,** and **teamwork.** Did you note the juxtaposition of **"change"** and **"constancy?"** One term seemingly conflicts with the other. One paradigm might insist that you can't achieve both. My paradigm is:

> Change is a constant.

Change never ceases; it keeps coming at us, knocking us off course, confusing us, and fatiguing us. When we understand the paradigm effect, we learn that **the only constant in our life is change**.

Our values, ethics, and visions flow through paradigms and are automatically subjected to incoming considerations for change. Once a set of values, a code of ethics, or a vision statement has tested valid by the paradigm effect and supported by the staff of a work unit or the police department, then constancy of vision is established.

The police supervisor-as-leader is in a pivotal position for conceiving, refining, and implementing a paradigm—a vision that others are able to get excited about working on. Revisit the opening story about the three stonecutters. Which paradigm/vision would compel you as a police supervisor to become a supervisor-as-leader? To do everything possible to meet and even exceed the 15 responsibilities that we'll explore together in this book?

Everything Changes

When police employees at any level have had an opportunity to actively consider what vision and purpose have real meaning for them, everything changes. Having gone through the hard work and ultimate satisfaction of creating a shared vision for their immediate team, they become more devoted to building shared vision and shared meaning for the entire police organization. As that process is repeated among many teams and multiple pairings, the whole department is engaged and enriched, and multiple strands of shared meaning begin to bind the organization together.

Many police departments have vision statements. Sometimes they are labeled **value** or **mission** statements. Regardless of the title:

- All contain values.
- All express the purpose of the organization.
- Frequently they will inform you about how they intend to make their vision a reality, and sometimes they will cast the values into measurable goals.

Vision: The Constancy of Purpose

Responsibility One dealt with individual values and personal vision. Here we will focus on group values and organizational visions.

Since a vision usually consists of several values, it is relatively stable over time. If an organization frequently changes its vision, it can cause chaos for the participants.

Visions, like values, are enduring. They will change, but only with considerable time and an enormous amount of thinking. Visions create a consistency of purpose for a police organization.

Vision: An Image of Our Desired Future

A vision is a paradigm of the future you seek to create, described in the present tense as if it were happening now. A statement of "our vision" shows where we want to go and what we will be like when we get there. The better you see it, the more richly detailed and visual the image is, and the more compelling it will be.

Because of its tangible and immediate quality, a vision gives shape and direction to the department's future or the future of a division, bureau, or work team. And it helps people set goals to take the organization closer to reality.

A vision is not idle daydreaming or casual reflection on the "what if." It reflects a lot of practical thinking about why we're here (purpose) and where we should be headed.

Values: What We Are Doing to Get Where We Want to Go

Values describe how we intend to operate on a day-by-day basis as we pursue our vision. A set of governing values might include how we want to behave with each other, how we expect to regard our community, and the lines that we will and will not cross. Values are best expressed in terms of behavior: If we act as we should, what would an observer see us doing? How would we be thinking?

When values are articulated but ignored, a critical part of the shared vision is destroyed. By contrast, when values are made a central part of the police organization's shared vision effort and put out in full view, they become a guiding symbol of the behavior that will help the organization's members move toward the vision.

Purpose or Mission: What the Organization Is Here to Do

Whether you call it a mission or a purpose, it represents the fundamental reason for the organization's existence. What are we here to do together? You will never get to the ultimate purpose of your organization, but you will achieve many visions along the way.

Goals and Objectives: Milestones We Expect to Reach before Too Long

Every shared vision effort needs not just a broad vision, but also specific, realizable goals. A goal is long-range—one to five years. An objective is short-range—something we seek to accomplish within a year's time frame.

TWO APPROACHES FOR BUILDING A VISION STATEMENT

First, note the word in the above heading—"vision." I use the term "vision" to encompass vision, value, and mission statement.

Second, conceiving a vision is rigorous work, often perplexing and sometimes frustrating. Once you've got it, building a written vision statement is relatively easy. The vision thinking is tough; vision writing is straightforward.

Third, your department may not have a vision statement, or it may have one that is corny or that does not reflect the shared vision that you and your staff have of your duties. If so, lead your employees in the creation of one to meet your specific desires. In other words, a vision statement is not the sole property of the top brass.

Approach A: Top Down

The "A" in this approach denotes "above." Since the mid-1980s, many police management teams have created vision statements and worked hard on communicating them down to their employees. Many of us have accepted the notion that vision must come from the top. In that case, a meeting is convened so the top managers can develop a vision statement and plan for its distribution. The intent is sincere, and the content is always appealing. Each police management team affirms its uniqueness by declaring that it:

- Is committed to being a professional department
- Believes in its people
- Stands firm for quality
- Cares for customers
- Affirms honesty and integrity
- Supports teams
- Is innovative

But there are problems—ownership and implementation!

OWNERSHIP.   The buy-in resides with those who create a vision and with them alone. The employees do not own a statement created for a police agency to endorse. An even more fundamental defect is that, in most cases, the vision statement is created for the rest of the organization to implement. Notice that the top-down vision is used to define a set of values to be lived. This is different from top management's rightful task of defining and setting operational goals.

The belief that brainstorming the vision is primarily a leadership-at-the-top function defeats, right at the beginning, the intent of empowering those close to the work and the community. Creating vision is an ownership function, and if we want ownership widely dispersed, then each person needs to struggle with articulating his or her own vision for the police function or work unit.

IMPLEMENTATION.   There is something in us that wants a common vision articulated by those at the top. This longing for a common vision is the wish for someone else to create the unity and purpose we seek. We continue to want strong leadership from police management even though it steals accountability from those below. Visions are implemented when each police supervisor and assigned staff define vision for their area of responsibility.

The desire for vision from the top is a subtle way of disclaiming any responsibility for its implementation. If your assigned police team were your own business, it is unlikely you would allow someone else to define your values for you.

Approach B: Bottom Up

Moving from approach A to approach B hinges on shared ownership and accountability. The operative word is "shared." I know of police agencies that reinforce ownership and accountability by conforming their performance appraisal system to their vision statement. They link the envisioned ideals to the measurement of performance. The department vision becomes an operational reality (more on this in Responsibility Twelve, Performance).

Structured Exercise 3–2

Objectively assess which stage best describes your police organization now. The five stages are as follows:

1. *Telling.* The "chief" knows what the vision should be, and the organization is going to have to follow it.
2. *Selling.* The chief knows what the vision should be, but needs the organization to "buy in" before proceeding.
3. *Testing.* The chief has an idea, or several ideas, about what the vision should be and wants to know the organization's reactions before proceeding.
4. *Consulting.* The chief is putting together a vision and wants creative input from the organization before proceeding.
5. *Sharing.* The chief and members of the police department, through a collaborative process, build a shared vision together.

Top police managers surely need a vision statement, but not for themselves alone to live out and be accountable for.

> Unless a vision statement has a shared beginning and ending, it will remain an ignored and lofty set of well-intentioned values that fail to materialize.

BUILDING A SHARED VISION

The following recommended steps will prove helpful as you create a vision and cast it into a vision statement.

Although your agency or division may have a vision/mission statement, this should not discourage you and your staff from generating your own. As a supervisor-as-leader, you are responsible for doing so.

- *Listening.* Choosing to continually listen for a sense of emerging purpose is a critical decision that shifts a supervisor and his or their crew from a reactive orientation to creative one.

- *Linking.* Police mission or purpose statements often lack depth because they fail to connect to the agency's overarching reason for existence. When this connection is made forcefully, an employee's commitment and energy can be increased for fulfilling the department's purpose.
- *Inclusiveness.* To be genuinely shared, visions must emerge from everyone reflecting on the department's purpose.
- *Openness.* At the heart of building shared vision is the task of designing and implementing ongoing processes in which police employees at every level of the agency, in every role, can speak from the heart about what really matters to them and be heard—by police management and each other.
- *Personal.* When a shared vision project begins with personal vision, the police organization becomes a tool for the employees' self-realization, rather than an impersonal structure to which they are subjected. They stop thinking of the organization as a thing to which they are subjugated.
- *Equality.* In the department, the top brass wield the policy-making power, but in this exercise, a boss should get only one vote. Similarly, no one team should get more votes than any other. During these exercises, discourage status differences.
- *Unity.* By interface and dialogue, all issues, concerns, and views should be brought to the surface and resolved. Do not expect uniformity; that is groupthink, and will produce a seriously flawed vision.
- *Interdependence.* When team members begin talking about their vision, avoid telling them what other teams have said. Instead, ask each team first: "What do we really want?" As teams become curious about each other's visions, two or more teams may discover a strategic value in meeting together, comparing notes, and creating a shared vision.
- *Participation.* To conserve resources, many police chiefs opt to sample the thoughts of their employees. This undermines whatever opportunities people feel to take on ownership.
- *Self.* Participants are permitted to speak only of their ideas and not to allude to those that may be held by missing members.
- *Phasing.* A compelling vision takes time to craft. Cast it into phases, with pauses between each one.
- *Power.* The process is more important than the product. Participants actively instill meaning and inspiration into words and give them symbolic value; the words on their own mean nothing. That's why the benchmark of vision is not in the statement, but in the directional power it instills in the agency.

Structured Exercise 3–3

Examine the three vision statements that follow. First, highlight all of the values you can spot in each one. Second, look for any goals and record them. Third, write a single sentence that summarizes the expressed purpose of the agency.

Compare your findings. Are there similarities? Are there any unique concepts or values? What else did you deduce from this exercise? Finally, either alone or as a member of a group, develop a vision statement for your work unit.

———•◦×◦•———

GOAL-SETTING: THE CONSTANCY OF PROGRESS

Our beginning should be with an end in mind. In other words, before we start our journey, we should have a destination or goal set for ourselves. By keeping the end clearly in mind, you can make certain that whatever you do on any particular day does not stray from the goal you have set as supremely important, and that each day of your life contributes in a logical way to the vision you have of your life as a whole. Hence, we are able to maintain our constancy of progress.

A while ago I conducted a three-day team-building workshop for a large, full-service sheriff's department. The sheriff is a tall, rugged, red-headed, affable guy. At that time, he'd been the sheriff of the 1,800-person organization for 12 years. The workshop was attended by an undersheriff, four assistant sheriffs, a coroner, and 15 captains. The second day started with a discussion of a pending shift in the allocation of sworn personnel. Within a few minutes, the 15 captains were adamantly defending their assigned turfs. The sheriff sensed this and asked, "Hey, what are our goals?" No one said a word. I saw his face start to match the color of his hair. In a louder voice, he stated, "I guess there's no reason to ask you: What are our priorities?" Then there was silence—perhaps 60 seconds, which seemed like an hour.

Finally, one brave captain ventured, "Sheriff, in my opinion, our number one priority and goal is corrections. After all, about one half of our personnel are assigned to it." In a second, the sheriff's obvious anger switched to puzzlement. He dropped his head and then looked up and scanned the group. He proceeded to surprise us by saying, "I apologize. I thought you knew. It's my mistake for not telling you and then retelling you. Our goals, in order of their priority, are 1) drug abuse enforcement, 2) contract cities, 3) corrections, 4) county patrol areas, and 5) the coroner's office. Now, don't forget them." I'm confident no one has; I certainly haven't.

It is very easy to get in an "activity trap" in the business of police work, to work harder and harder at producing results only to discover that they're unnecessary. A police organization without goals can be highly efficient and very ineffective. The police organization that lives without goals will spend its future in the present.

> The police supervisor who supervises without goals is not in a position to lead.

Los Angeles County Sheriff's Department

Mission & Values

Our Mission

The quality of neighborhood life, its safety and welfare comes from the commitment to each of its citizens. The **Los Angeles County Sheriff's Department** takes pride in its role as a citizen of the community; partners with its members in the delivery of quality law enforcement services. We dedicate our full-time efforts to the duties incumbent upon every community member. As we act, we are universal citizens deriving our authority from those we serve. We accept our law enforcement mission to serve our communities with the enduring belief that in so doing, we serve ourselves. As professionals, we view our responsibilities as a covenant of public trust, ever mindful that we must keep our promises. As we succeed, our effectiveness will be measured by the absence of crime and fear in our neighborhoods and by the level of community respect for our efforts. In accomplishing this all important mission, we are guided by the following principles:

To recognize that the primary purpose of our organization is not only the skillful enforcement of the law, but the delivery of **humanitarian** services which promote community peace.

To understand that we must maintain a level of professional **competence** that ensures our safety and that of the public without compromising the constitutional guarantees of any person.

To base our decisions and actions on **ethical** as well as practical perspectives and to accept **responsibility** for the consequences.

To foster a collaborative relationship with the public in determining the best course in achieving **community order.**

To strive for **innovation,** yet remain **prudent** in sustaining our fiscal health through wise use of resources.

To never tire of our **duty,** never shrink from the difficult tasks and never lose sight of our own humanity.

Our Core Values

We shall be service oriented and perform our duties with the highest possible degree of personal and professional integrity.

Services Oriented Policing means:

Protecting life and property

Preventing crime

Apprehending criminals

Always **acting lawfully**

Being **fair and impartial** and treating people with dignity

Assisting the community and its citizens in solving problems and maintaining the peace.

We shall **treat every member** of the Department, both sworn and civilian, as we could expect to be treated if the positions were reversed.

We shall **not knowingly break the law** to enforce the law.

We shall be **fully accountable** for our own actions and failures and, when appropriate, for the actions or failures of our subordinates.

In considering the use of deadly force, we shall be guided by **reverence for human life.**

Individuals promoted or selected for special assignments shall have a history of **practicing these values.**

Something We Desire

A goal is something we desire; it is something we hope for in the future. An objective is a goal that is more finite and time-certain. For example, a police supervisor may set a goal of developing his or her assigned personnel to the maximum of their innate strengths. An objective that would support fulfillment of this goal could be this: All personnel within my purview will have attended an officer survival course within the next six months. Note that the goal is broader in scope, while the objective is specific with an assigned time frame.

The MISSION of the New York City Police Department is to enhance the quality of life in our City by working in partnership with the community and in accordance with constitutional rights to enforce the laws, preserve the peace, reduce fear, and provide for a safe environment.

IN PARTNERSHIP WITH THE COMMUNITY, WE PLEDGE TO:

- *Protect the lives and property of our fellow citizens and impartially enforce the law.*
- *Fight crime both by preventing it and by aggressively pursuing violators of the law.*
- *Maintain a higher standard of integrity than is generally expected of others because so much is expected of us.*
- *Value human life, respect the dignity of each individual and render our services with courtesy and civility.*

Multiplicity of Goals

At first glance, it might appear that organizations have a singular objective—for police departments to apprehend criminals. But closer analysis demonstrates that all organizations have multiple goals. Police agencies also seek to increase public safety and provide general government services. No one measure can effectively evaluate whether an organization is performing successfully. Emphasis on one goal, such as reducing crime, ignores other goals that must also be achieved if long-term safety is to result. Additionally, the use of a single goal almost certainly will result in undesirable practices, since supervisors will ignore important parts of their job in order to look good on the single measure.

Real versus Stated Goals

Stated goals are official statements of what an organization says and what it wants various publics to believe are its objectives. But stated goals, which can be pulled from the organization's charter, annual report, public relations announcements, or public statements made by a police chief, are often

home
chief's message
terms of use
news releases
mission statement
hpd divisions

contact hpd
crime stats
hpd heroes
hpd history

a career with hpd
positive interaction
crime prevention

what's new
search
links

city of houston
houston weather
houston traffic
houston culture
texas laws
city ordinances

houston police online
the official website of the houston police department

MISSION STATEMENT: The mission of the Houston Police Department is to enhance the quality of life in the City of Houston by working cooperatively with the public and within the framework of the U.S. Constitution to enforce the laws, preserve the peace, reduce fear and provide for a safe environment.

Values

Preserve and Advance Democratic Values

We shall uphold this country's democratic values as embodied in the Constitution and shall dedicate ourselves to the preservation of liberty and justice for all.

Improve the Quality of Community Life

We shall strive to improve the quality of community life through the provision of quality and equitable services.

Improve the Quality of Work Life

We shall strive to improve the working environment for the department's employees by engaging in open and honest communication and demonstrating a genuine concern for one another.

Demonstrate Professionalism

We shall always engage in behavior that is beyond ethical reproach and reflects the integrity of police professionals.

Principles

Life and individual freedoms are sacred.

All persons should be treated fairly and equitably.

The role of the police is to resolve problems through the enforcement of laws - not through the imposition of judgement or punishment.

The neighborhood is the basic segment of the community.

Because law enforcement and public safety reflect community wide concern, the police must actively seek the involvement of citizens in all aspects of policing.

The fundamental responsibility of the police is provision of quality services.

The department's employees are its most valuable asset.

Employee involvement in departmental activities is essential for maintaining a productive working environment.

Employees should be treated fairly and equitably in recognition of basic human dignity and as a means of enriching their work life.

conflicting and excessively influenced by what society believes police organizations should do.

The conflict in stated goals exists because organizations respond to a vast array of constituencies. Unfortunately, these constituencies frequently evaluate the organization using different criteria. As a result, police management is forced to say different things to different audiences.

Given the diverse constituencies to which police management is required to respond, it would be a surprise to find a department with a set of objectives stated to everyone that actually describes what the organization seeks to achieve.

There is visible evidence to support the fact that police managers give much attention to their social responsibilities in the decisions they make and the actions they take. The overall goals that top management expresses can be actual or real, or they can be fiction. If you want to know what a police department's real objectives are, closely observe what members of the organization actually do. It is behavior that counts.

If we are to develop comprehensive and consistent plans, it is important to differentiate between stated and real objectives.

The police supervisor-as-leader will quickly and easily be able to assert the real goals of the department. He or she understands existing values and possesses a clear vision of the incoming future. This assures the consistency of progress.

Structured Exercise 3–4

This is a simple but powerful exercise to help you understand the significance of distinguishing between real and stated goals.

- Imagine learning that you have to retire in one year. List three things you'd like to accomplish during this last year.
- Assume 11 months have passed, and you have one month left. Again, list three things you would like to do.
- Make a new list assuming you have one week left, and another assuming you have only 48 hours left.
- Examine what you've written. If your list includes activities you're not currently pursuing, what's stopping you from pursuing them now? Get on track!

(Note: This exercise can be easily modified to focus on your personal life. Merely assume that you have one year to live. List three things you'd want to do within the year and so on to 48 hours.)

STRATEGY: THE CONSTANCY OF CHANGE

> The 20th century began by changing the old constancies, while the 21st century begins by change being the only constant.

All police departments are confronted by change. How well a police agency negotiates the hurdles of change is the key to its survival and success. Some change is external (e.g., Americans with Disabilities Act, terrorism, population mix). Some is internal (e.g., organizational structure, management style, labor relations). Regardless of its source, any change poses two questions:

- Does it challenge our vision?
- How does it affect our goals?

Incessant and avalanching changes can modify a goal, which means reexamining and perhaps recasting it. Or these changes may alter how the goal will be implemented. In both cases, the police supervisor must think strategically.

Strategic thinking is the basis for developing strategic plans and operational plans. It is a supervisory tool for making better choices about how to implement departmental goals in the face of chronic and random changes. And it always:

1. Uncovers the causes versus the symptoms of problems
2. Hammers conventional thinking
3. Depends more on intuition than on intellect
4. Seeks to anticipate
5. Points out more than one approach for accomplishing a goal

Step 1: Recognizing Insight

Recognizing insight in yourself or others begins with increased comprehension of the characteristics that insightful police leaders share. Don't look for once-in-a-lifetime brilliant flashes! Deep insight is a basic and abiding skill that continually guides the thinking of a winner. Most often you'll find insightful police leaders engaged in the following behavior:

- They prefer tackling problems that do not have precise answers, asking questions like "In what ways can we improve our police services for our clientele?"
- They spend more time synthesizing information than gathering it, relishing the process of breaking information down into its component parts and then reconfiguring those parts to expose the essence of a problem.

- They can easily drop an approach to a problem that isn't working, forcing their way out of habitual methods of thinking or analyzing.
- They doggedly pursue difficult problems over long periods of time, never feeling frustrated when the solution isn't readily apparent.
- They don't worry about asking questions that might display their ignorance.
- They usually think up more ideas more rapidly than anyone else in brainstorming sessions, because their disciplined but flexible minds thrive on such exercises.
- They have made meditation a habit, not an occasional exercise, and set aside time each day for such activity.
- They read voraciously to satisfy a thirst for knowledge and the experience of others.
- They entertain new ideas enthusiastically. They help their associates and staff come up with innovative approaches.

With these attributes in mind, you should be ready to test your own level of insight with the Leader Insight Self-Examination (Structured Exercise 3–5).

Structured Exercise 3–5

Leader Insight Self-Examination

	Always	**Often**	**Seldom**	**Never**
1. You are stimulated by complex problems and situations that tax your thinking.	4	3	2	1
2. You dislike the sort of rigid problem solving that attacks every problem with the same mechanical approach.	4	3	2	1
3. You encourage open discussion and disagreement in your work unit.	4	3	2	1
4. You read voraciously to expand your experience.	4	3	2	1
5. You entertain new ideas with enthusiasm, rather than skepticism.	4	3	2	1

	Always	**Often**	**Seldom**	**Never**
6. You ask numerous questions, never worrying about whether they reveal your ignorance.	4	3	2	1
7. You look at things from a variety of viewpoints before making a decision.	4	3	2	1
8. You surround yourself with people who promote distinctly different orientations and points of view.	4	3	2	1
9. You make decisions others call "innovative."	4	3	2	1
10. You search for new and better ways of approaching work within your organization.	4	3	2	1

How did you fare? A score of 40 marks you as a deeply insightful leader, while anything below 30 indicates a need for improvement. Your improvement will occur when you take the next two steps.

Step 2: Asking the Right Questions

The majority of us function daily with paradigms that constrain our creativity. There are six in particular that limit our powers of imagination:

- *Resistance to and avoidance of change.* Many of us who cling to the status quo for safety are consciously or unconsciously blocking new insights.
- *Dependence on rules and conformance.* Some supervisors emphasize conformance over performance by enforcing strict adherence to rules, procedures, and structures.
- *Fear and self-doubt.* Some police supervisors become immobilized by insecurity, lack of confidence, and fear of criticism.
- *Fixation on logic and hard data.* Some police supervisors have more of a commitment to mechanics than to results. Some expect problems and solutions to fit snugly into neat compartments. This hampers our intuitive powers.

- *Black-and-white viewpoints.* The maturity that comes with experience tends to change previously black-and-white judgments to varying shades of gray. Regretfully, some police supervisors hold to an either/or approach, which reduces their options to a few oversimplified solutions.
- *Narrow-minded dedication to practicality and efficiency.* Some police supervisors refuse to consider wild alternatives and ideas. Every idea for them must fit into some logical scheme.

I propose five exercises for you to free up your creativity and thus help you to be more innovative in your job.

CREATIVITY TRAINING.   Numerous training programs are available to you for increasing your creativity. For example, contact Princeton Creative Research in Princeton, N.J. An excellent guide on the subject is Roger Von Oech's "A Whack on the Side of the Head" (Warner Books).

ONE NEW IDEA A DAY.   Supervisors are usually idea-getters; hence, you should find it natural to get one more idea every day. At first, it may seem difficult, even frustrating. But once in motion, you'll find that ideas flow with ease. New visions of alternative futures for yourself and your department will outcrop.

WILD THINKING.   Wild thinking helps us break the locks of mechanistic approaches. Whenever you find yourself bogged down with formal, technical processes for solving problems, pause for a little wild thinking. Look for historical successes that can be retested. Look for other technologies, such as robotics, and see how they fit in your operation. Ask this question: What is impossible to do right now, but if it could be done, it would significantly change my work?

MAKE THE OBVIOUS STRANGE.   Instead of relying on the tried-and-true perspective on a problem, force yourself to see two or more strikingly different solutions. Before making any decision, step back to view the full richness of a situation. Look for multiple meanings and possibilities. Once a day for a month pick at least one situation or problem and make it complex and ambiguous. The quick and simple answer to a problem can be both quick and wrong!

PUSH THE ARTIST; RESTRAIN THE JUDGE.   An overdependence on being practical and getting to the bottom line hurries you into making an evaluation. At least once a week for three months, deliberately postpone a new idea, discussion, strategy, or plan by reserving judgment until it becomes unavoidable. Don't think you're procrastinating. Rather, allow a little further discussion, initiate an experiment, or demand a follow-up report. Once your creative juices have ebbed, the practical you—the judge—can step in to evaluate the ideas.

Step 3: Tuning In

In police supervision, "tuning in" means letting your intuition, your years of experience, your awareness of challenges, your sensitivity to the community, and your understanding of cold, hard facts flow together in a calm and natural way. Most of us seldom tap the full reserve of our knowledge and experience.

When we encounter problems, we suffer anxiety because problems pose dangers, as well as opportunities. In our anxiety, we forget to trust our most valuable intuitive resources. Insight, like great poetry, music, or art, arises from the quiet depths of the unconscious from a source that lies beneath words, deeds, thoughts, and figures.

With the integration of your insight, experience, and knowledge, you're armed to build an operational paradigm. An operational paradigm enables the supervisor-as-leader to accurately and quickly move to the heart of strategic issues confronting their work unit, meanwhile dodging bureaucratic barriers and vaulting mountains of minutiae.

THINK SLOWLY; ACT QUICKLY!

Police organizations and police supervisors are inclined to make two major blunders when it comes to crafting a vision, defining goals, and developing a strategy:

- Not making the three processes a shared or team effort
- Taking far too much time in their accomplishment

Both are killer bullets to vision statements, goal setting, and strategic plans. I underscored earlier the importance of everyone sharing in the three-part effort. In terms of time commitments, I concur with the Greek proverb "Think slowly." Only I would add, "Do it now!" Some believe that establishing a vision, goals, and strategies demands months of brainware. Nonsense. Get everyone into a room and do it! Allow 24 hours maximum.

To Be Continued . . .

Visioning, goal setting, and strategic thinking set the stage for planning and managing by objectives (MBO). The latter two move from thinking about who we are to showing others who we are. Hence, planning and MBO will be found in Responsibility Twelve, Performance.

KEY POINTS

- The way we envision our world and our job is determined by our paradigms.
- A key paradigm held here is that change is a constant.
- Without a vision, a supervisor will never be able to determine if he or she made a difference.
- The vision encompasses its values, purpose, and goals.
- There are two approaches for building a vision: top down and bottom up.
- The bottom-up or shared approach is, by far, preferable.
- Goal setting is an effort to translate a vision into measurable benchmarks of progress.
- Strategic thinking is intended to keep organizational goals operable.
- Act now on a vision, a set of goals, and a strategy for their realization.

DISCUSSION

1. What is the primary purpose of a local police department in today's modern world?
2. What is wrong with the top-down approach for building a vision statement?
3. Why build a shared vision of what you are and where you want to go?
4. Why are goals important? How do they relate to a vision?
5. How does strategic thinking impact goal attainment?
6. What does "Act quickly, think slowly" mean to you as an existing or a potential supervisor?
7. Examine the list of "Paradigms – Year 2000 and Beyond." Debate the accuracy of each one. Add five of your own to the list.

COMMUNICATIONS

The police supervisor is responsible for communication with others in such a manner that employee understanding, trust, and mutual support are engendered.

If you cannot express yourself on any subject, struggle until you can. If you do not, someone will be the poorer all the days of his life.

—Oswald Chambers

At this point, your values (Responsibility One) and ethics (Responsibility Two) have been explored for the purpose of developing your capacity to create a vision for your work team (Responsibility Three). The next step is to accurately convey it (Responsibility Four).

Communication is our most important human skill. Everything that we've done, are doing, and wish to do revolves around it. Everything a police supervisor does involves communicating. Not a few things, but everything! You can't make a correct decision without information. That information has to be communicated. Once a decision is made, again communication must take place. Otherwise, no one will know a decision has been made. Supervisors, therefore, need effective communication skills. I am not saying that solid communication skills alone make a successful police supervisor. I am saying, with confidence, that ineffective communication skills can lead to a continuous stream of problems for the supervisor.

The success of any relationship (work, marriage, friendship, etc.) hinges on trust. And trust depends on communication. As you read what follows, keep in mind that communication and trust are tied to one another—if one rises or drops, so will the other. As a supervisor you've got to be trusted; hence, you've got to communicate.

We'll start here by asking "why?" and eventually conclude this chapter by asking an additional "why?"

WHY DO WE COMMUNICATE?

> Our ability to communicate effectively and directly determines our success on becoming a leader, our success in making accurate decisions, and our success in being trusted.

When I use the term "communications," I am referring to it in its most dynamic, pervasive, and expansive dimensions: Words written, spoken, and not spoken, and nonverbal cues. Now, why do we communicate?

- To be a leader
- To make decisions
- To establish trust

Leadership

Communication is the vehicle for supervisory leadership. The police supervisor is a key person in building and maintaining effective organizational communications, as he or she interacts with subordinates, peers, superiors, and the citizenry.

Decision-Making

A police supervisor assesses issues based on information received in conjunction with previously developed strategies, procedures, or rules. Consequently, the communication process is necessary because the flow of proper information to the decision points throughout the organization is such a vital requirement for task accomplishment. In fact, if supervision were thought of primarily as decision-making, and if the decision process were considered essentially a communication process, including a network of communication systems, then supervision could be viewed as a communication process. The closer we look at leadership and decision-making, the more we become aware of the significance of information exchange.

Trust

Later on I'll cover the concept of a trust bank account (TBA). The most important ingredient we put into any relationship is not what we say or what we do, but what we are. We do this by communicating. How do you react to the person who does not share with you his ideas, values, hopes, and ethical standards? Do you grow to trust him? Probably not. He either refuses to make or is incapable of making deposits into your TBA. In fact, if this individual persists in being closed, he'll likely make withdrawals from your TBA. Trust and communication are linked. For one to be high, the other must be high. You lower one (reduced communication), and you'll lower the other (reduced trust).

WHAT IS IT?

Communications is the:

- Transfer of meaning between two or more people in order that . . .
- Understanding will occur within an . . .
- Environment—in this case a police organization.

Transfer of Meaning

Communication is the transfer of meaning. If no information or ideas have been conveyed, communication has not taken place. The supervisor who is not heard or the writer who is not read does not communicate. For communication to be successful, the meaning must be not only sent, but also comprehended. Therefore, communication is the movement and understanding of meaning. Perfect communication, if such a thing were possible, would exist when a transmitted thought was perceived by the receiver exactly the same as envisioned by the sender.

Understanding

Good communication often is erroneously defined by the communicator as agreement, rather than clarity of understanding. If someone disagrees with us, it's not unusual to assume the person just didn't fully understand our position. What happens is that many of us define good communication as having someone accept our views. But a supervisor can very clearly understand what you mean and not agree with what you say. In fact, often when observers conclude that a lack of communication must exist because a conflict has continued for a prolonged time, a close examination reveals that there is plenty of communication going on.

Yes, a lot of communication, but little or no understanding. First, there must be understanding; then there is a basis for agreement. Without mutual understanding two people may actually agree and not know it. Worse yet, without it two people may think they agree but be on opposite sides of an issue.

Environment (The Setting)

A communication—or, in terms of an organizational setting, a communication system—provides the means by which information, statements, views, and instructions are transmitted through a department. Although one often speaks of the "flow" of communications, this flow actually consists of a series of discrete messages of different length, form, and content. These messages are transmitted through certain channels (or lines of communication), which make up the communication system or network. Each message is sent by a transmitter (an individual, a group, a division, a computer) to a receiver or several receivers. The supervisory role and functions are filled with an excessively heavy volume of transmissions and receptions.

What We Know about Communications

What knowledge exists about communications is scattered over numerous disciplines and fields and is often contradictory. In many ways, what we know about communications has been derived from our failures, rather than from our successes. Sufficient evidence is now before us to conclude that communications 1) is perception; 2) is expected; 3) makes demands; 4) is related to, but different from, information; 5) is marginal when one-way; and 6) is best when accomplished by example. These six premises are explained next.

1. *Perception.* Paradoxically, it is the recipient who communicates, rather than the person who emits the message. (Therefore, the truism—a leader cannot lead until he or she has a follower.) While the communicator speaks, writes, or gesticulates a message, communication does not occur until the receiver perceives it. Keep in mind that perception is a total experience, as opposed to logic. And receivers vary in their sensory and mental capacities to perceive data inputs. Hence, the first question that the communicator must ask prior to the sending of a message is, "Can the receiver perceive it?" That is, is the receiver sensorially and cognitively capable of ingesting and conceptualizing the message? The second question concerns the values, attitudes, and emotions of the recipient. Thus the query, "What is the receiver's particular mental set at this time?" The communicator is, therefore, dealing with psychophysiological paradigms that determine *if* the message is received and how it is interpreted.

2. *Expectations.* In most instances, we perceive what we expect to find in the message. The unexpected or unwanted data are frequently ignored or filtered in line with our expectations. Basically, our human mind seeks to fit incoming data into a pre-established pattern of expectations. Consequently, before we attempt to communicate, we must predict what the recipient expects to hear or see. And we should keep in mind that minor incongruities will probably be rejected or distorted to fit the pattern. Thus, if the data are important, the communicator may find it necessary to apply sufficient "shock" or drive to the message so that it disturbs the pattern and alerts the recipient that the unexpected is occurring.

3. *Demands.* The prime usage of communications is to influence or control. Therefore, it is always making demands on us to change or continue to do what we are doing, believe or not believe, and act or not act. Usually, such demands are gradual or subliminal in that major demands are frequently resisted because they do not comply with the existing pattern of expectations.

4. *Information.* Information and communication, although different, are nevertheless interdependent. Information is formal and logical. Conversely, communication is personal and psychological. Indeed, communications can occur without information. As an example, we can share in an experience while not receiving the logic of information. Also of interest is the difference between effective information and effective communication. The former is specific, terse, and structured; the latter is subjected to varying perceptions, expectations, and demands. It is debatable whether information, once freed from these three conditions, becomes more informative or whether, on the contrary, it tends to lose its meaning.

5. *Two-way is good.* One-way communication typically fails. It is ineffective for the obvious reason that we do not know if or how the recipient has perceived the message. Listening is important, but not sufficient to ensure that one has communicated. Moreover, the answer to better communications is clearly not more information. Usually, more information tends to widen the communications gap between the sender and the receiver (information overload). Are not most of us today in need of more communication and less information?

(Note: E-mail and fax messages are one-way communications!)

6. *By example is much better.* The clearest, most convincing message to the receiver is the one conveyed by an example. The supervisor-as-leader relies on furnishing examples of what is intended. The message in some way is demonstrated. It is experienced. If the subject matter is a complete and well-written crime report, then the supervisor will show the officer what one looks like along with an explanation and a two-way conversation. There are hundreds of written procedures but rarely do they impart precisely what is expected. Good and bad police officer behavior is learned. Much of it is learned—by example—from the person's supervisor.

Producing examples today is more and more difficult and frustrating for the supervisor-as-leader. Mounds of paperwork, pervasive technology, and invasive procedures dictate the supervisor's time and attention. Field supervisors are being tied to their desks and captivated by their computers. Simultaneously they will know that first-line leaders, to be leaders, must be visible. Examples of what is expected are next to impossible to convey by e-mail, fax, telephone, or roll-call conversations. Tell-me doesn't cut it; show-me does.

It is the courageous supervisor-as-leader who assiduously battles bureaucratic baloney and technological entrapments. This person realizes that to communicate and therefore provide leadership, you must provide examples. Being visible is a prerequisite for leadership by example. Being visible today is not easy, but then again neither is supervision, per se. If you're going to lead, then you've got to successfully communicate with your potential followers. This can't be accomplished from behind your desk while fixated on a computer screen and processing paper. If your priority is to be a leader, then do something about it right now!

WHERE WE COMMUNICATE

Supervisors communicate in two channels that flow in four different directions. The channels are:

- Formal
- Informal

  The directions are:

- Down
- Up
- Across
- Diagonal

Formal channels are primarily configured for the **downward** and **upward** movement of information, although there is some across and diagonal movement of formal information. Informal channels use all four directions equally.

Formal Communication Channels

All organizations develop formal communication channels as a response to large size and the limited information-handling capability of each individual. The formal channels adhere to the recognized official structure of the organization. Accordingly, the formal communication channels transmit messages expressive of the legitimate structure of authority. Hence, one usually sees formal orders and directives, reports, official correspondence, standard operating procedures, and so on. Those persons who emphasize going through channels are doing so in deference to the unit of command principle within the formal hierarchy.

Strict compliance with formal channels can be disruptive. These are disruptions primarily of time, creativity, and experience. First, it takes a long time for a formal message from a supervisor in one division to pass to another supervisor in another division. Second, formal messages are on the record and thus restrict the free flow of ideas. As an example, police officers may not want to expose their ideas to their supervisors for the time being, even in rough form; yet any formal communication is immediately routed through the originator's supervisor. Third, in practice a formal communication system cannot cover all informational needs. Informational needs change quite rapidly, while the formal channels change only with considerable time and effort. The most urgent need for informal communication channels is to plug the gaps in the formal channels.

Informal Communication Channels

Regretfully, there are some who consider formal communication channels as the only way to transmit information necessary to the functioning of the organization. However, this precept is no longer as sacred as it once was. We are witnessing an interest in acquiring a better understanding of the informal organization along with its potential use. This interest and awareness quite naturally lead to a different perspective on the structuring of communication flow. This perspective does not confine organizationally useful communication to purely formal channels. It includes all the social processes of the broadest relevance in the functioning of any group or organization. Consequently, we now treat informal and personal communications as a supportive and frequently necessary process for effective functioning.

It is futile for police administrators to establish formal channels and assume that those channels will carry most of the messages. Ironically, the more restricted the formal channels, the greater the growth of informal ones.

We next proceed to an analysis of three kinds of informal communication channels:

SUB-FORMAL.   Sub-formal channels carry those messages arising from the informal power structure existing in every police organization. Every member of the department must know and observe informal rules and procedures about what to communicate and to whom. Such rules are rarely written down and must be learned by experience and example, a necessity that causes difficulties for newcomers.

There are two types of subformal communications: those that flow along formal channels, but not as formal communications, and those that flow along purely informal channels. Both types have the distinct advantage of not being official; therefore, they can be withdrawn or changed without any official record being made. As a result, almost all new ideas are first proposed and tested as subformal communications. The vast majority of communications in police organizations are sub-formal.

Sub-formal channels become all the more necessary under certain conditions. First, the greater the degree of interdependence among activities within the department, the greater the number and use of sub-formal channels. Second, the more uncertainty about the objectives of the department, the greater the number and use of sub-formal channels. When the environment is relatively unpredictable, people cannot easily determine what they should be doing simply by referring to that environment. Consequently, they tend to talk to each other more to gain an improved understanding of their situation. Third, when a police organization is operating under the pressure of time, it tends to use sub-formal channels extensively because there is often no time to use the formal channels. Thus, police administrators reach out for information whenever they can get it from whatever channel is necessary. Fourth, if the divisions of a police organization are in strong competition, they tend to avoid sub-formal channels and communicate only formally. Conversely, closely cooperating sections rely primarily upon subformal communications. Fifth, subformal communication channels are used more frequently if departmental members have stable, rather than constantly changing, relationships with each other.

PERSONAL TASK-DIRECTED.   A personal task-directed communication is one in which an organization member deliberately reveals something of his own attitude toward the activities of his own organization. While personal, this communication also relates to the goals or activities of the organization. Thus, we can refer to it as task directed. It possesses the following characteristics: First, task-directed personal channels are nearly always used for informing, rather than for directing. Second, before a person acts on the basis of information received through personal channels, he or she usually verifies that information through either subformal or formal channels. Third, this channel transmits information with considerable speed because there are no formal mechanisms to impede its flow. Fourth, because task-directed personal messages are transmitted by personnel acting as individuals, they do not bear the weight of the position emitting them. To this extent, they differ from subformal messages, which are transmitted by individuals acting in their official capacity—but not for the record.

PERSONAL NON-TASK-DIRECTED.   As suggested by its title, this form of communication apparently does not contain information related to the task of the organization. Note the word "apparently." Paradoxically, this channel may on occasion handle information far more valuable to the achievement of organizational goals than does any other channel, including the formal ones. An example of this channel is the supervisor learning through a friendly subordinate of the reasons for growing job dissatisfaction. First, non-task-directed channels furnish a vehicle for an individual to satisfy his or her social needs. In doing so, a person experiences a certain degree of need fulfillment that carries over into the job. Second, this channel provides a way for an individual to blow off steam over things that are disturbing. Third, non-task-directed channels frequently supply useful feedback information to the management and supervisory levels. This feedback is normally comprised of unexpected information not obtainable in any other way. Fourth, personal channels offer the best medium for a person to become socialized in the organizational setting. Unwritten standards, group values, and "the way we do things here" are conveniently expressed through non-task-directed channels.

Downward

Communications from supervisor to staff are primarily of five types:

1. Specific task directives: job instructions
2. Information needed to produce the understanding of the task and its relation to other organizational tasks: job rationale
3. Information concerning organizational procedures and practices
4. Feedback to the subordinate officer about his or her performance
5. Information to instill a sense of mission: indoctrination of goals

   1. *Job instructions.* The first type of message is most often given priority in police organizations. Instructions about the position of police officer are communicated to the person through direct orders from the supervisor, training sessions, training manuals, and written directives. The objective is to ensure the reliable performance of every police officer in the organization.

2. *Job rationale.* Less attention is given to the second type, which is designed to provide the police officer with a full understanding of his or her position and its relation to related positions in the same organization. Many police officers know what they are to do, but not why. Withholding information on the rationale of the job not only reduces the loyalty of the member to the organization but also means that the organization must rely heavily on the first type of information, detailed instructions about the job. If a person does not understand why he or she should do something, or how his or her job relates to other jobs performed by co-workers, then there must be sufficient repetition in the task instructions so that the individual behaves automatically.

3. *Procedures and practices.* Information about organizational procedures supplies the role requirements of the organizational member. In addition to instructions about the job, the police officer is informed about other duties and privileges as a member of the police organization.

4. *Feedback.* Feedback is necessary to ensure that the organization is operating properly. It is also a means for motivating the individual performer. However, feedback to the individual about how well he or she is doing in the job is often neglected or poorly handled, even in police organizations in which the managerial philosophy calls for such evaluation.

5. *Organizational goals.* The final type of downward-directed information has as its purpose to implant organizational goals, either for the total organization or for a major unit of it.

SIZE OF THE LOOP. The size of the loop in downward communication affects organizational morale and effectiveness. In terms of morale, communications about the goals of the police organization cover in theory a loop as large as the organization itself. In practice, however, the rank-and-file officers are touched only minimally by this loop. Their degree of inclusion within the loop depends mainly upon how they are tied into the police organization. If they are tied in on the basis of being rewarded for a routine performance, information about the goals and policies of the overall structure will be of no interest to them.

Next, the size of the loop affects the degree of understanding contained in a communication. Messages from top management addressed to all organizational personnel often are too general in nature and too far removed from the daily experiences of the line police officer to convey their intended meaning.

Upward

Communications from subordinate to supervisor are also of chiefly five types:

1. Information about his or her *performance* and *grievances*
2. Information about the *performance* and *grievances* of others

3. Feedback regarding organizational *practices* and *policies*
4. Feedback concerning what needs to be *done* and the *means* for doing it
5. Requests for *clarification* about goals and the mission

1. *Performance and grievances—me.* By our very nature, we want to know "why?" This is especially so when it comes to performance evaluations. Good, bad, or standard, we want to know the reasons for such judgments about our work. We want examples, the facts about our rating. To get this information, we have to communicate upward. Similarly, when it comes to feeling unfairly treated, we seek an upward appeal—a second opinion—about what befell us.

2. *Performance and grievances—others.* We likewise want to ask similar questions about our co-workers. This is a touchy one because in some cases it may not be any of our business. However, if we're reprimanded for a mistake, and someone else commits the same one and is not reprimanded, we'll want to know why.

3. *Feedback on policies and practices.* Feedback is one form of two-way communication. Indeed, it may be the most important. "Do I understand this policy/practice correctly?" is a critical inquiry deserving the singular attention of the person being asked.

4. *Feedback on objectives and methods.* Later on I'll be covering managing by objectives (MBO) and how it motivates people into action. You'll find that without feedback, it crashes. The supervisor should be in a position to clarify, explain, and justify the objectives of the work unit and how the employees ought to proceed in their accomplishment of these objectives.

5. *Goal clarification.* Similar to the above, the police supervisor should be able to clarify, explain, and justify the overall goals and mission of the department.

UPWARD IS TOUGH. There are enormous constraints on free upward communication, for a variety of reasons. Most prominent is the structure itself. Simply stated, bureaucracies or highly formalized organizations tend to inhibit upward informal communications. In doing so, a tremendous amount of important information never reaches the upper-level decision centers.

Other factors adversely affecting the upward flow of messages are as follows: Superiors are less in the habit of listening to their subordinates than of talking to them. Furthermore, information fed up the line is often used for control purposes. Hence, the superior is not likely to be given information by subordinates that would lead to decisions adversely affecting the subordinates. They tell the superior not only what they want to hear, but also what they want the supervisor to know. Employees do want to get certain information up the line, but generally they are afraid of presenting it in the most objective form. Full and objective reporting about one's own performance and problems is difficult.

For all these reasons, the upward flow of communication in police organizations is not noted for spontaneous and objective expression, despite attempts to formalize the process of feedback up the line. Importantly, it is a problem not of changing the communication habits of individuals, but of changing the organizational conditions responsible for these habits.

Across and Diagonal

Communications between employees must occur out of necessity between work units that are located in different divisions. Across means a sergeant in patrol speaking to a sergeant in investigations. It also means a dispatcher in communications talking to a lieutenant in training. *Communicating across and diagonally in a police organization assures it of seamless operations.* There are four reasons for across and diagonal communications:

1. Information necessary to provide task teamwork
2. Information for identifying and defining common problems to be solved through cooperation
3. Feedback from co-workers that fulfills individual needs
4. Information needed to provide professional (not organizational) guidance for a group so that it can maintain the members' compliance with its standards and values

1. *Teamwork.* Confusion, conflict, and frustration result from a lack of coordination between work units. If not emphasized, detectives and narcotics could be investigating the same crime, one patrol unit could be messing up the operations of another, and so on.

2. *Common problems.* Weak horizontal and diagonal communications nearly guarantee that the root causes of a police problem will go undetected. When I discuss problem-oriented policing in a subsequent chapter, you'll gain an appreciation for a comprehensive (versus narrow) view of a police problem.

3. *Feedback on individual needs.* Most of us want to know what others think about our efforts. "Am I doing a good job?" "Am I trusted?" The answers to questions like these are of concern to us. Some of this feedback occurs within the work unit. Clearly, it is also valued from co-workers in other work units.

4. *Professional guidance.* The sharing of information among work units increases the probability that the various groups are acting in concert with approved service values and quality standards.

A BALANCE. Organizations face one of their most difficult problems in procedures and practices concerned with lateral communication. A working balance must be found between unrestricted and over-restricted communications among peers in an organization. To explain, unrestricted communications of a horizontal and diagonal character can detract from maximum efficiency because too much irrelevant information may be transmitted. At the opposite extreme, efficiency suffers if an employee receives all his or her instructions from the person above, thus reducing task coordination.

Communication across boundaries is usually over-restricted. If I had to choose between too much or too little, I would opt for the former. Teamwork depends on the speed and ease of movement of information from one departmental sector to another.

The type and amount of information that should be circulated on a seamless basis are best determined by answering the question "Who needs to know and why?" To put it another way, the information transmitted should be related to the objectives of the various units in the police organization, with primary focus on their major task. An interesting hang-up in horizontal communications occurs when people overvalue peer communication to the neglect of those below and above them. Sergeants talk only to sergeants, and lieutenants only to lieutenants.

How We Communicate

The four major ways that we endeavor to communicate messages are:

1. Spoken words
2. No words
3. Written words
4. Infotech words

The above four words combined produce the total volume of messages received and sent by a police supervisor. To conclude this section we'll discuss the:

Volume of Words

Spoken

The method most used by people to communicate with one another is the spoken word. Popular forms of oral communication include speeches, formal one-on-one and group discussions, and the informal rumor mill or grapevine.

The advantages of oral communications are speed and feedback. A verbal message can be conveyed and a response received in a minimal amount of time. If the receiver is unsure of the message, rapid feedback allows for early detection by the sender, and for correction.

The major disadvantage of oral communication surfaces whenever the message has to be passed through a number of people. The more people a message must pass through, the greater the potential for distortion is. In a police agency where decisions and other information are verbally passed around the hierarchy, considerable opportunity exists for messages to become distorted.

ORAL MESSAGES.   Oral messages are of two varieties: meetings (face-to-face) and telephone conversations (ear-to-ear).

- *Meetings.* A meeting involves a discussion among two or more people. Meetings have four purposes: 1) to provide a means for exchanges to take place quickly; 2) to provide a job environment in which members are stimulated to new ideas by the rapid exchange of views between individuals; 3) to reduce the amount of semantic difficulties through face-to-face interaction; and 4) to get the members attending the meeting committed more strongly to given proposals or procedures than they would be otherwise.

    There are two types of meetings: routine meetings, such as those of permanent committees, and ad hoc meetings, called to discuss particular issues. The difference between a routine meeting and an ad hoc meeting is similar to that between a routine report and a memorandum. Like a routine report, a routine meeting can be either time- or event-triggered, whereas an ad hoc meeting may either be called in regard to a request to consider a particular problem or be event-triggered.

- *Telephone conversations.* Many of the comments made on meetings are pertinent to telephone communications. The distinction made earlier between routine and ad hoc communications may be useful here. There are, however, some noteworthy differences between the two media: 1) A telephone conversation is generally confined to two participants, and 2) it lacks certain unique characteristics of interaction that take place in a face-to-face exchange. The preceding two differences are being rapidly erased by technology that supports videoconferencing.

Written

Written communications include memos, letters, organizational periodicals, bulletin boards, and any other device that transmits information via written words or symbols.

Written messages have advantages because they are permanent, tangible, and verifiable. Typically, both the sender and the receiver have a record of the communication. The message can be stored. If there are questions concerning the content of the message, it is physically available for later reference. This is particularly important for complex or lengthy communications. A final benefit of written communications comes from the process itself. More care is taken with the written word than with the spoken word. Written communications are more likely to be well thought out, logical, and clear.

Of course, written messages have their drawbacks. They're time-consuming. You could probably say the same thing in 10 to 15 minutes that it takes you an hour to write. Thus, while writing may be more precise, it also consumes a great deal more time. The other major disadvantage is feedback, or lack of it. Oral communications allow the receivers to respond rapidly to what they think they hear. However, written communications do not have a built-in feedback mechanism.

WRITTEN REPORTS.   There are six basic characteristics of a well-written report. Each of these is equally important to the completion of a well-written report:

1. *Accurate.* Accurate means in exact conformity to fact.
2. *Clear.* Clear means the report is plain or evident to the reader; the meaning is unmistakable.
3. *Complete.* Reports must have all the necessary parts and include the who, what, when, where, why, and how. Crime reports must include the elements of the crime.
4. *Concise.* Concise means to express all the necessary information in as few words as possible. It does not imply leaving out part of the facts in the interest of brevity.
5. *Factual.* A fact is something real and presented objectively. Facts are things the officer can prove or disprove. Inference and unsubstantiated opinion are not facts and must not be written in police reports. Unsubstantiated opinions are usually based on premises; however, sometimes they are based on prejudice and bias.
6. *Objective.* Objective police reports are not influenced by emotion, personal prejudice, or personal opinion. Officers should record all the facts, remembering there is more than one side to each story.

There are six types of written reports:

1. *Routine report.* A routine report is a message that supplies information as part of a standard operation. There are two ways in which a report can be created: 1) If it is time-triggered, a report is called for at set time intervals (e.g., a police supervisor is required to send weekly reports on the activities of subordinates); 2) if it is event triggered, a report is called for when certain tasks are completed (e.g., a report is to be sent when a case is finished or when certain training has been provided to subordinates).

   In each of these examples, the initiative to make a report does not lie with the supervisor; the circumstances under which a report is issued are clearly specified by organizational procedures. Frequently, the contents of the report are prescribed, either in the format the report is to take (as in the case of a pre-designed form) or in the information it is expected to furnish, although the supervisor can exercise initiative as to the content and coverage.

2. *Memorandum.* A memorandum also supplies information, but not as a part of a routine procedure. A memorandum can be 1) a statement of fact, submitted in response to an inquiry, to aid in evaluating a problem or to prepare proposals for action; 2) a statement that is event-triggered, released when circumstances have changed in an non-prescribed manner, calling for some initiative by the transmitter in drawing attention of others to the change so that a plan of action can be formulated; or (3) a comment, made

in response to some other statement to add information or to give a different interpretation of data.

3. *Inquiry.* An inquiry is a message requesting information to assist in evaluating a given problem, usually before making recommendations for action. The response to such a request would be a memorandum, which would include a statement with the necessary information and an analysis of the data. An inquiry usually involves information not included in reports, unless the reports are time-triggered and the information is required before the next report is due.

4. *Query.* A query is a message defining the characteristics of a problem and asking for instructions or proposals about courses of resolution. A query is often made by a subordinate concerning a problem not fully covered by standing regulations, either because of the novelty of the situation or because of ambiguities or inconsistencies in procedures. Furthermore, a query may be generated by a supervisor seeking advice and direction from peers or subordinates.

5. *Proposal.* A proposal describes a course of action the writer feels should be taken. It can be the result of several exchanges of queries, inquiries, reports, and memoranda. It may be generated by a subordinate on her or his own initiative or at the instigation of a supervisor, or it may be created by a supervisor wishing to test the reactions of peers or subordinates. A response to a proposal may take the form of a comment or a counterproposal.

6. *Decision.* A decision states the action to be taken. This message may be 1) a decision that affects recurrent events, which provides direction not only on how to handle the particular event that caused the discussion prior to the decision, but also on similar events in the future; or (2) a decision on an ad hoc problem, which does not formally affect future procedures.

   A decision can take a number of forms. It may begin with a request to review the causes that necessitate making a decision to resolve certain problems; it may continue by outlining alternative courses of action and explaining the reasons for the rejection of some; it may then specify what has been decided and how the decision is to be implemented; next, it may indicate what feedback is expected to keep the decision-maker informed of progress in implementation.

Nonverbal

Some of the most meaningful communications are transmitted neither verbally nor in writing. These are nonverbal communications. A loud siren at an intersection tells you something without words. A supervisor teaching a group of officers doesn't need words to tell when the trainees are bored. The size of a person's office and desk and the clothes a person wears also send messages to others. However, the most well-known areas of nonverbal communication are verbal intonations and body language.

- Verbal intonations are how we use the voice to emphasize words or phrases. A pleasant, smooth tone creates a different meaning than an intonation that is abrasive with strong emphasis placed on the last word.
- Body language includes everything from facial expressions to our sitting or standing posture.

UNDERSTAND FIRST—EMPATHIC LISTENING.   The key to influencing another person is first to gain an understanding of that person. As a supervisor, you must know your staff to influence them. Most of us are prone to want the other person to open their mind to our message. Wanting to understand the other person requires that we open our mind to him or her.

Consider this scenario. Sergeant Ker says to Sergeant Paulson, "I can't understand Officer Hooper. He just won't listen to me." Sergeant Paulson replies, "You don't understand Hooper because he won't listen to you?" Ker answers, "That's what I said." Paulson remarks, "I thought that to understand another person, you needed to listen to him!" Ker realized that he didn't communicate with Hooper because he didn't understand him.

When we seek to understand, we are applying the principle of "empathy." Empathy is a Greek word. The "em-" part of empathy means "in." The "-pathy" part comes from pathos, which means "feeling" or "suffering." Empathy is not sympathy. Sympathy is a form of agreement, a form of judgment. We have empathy, then, when we place ourselves within the other person, so to speak, to experience his feelings as he experiences them. This does not mean that we agree, but simply that we understand the other viewpoint.

Once we understand, we can proceed with the second step of the interaction: seeking to be understood. But now it is much more likely that we will actually be understood, because the other person's drive to be understood has been satisfied.

- To understand another person, we must be willing to be open to that person's thoughts.
- When we are open, we give people room to release their fixed positions and consider alternatives.
- Seeking first to understand lets us act from a position of knowledge.
- By seeking to understand, we gain influence in the relationship.
- Seeking first to understand leads us to discover other options.

When we seek to understand, people become less defensive about their position. They become more open to the question "How can we both get what we want?" As they get their position out of the way, they begin to see their values more clearly so that they can use them as guidelines for creating and evaluating other options.

Empathic listening is particularly important under three conditions:

- When the interaction has a strong emotional component
- When we are not sure that we understand
- When we are not sure the other person feels confident that we understand

The following three steps, if practiced, will measurably assist you in listening with an empathetic ear:

LISTENING WITH THE EYES.   To truly understand, we must listen to more than words. Words are weak compared with the richness and complexity of the ideas that we need to express. They are particularly poor at expressing feelings, for example, and yet feelings are often the thing that people most want us to understand. So when we seek to understand, we must look beyond the surface issues that the words describe, to consider how people feel.

WIN-WIN.   The most vital part of empathic listening is developing a win-win attitude. Win-win requires a nexus of courage and consideration. It will give us success even when we are not adept at the skill. As we learn the skill, we will be that much better.

Empathic responses will destroy understanding if the attitude behind them is wrong. The danger of empathic listening is that we may use it because we believe that it "works." We may see it as a tool for getting what we want, or for manipulating people. If we use it with wrong intentions, we corrupt the skill. Empathic listening creates positive results only when we accept it as a useful principle and use it solely with the intent to understand.

NOW TO BE UNDERSTOOD.   Once we understand, we can then proceed to be understood. This is related to the earlier comment that win-win is a balance between courage and consideration. Understanding the other person shows consideration. Being understood takes courage. Both are necessary conditions for win-win agreements.

If, in the course of being understood, we sense resistance, we have another opportunity to choose again either to be defensive or to seek to understand. So we may find ourselves moving back and forth between seeking to understand and seeking to be understood. The process is complete when both parties feel understood and when their interaction has given them a foundation for discovering other options. This is what empowerment is all about (see Responsibility Eight).

Structured Exercise 4–1

Complete this exercise by yourself. Then, if others are available, brainstorm the possible answers as a group.

1. Identify a situation in which you should use the skill and attitude of empathy.
2. What benefit might occur from your use of empathy in this situation?

3. What may happen if you don't use empathy?

4. Would it be helpful to inform the other person of your intention to try to be a better listener and to ask for his or her support as you try out this approach? Why or why not?

———◆·◆·◆———

INFOTECH

Old communication paradigms are being replaced by new technologies and application dynamics. The Internet is generating unprecedented data traffic, and customers are no longer tolerant of routine network downtime. But this evolution is about more than data. It's about optical networking, which is creating virtually unlimited capacity and mind-boggling speed. It's about wireless systems that offer mobility without sacrificing quality or reliability. And it's about the need for networks of networks that can handle data or voice, wired or wireless, and optical or electronic signals with equal aplomb. It's not just a data networking revolution or a voice networking revolution. It's a communications networking revolution, and police agencies are at the center of it.

The communications revolution is really about liberating communications from the confines of one medium or protocol. It's about how and where and why we communicate, and it will change forever the way we work, play, shop, and socialize.

The industrial age manufactured things, whereas the communications age is intended to provide knowledge. The computer, and especially the personal computer (PC), is presently the driving force. The PC has given us new applications, online systems, Internet connections, electronic mail, multimedia titles, and a host of games.

Technological advancements are racing toward us all, creating a world in which information is both advantage and freedom. This is a world where time and space are decreased, where computers operate faster, taking up a fraction of the space and communicating across networks without borders. We hear it every day: "cyberspace," "wired," "on demand," "seamless access," "virtual reality," and "fun." But what does it all really mean to you? Does it make your job easier? Does it make your life better? We are becoming a society that is in touch, but . . . not touched!

Microsoft's Bill Gates asserts that the current information revolution, with all of its unresolved confusion and challenges, is but a porous foundation for the incoming second revolution in communications. (In fact, he refers to the present global information highway as more like a lot of country lanes.) The dimensions of the second revolution are still vague, but are likely to involve increasing speeds, inexpensive communications, global interconnections, and customer-driven applications. The most fundamental difference we'll see in future information is that almost all of it will be digital. The latter point means that the cyber-executives will ask us what we want and then they'll build it for us. Bill Gates sees technology as responsible for providing us with more flexibility and efficiency.

Forward-looking police supervisors-as-leaders will have numerous opportunities to perform better in the years ahead if they are able to strike a balance between "high-tech" and "high-touch." An over-concentration on high-tech will cost them leadership; an overemphasis on high-touch will cause them obsolescence. While the Internet, e-mail, and fax machines have enhanced the movement of information, they in turn are impeding interpersonal communication. There is no substitute for face-to-face communications. We see "fax potatoes" emerging. They'll fax or e-mail you a message, rather than walk a few feet to communicate with you in person. We're getting tons of information with only a few pounds of knowledge. Technology is frequently sold as the panacea of all work-related problems. It is alluring and habit-forming to the detriment of much-needed person-to-person contacts. (I would urge that all computers be programmed to periodically shut down, thus ensuring the supervisor prime time for two-way, face-to-face conversations with his staff.)

Volume

Communication is costly. Every message involves the expenditure of time spent deciding what to send, the time spent composing the message, the cost of transmitting the message (which may consist of time or money, or both), and the time spent receiving the message. Consequently, the volume of messages in an organization is of real concern to everyone. *The more information there is, the more difficult it is for communication to succeed.*

Every individual has a saturation point regarding the amount of information that can be usefully handled in a given time period. In this case, both the volume and the length of the message can overload an individual beyond the saturation point. When overloaded, a person will be unable either to comprehend the information provided or to use it effectively. All of this means that the particular methods used by a police organization to collect, select, and transmit information are critically important determinants of its success.

The volume of messages in a police organization is determined by seven basic factors:

- The total number of members in the organization
- The nature of its communication networks (downward, upward, or seamless)
- The transmission regulations controlling when and to whom messages are sent
- The degree of interdependence among the organization's various activities
- The speed with which relevant changes occur in its external environment
- The search mechanisms and procedures used by the organization to investigate its environment
- The amount (e.g., everyone has a portable radio) and type (e.g., e-mail) of communications technology in the department

High message volume usually results in overloading. Attempts are automatically made to reduce any overloading. Police supervisors can react to this situation in one or more of the following ways. First, they can slow down their handling of messages without changing the organization's network structure or transmission rules. This action will cause the police department to reduce its speed of reaction to events and thereby lessen its output. Second, they can change the transmission rules so that their subordinates screen out more information before sending messages. This reaction also reduces the quantity of the department's output. Third, they can add more channels to the existing network to accommodate the same quantity of messages in the same time period. This reaction provides more opportunities for message distortion and is more expensive. Fourth, they can relate tasks within the organization so that those units with the highest message traffic are grouped together within the overall communications system. This action reduces the volume of messages sent through higher levels in the network and facilitates the coordination of effort. Fifth, they can improve the quality of the messages in order to reduce the time needed for receiving, composing, and transmitting them. Furthermore, besides bettering the content and format of messages, the supervisor can decide on more advantageous methods for handling them.

The supervisor's energy is being suffocated and his time trapped by Infotech. They're being buried in an avalanche of paper, accosted by more and more telephone calls, and bombarded by incessant e-mail. Many are also being burdened by "collateral" assignments. Now the kicker—they're expected to lead others, which means being visible, being in front, and serving as an example to their team members. Something's got to give here.

Why Don't We Communicate Better?

We started this chapter with the three main reasons that we communicate with one another. In review, they are:

- To be a leader
- To make decisions
- To establish trust

After covering what it is, what we know about it, where and how we do it, we've arrived at an end point of again asking "why?" In this instance, "Why aren't we doing a better job of understanding one another?" We have the need; we have the training and education; we know it's vital for the supervisor-as-leader, and we have incredible technology. But we're not as successful as we should or could be.

There are a few reasons and hundreds of excuses. I'll cover the reasons:

Listening

Now you may be an active and empathetic listener; I'm not. I try, but I must work harder at it. Many of us will proudly and confidently assert, "One of my strongest skills is I'm a good listener." Really? Have you ever asked anyone? If a supervisor fails in his job, most often, not listening is the major underlying cause. You and I must become better listeners.

Infotech

It's not easy to develop trust and sometimes understanding in an e-mail or fax message. One-way messages are typically one-way and impersonal. Worse still, such Infotech encourages us to be the great communicator. "With one touch of a key I can send my message to tens, hundreds, or more people." This thinking is the cause of information high and low understanding. Infotech has its place. If used properly, it promises many advantages. If abused, it reduces the supervisor's chances of becoming a leader. Use Infotech as necessary, but remember—it is not leadership.

Race

I believe that one's race per se is not the significant reason for being unable to communicate with a person of another race. It is convenient and a common practice assume so. Unfortunately, it is frequently proffered as a reason we fail to understand one another, when in fact, the other culprits of communication are: culture, gender, and generations.

Culture

One's culture consists of such prominent factors as: language, mores, art, music, and religion. In this case, one's culture may and usually does present a challenge to achieving mutual understanding. Think about it; you're a police supervisor, and your new team member is from a different culture. English is a second language, and the mores, music, and art are "different." Now, add religion to this mix. The supervisor-as-leader has a definite challenge here. Supervisors-as-leaders pursue a capability for bridging cultural gaps while cementing foundations of understanding.

Gender

In respect to gender differences, the French refer to it by "vive la difference." Yet the entire world always has and continues to grope for answers to our inability to effectively understand each other. Researchers are concentrating on the reduction of eons of confusion. (See for example: John Grey, *Men Are From Mars, Women Are From Venus*.) As more females engage in police work, supervision, and management, this dimension is exacerbated. Many of us are prone to rationalize or outright ignore the situation. By now you may be looking for a pat answer to centuries of gender-driven misunderstanding. I don't have an answer. I am, however, sincerely attempting to better understand and thus be understood by my female colleagues.

Generations

Little attention is paid to the several generations that must co-exist in our world as being not just an issue but a major problem in our quest for better understanding. We hear and read about such generations as "Baby Boomers,"

"Baby Busters," "Gen-X," and the venerated "Great Generation." Each one has its own paradigms on values, ethics, family, success, and so on. The older generations typically disparage the younger ones. At times it seriously injures mutual understanding.

The police sergeant of one generation thinks, "The new officers are all screwed up." The officer thinks, "Wow, are these supervisors out of touch." Each generation reaches for the easy explanation; it must be a difference (conflict) in our race, gender, or culture. Thus ignored is how deeply enormous and incredibly complex our generational differences are. And how powerful they are in messing with our need and ability to communicate with and understand one another.

Structured Exercise 4–2

This is an awareness exercise. The questions asked require thoughtful and hard answers. No rationalizations, wishes or "sounds good to me" allowed. It also encourages feedback. (Supervisors-as-leaders thrive on feedback.) Circle the number that reflects where you are now on a particular dimension, and box the number where you hope to be in 12 months.

	Miss A Lot						Very Active
Listening	1	2	3	4	5	6	7
	Misuse It						Proper Use
Infotech	1	2	3	4	5	6	7
	Unaware						Very Aware
Race	1	2	3	4	5	6	7
	Unaware						Very Aware
Culture	1	2	3	4	5	6	7
	Unaware						Very Aware
Gender	1	2	3	4	5	6	7
	Unaware						Very Aware
Generation	1	2	3	4	5	6	7

The next step is equally important. Ask someone who you respect and is candid to orally respond with a number to each one of the above questions. Compare your responses with theirs. What have you learned about your ability to communicate with other people?

KEY POINTS

- Communication is our most important human skill.
- The supervisor communicates to: be a leader; make decisions; and establish trust.
- Communication is the transfer of meaning so that understanding will occur within a particular environment.
- Communication is influenced by our perceptions and expectations; makes demands on us; is related to but different than information; and is best when not "one-way," and better still by example.
- Communication channels are of two types, formal and informal, and they flow in directions: down, up, and across/diagonal.
- We transmit messages four ways: orally, in writing, via nonverbal cues, and electronically.
- The volume of messages received and sent by a supervisor impacts their effectiveness. Too many is as harmful as not enough.
- The barriers to improved understanding within a police agency center on: listening; Infotech; race; culture; gender; and generations.

DISCUSSION

1. What are other reasons we communicate besides those cited in the section "Why Do We Communicate?"
2. What information do we usually find moving in a formal channel as compared with informal channels?
3. Of the four main methods for communicating, which is best? Why?
4. In which direction is it most difficult for a supervisor to communicate (up, down, across/diagonal)? Why?
5. Of the five communication networks, which is best? Why?
6. What have you or your organization done recently to improve the human communication process?
7. When have you either performed or observed empathic listening? What did the listener actually do?
8. How has communication technology helped you in your job? How has it caused you problems?
9. Review with others the results of Structured Exercise 4–2. Afterward, generate an action plan for correcting any deficiencies in the group's ability to understand one another.

TIME MANAGEMENT

The police supervisor is responsible for self-management, which assures precious time for making prudent decisions on job-related matters.

Nine-tenths of wisdom is being wise in time.

—Theodore Roosevelt

Now that you have acquired a greater understanding and appreciation of your values (Responsibility One) and ethics (Responsibility Two), and of how to communicate (Responsibility Four) a vision (Responsibility Three), you are prepared to manage yourself, and in turn your time (Responsibility Five), in their application.

My time is very important to me. I'm sure you feel the same. When I waste my time, I'm frustrated, even sore. I'm sure you feel the same. Time is one of our top priorities. Yet it seems we have so little of it. This chapter will help you as a supervisor-as-leader to master it.

Imagine there is a bank that credits your account each morning with $86,400. It carries over no balance from day to day. Every evening the bank deletes whatever part of the balance you failed to use during the day. What would you do? Draw out every cent, of course!

Each of us has such a bank. Its name is "TIMES." Every morning it credits you with 86,400 seconds. Every night it writes off, as lost, whatever of this you have failed to invest to good purpose. It carries over no balance. It allows no overdraft. Each day it opens a new account for you. Each night it burns the remains of the day. If you fail to use the day's deposits, the loss is yours. There is no going back. There is no drawing against "tomorrow." You must live in the present on today's deposits. Invest it so as to get from it the utmost in health, happiness, and success! The clock is running.

Have you ever heard or used the expression "I'll save some time by taking this approach?" Or "I really lost a lot of time by doing it that way?" Time is not ours to bank or spend. It is a precisely measured period of seconds, minutes, and hours that eventually become a day, and with a great deal of time, we arrive at a new millennium.

> *On May 6, 1954, Roger Bannister achieved a major breakthrough in time—he ran a 3:59:6 mile. Now, many track athletes have run a sub-four-minute mile. Will the year 2003 see a sub-three-and-a-half-minute mile or a sub-two-minute-mile marathon? The athletes that eventually will succeed in doing so will not be managing time; they'll be managing themselves.*

Once you've finished this chapter, you'll be managing your time by better managing yourself. This responsibility will, if you truly intend to manage your time, require much more thought and effort than the mere number of pages would suggest. You'll discover that much of what you will do depends on the accomplishment of the four prior responsibilities. If you have those well in mind, you'll find the steps necessary for fulfilling Responsibility Five to be richly rewarding and even fun. Moreover, you'll be closer to what we earlier assumed you sought to become—a police supervisor-as-leader.

A COUPLE OF QUESTIONS FOR YOU

On a sheet of paper, write down short answers to the following questions. (Later on you'll find that your responses are important—be certain to write your answers.)

First, what one thing could you do consistently (but are not doing now) that would make a significant change in your personal life?

Second, what one thing in your career life would cause similar results?

OUR MISSION

> We gain control of time and events by understanding how they relate to our mission.

Responsibility Five is the exercise of our independent will for becoming a more effective supervisor, which automatically means a more effective person. We do not lead a compartmentalized life. The various roles that we play out in life definitely overlap and influence one another. If you spot a wise time manager at work, you'll probably discover that this individual also prudently manages time as a father or mother, family member, sports participant, hobby enthusiast, and so on. Conversely, the worker who is managed by time, who misses deadline dates, is late for work, or is unprepared to do the tasks is probably the same way in attempting to fulfill other life roles.

Hence, our approach to time management must involve the total you. Dealing with your role of supervisor exclusively would be meaningless, or at best a long list of "to-do's," many of which would never get done. Obviously, we'll concentrate on making your time at work more productive. At the same time, remember when I use the term "mission," I mean your comprehensive mission in life—the total you.

PEOPLE, PEOPLE, PEOPLE

A nationally recognized business leader wrote, "My firm basically is comprised of manufacturing, service, and people. In order of importance they are: people, people, people."

If you accept the preceding premise that people are a police agency's greatest asset, then supervisors must understand how to bind them together in a culture wherein they feel truly motivated to achieve high goals. Face-to-face communication, ongoing training and development, creative incentive programs, and job security all display the sort of sensitivity that nurtures strong departmental cultures. Every strong culture derives from management's sensitivity. Without it, police employees feel unmotivated, underused, and even exploited. Building the kind of work culture and work team you want obviously takes time. Quality time. PRIORITY TIME.

TIME DIMENSION

Time\tim\n[Me,fr]: the measured or measurable period during which an action, process, or condition exists or continues.

One complexity is ever-present in every supervisory job: Every decision, every action demands due consideration of the time dimension. Supervisors have to assess both today and tomorrow—the present and the future. Little Orphan Annie sang in the musical of the 1980s, "Tomorrow, tomorrow, tomorrow is only a day away."

The challenge of harmonizing today and tomorrow exists in all areas, and especially with people. The time dimension is inherent in supervision because supervision is concerned with decisions for action. The time dimension influences decisions for progress (e.g., crime reduction, crime prevention). Finally, the supervisor's time dimension entails the future. One international airline's motto is "Being prepared in everything." The successful police supervisor is in constant preparation for the incoming unnecessary future—the next event, the next decision, the next risk, all the while knowing that they'll be different.

Again, a time for action, a time for progress, and a time for tomorrow—you've got to get a grip on this threefold time dimension.

SELF-MASTERY OF TIME

One of Albert Einstein's brilliant contributions to modern physics was his intuition that linear time, along with everything happening in it, is superficial. Time seems to flow and move; clocks tick off their seconds, minutes, and hours; eons of history unfold and disappear. But ultimately, Einstein held, this vast activity is all relative, meaning that it has no absolute value.

Einstein displaced linear time with something much more fluid—time that can contract and expand, slow down and speed up. He often compared this to subjective time, for he noted that spending a minute sitting on a hot stove seems like an hour, while spending an hour with an attractive companion seems like a minute. What he meant by this is that time depends on the situation of the observer.

We all have a sense that time expands and contracts, seeming to drag one moment and race the next, but what is our constant, our absolute? It is "me," our core sense of self. The clock doesn't lie about how much linear time has elapsed "out there." But subjective time, the kind that exists only "in here," is a different matter. If you're bored, time hangs heavy; if you're desperate, time is running out; if you're exhilarated, time flies; when you're in love, time stands still. In other words, whenever you take an attitude toward time, you are really saying something about yourself. Time, in the subjective sense, is a mirror.

Time Pressure = Stress

Time pressure causes stress hormones to be released into the body, which in turn elevates heartbeat. If the person struggles against this reaction, his situation only gets worse. Now his heart has to put up with time pressure and frustration. When heart patients are given demanding tasks under a deadline, a significant number grow so agitated that their heart muscles actually suffer "silent" heart attacks ("silent" meaning that damage is occurring, but without any sensation of pain).

The element of time pressure also alters behavior, attitudes, and physiological responses. So subjective time can be an incredibly powerful force. It's no accident that the word "deadline" contains the word "dead."

Some people are much more sensitive to stress than others. One feels time pressure as a threat; the other feels it as a challenge. One feels thrown out of control; the other feels impelled to test his or her sense of control and improve upon it.

Boundaryless Time

We are the only creatures on earth who can change our biology by what we think and feel. Being able to identify with a reality that is not bounded by time is extremely important; otherwise, there is no escape from the tyranny that time inevitably brings. Linear time (the clock) fools us into thinking that one minute follows another with equal spacing, but change your reference for a moment to *subjective time*. You can catch a glimpse of timelessness with a simple mind-body exercise.

Structured Exercise 5-1

Choose a time of day when you feel relaxed and unpressured. Sit quietly in a comfortable chair and take off your watch, placing it nearby so that you can easily refer to it without having to lift or move your head very much. Now close your eyes and be aware of your breathing. Let your attention easily follow the stream of breath going in and out of your body. Imagine your whole body rising and falling with the flow of each breath. After a minute or two, you will be aware of warmth and relaxation pervading your muscles.

When you feel very settled and quiet inside, slowly open your eyes and peek at the second hand of your watch. What's it doing? Depending on how relaxed you are, the second hand will behave in different ways. For some people, it will have stopped entirely, and this effect will last anywhere from one to perhaps three seconds. For other people, the second hand will hesitate for half a second and then jump into its normal ticking. Still other people will perceive the second hand moving, but at a slower pace than usual. Unless you have tried this little experiment, it seems very unlikely, but once you have had the experience of seeing a watch stop, you will never again doubt that time is a product of perception. The time you are aware of is the only time there is.

Eastern philosophy and Western science together inform us that:

- While perception appears to be automatic, it is, in fact, a learned phenomenon. The world you live in, including the experience of your body, is completely dictated by how you learned to perceive it. If you change your perception paradigm, you change the experience of your body and your world.
- Time does not exist as an absolute, but only in relationship to eternity. Time is quantified by eternity, timelessness chopped up into bits and pieces (seconds, hours, days, years) by us. What we call linear time is a reflection of how we perceive change.

TIME AND PRODUCTIVITY

Most of us want to feel productive. Those who do feel this way do not want to waste their time. After all, time is our most perishable resource. There is nothing less productive than idle time of capital equipment (patrol cars) or wasted time of highly paid and able police employees. Equally unproductive—even counterproductive—may be jamming more work effort into time than it will comfortably hold—for instance, the attempt to provide full patrol coverage by repeatedly paying overtime to officers who are daily becoming more fatigued and less quality-conscious.

Time and productivity are causally linked. You have to pay attention to both factors. However, solid time management is the forerunner of highly productive supervisors.

OVERLOADS

Many years ago you would hear police supervisors complain, "I don't get enough information to do my job." The 1950s started to flip such statements to where today we hear "Good grief, there's just too much information. I don't have the time to process it!"

There have never been more media—new television networks and channels, video and film, record numbers of new magazines, newsletters, journals, and newspapers—dedicated to delivering you the changing news of the day. Compounding this is the computer—desktops, laptops, in-car terminals, and even wrist-tops. You don't have to look for a telephone today—they're in airplanes, trains, and automobiles and frequently on a person's hip. We have e-mail and voice mail. Then there is the omnipresent fax. Finally, we have the advanced photocopying machines—"Let's make a copy for everybody!"

What are you absorbing? Do you have the time to process the multitude of incoming messages, much less add yours to the information glut? Incidentally, have you noticed that the so-called paperless society actually has more paper than before? And while you're receiving and sending more information much faster, much of it doesn't make sense, or you haven't the time to make sense out of it.

> Without a structure, a frame of reference, the vast amount of data that comes your way each day will probably whiz right by you.

Probably in reaction to the overloads of his day, Lao Tzu wrote nearly 4,000 years ago to the leaders of China:

Endless drama in a group clouds consciousness. Too much noise overloads the senses. Continual input obscures genuine insight. Do not substitute sensationalism for learning.

Allow regular time for silent reflection. Turn inward and digest what has happened. Let the senses rest and grow still.

Teach people to let go of their superficial mental chatter and obsessions. Teach people to pay attention to the whole body's reaction to a situation.

When group members have time to reflect, they can see more clearly what is essential in themselves and others.

It takes time for reflection. Overloads attempt to block such time allocation. The supervisor must assign reflection a high priority. Otherwise, any endeavor to manage one's time is doomed to fail.

Structured Exercise 5–2

Questionnaire: How Do You Experience Time?

Read the following sentences and check off each one that applies to you fairly often or that you generally agree with. Some of the statements in Part I may seem to contradict others in Part II, but that doesn't matter. Even if you have seemingly opposed traits and opinions, answer each statement on its own.

Part I

_____   **1.** There's barely enough time in the day to do all the things I have to do.

_____   **2.** I'm sometimes too exhausted at night to get to sleep.

_____   **3.** I've had to abandon several important goals I set for myself when I was younger.

_____   **4.** I'm less idealistic than I used to be.

_____   **5.** It bothers me to let unpaid bills sit around.

_____   **6.** I'm more cautious now about making new friends and entering serious relationships.

_____   **7.** I've learned a lot from the school of hard knocks.

_____   **8.** I spend more time and attention on my career than on my friends and family.

_____   **9.** I could be a lot wiser about how I spend my money.

_____   **10.** Life is a balance of losses and gains; I just try to have more gains than losses.

_____   **11.** In a loving relationship, the other person should be counted on to meet my needs.

_____   **12.** It sometimes hurts to remember the people I have let down.

_____   **13.** Being loved is one of the most important things I can think of.

_____   **14.** I don't like authority figures.

_____   **15.** For me, one of the most frightening prospects about old age is loneliness.

Part I score _____

Part II

_____ **1.** I do what I love. I love what I do.

_____ **2.** It's important to have a greater purpose in life than just family and career.

_____ **3.** I feel unique.

_____ **4.** Near-death experiences are very real.

_____ **5.** I often forget what day it is.

_____ **6.** I would describe myself as a carefree person.

_____ **7.** It's a good thing to bring sexual issues out in the open, even when they are disturbing.

_____ **8.** I work for myself.

_____ **9.** It doesn't bother me to miss reading the newspaper or watching the evening news.

_____ **10.** I love myself.

_____ **11.** I've spent time in therapy and/or other self-development practices.

_____ **12.** I don't buy into everything about the New Age, but it intrigues me.

_____ **13.** I believe it is possible to know God.

_____ **14.** I am more leisurely about things than most people.

_____ **15.** I consider myself a spiritual person: This is an area of my life I work on.

Part II score _____

EVALUATING YOUR SCORE.   Although everyone usually checks at least a few answers in both sections, you will probably find that you scored higher in one section than the other.

If you scored higher on Part I, you tend to be time-bound. For you, time is linear; it often runs short and will eventually run out. Relying on outside approval, motivation, and love, you have not grappled with your inner world as much as with the external one. You are likely to value excitement and positive emotions more highly than inner peace and non-attachment. You may cherish being loved by others too much and lose the opportunity to find self-acceptance.

If you scored higher on Part II, you tend to be timeless in your awareness. Your sense of loving and being loved is based on a secure relationship with yourself. You value detachment over possessiveness; your motivations tend to be internal, rather than external. At some time in your life, you developed a sense of being larger than your limited physical self; your life may have been shaped by decisive experiences of a spiritual nature or your higher self. Where others fear loneliness, you are grateful for your aloneness—solitude has developed your ability to know who you are.

————◆◦◆◦◆————

IF IT'S WORTH DOING, IT'S WORTH DOING POORLY

Take a moment and reread the title of this section. This comment was made by a very successful person. Think about it. Before reading further, attempt to develop some type of a rationale for refuting or confirming "If it's worth doing, it's worth doing poorly."

Let us now add—to make the best use of your time, you have to make a habit of using it flat out. Conversely, do you not agree with the proposition that working hard is not necessarily the same as working smart? One more thought—are working hard and working fast synonymous?

Many of us prefer fast decisions to slowness and wrong ones to none at all. Throughout his writings, Tom Peters challenges us to "move, move, move." The preceding heading essentially means that if something is vitally important, make a decision quickly. It may cause less-than-perfect results (even poor results), but the fact remains that someone is taking on the problem. It's the quick and timely response, with the underlying knowledge that you're doing the best you can. Now the big but—slow decisions are usually better than fast ones. It has been demonstrated again and again that shared or participative decision-making produces significantly better results. Further, shared decision-making typically builds in a commitment on the part of those involved to implement it.

Fast or slow—which should it be? No doubt both approaches impact on your truly irreplaceable commodity—time. I believe the answer to this puzzle is both—sometimes a fast, sometimes a slow application of time. Both have their place in police organizations. An emergency situation (e.g., a robbery in progress) obviously requires fast decisions, a fast time frame. Many supervisors make all decisions quickly, when in most cases there is ample time to involve those who are going to be affected in the decisions. Getting one or two really good ideas normally requires getting a lot of ideas at first. Later we'll consider "empowerment." Fast decisions impede empowerment.

I'm not against fast decisions. At times they're needed. What I am arguing for is flexibility. Sometimes fast, sometimes slow—it all depends on the situation.

FOUR GENERATIONS OF TIME MANAGEMENT

According to Steve Covey, a management consultant, there are four generations of time management. Each one builds on the other. The first three conform to this axiom: Organize and execute around priorities. The first generation is characterized by notes and checklists. It essentially recognizes the varying demands made on our time. The second generation is epitomized by calendars and appointment books. Here we see an endeavor to schedule ahead. The third generation portrays the most prevalent form of time management. It takes the above two and adds the dimension of prioritization. It focuses on values toward which time and energy are allocated. (The higher the priority of a value, the more time spent.) It is planning with a purpose. The emerging fourth generation recognizes that "time management" is misconstrued! The challenge is not to manage time; after all, time by its very nature manages itself. Rather than concentrating on activities and time, the fourth generation emphasizes preserving and enhancing relationships and getting results through teamwork.

Time Management Matrix

The matrix in Table 5–1 categorizes activities or things as fast or slow and as critical or non-critical. Fast activities press us to respond now. Critical matters have to do with results, the fulfillment of our job duties.

Category I is both fast and critical. All of us operate on occasion in this area. Regretfully, some become habitual crises persons. Push, push, faster, faster. These people are frequently task-driven and aggressive. Unfortunately, they beat themselves up while tackling the crises (e.g., experience stress, burnout, overloads; are always putting out fires). When exhausted, they often retreat to Category IV, with little attention paid to Category II. There are others who spend a lot of time in Category III, believing that they're in Category I. They are confronting crises all right, only the issues are relatively unimportant in terms of their mission. In fact, they are likely responding to the values and expectations of others. Those of us who spend most of our time in Categories III and IV basically lead irresponsible lives.

Category II is the crux of managing ourselves. It deals with things that do not require a fast response, but are critical, such as trust-building, enhancement of candid communications, long-range planning, physical exercise, preparation, and renewal. These are high-leverage, capacity-expansion activities.

Table 5–1 Time Management Matrix

	Fast	Slow
	Critical	
	I	II
	Activities	Activities
	Crises (shots fired)	Prevention of conflicts
	Pressing problems (computers down)	Relationship-building
	Deadline-driven projects (staff reports)	Recognition of new opportunities
		Planning, recreation
		Team building
	Non-critical	
	III	IV
	Activities	Activities
	Interruptions, some calls (open door)	Trivia, busy work
	Some mail, some reports (In basket)	Some mail
	Some meetings (roll call)	Some phone calls
	Proximate, pressing matters (evaluation)	Time-wasters
	Popular activities (code 7)	Pleasant activities

Stop—now take a look at the two answers you wrote down earlier. What category do they fit in? They probably relate to Category II. But because they do not require a ready-aim-fire response, we neglect them. Your effectiveness will measurably grow if you focus on them. They will make a tremendous, positive difference in your professional and personal lives.

Just Say No

The only place to get time for Category II in the beginning is from Categories III and IV. You can't ignore the urgent and important activities of Category I, although it will shrink in size as you spend more time with prevention and preparation in Category II. But the initial time for Category II has to come out of III and IV. You have to be proactive to work on Category II because Categories I and III suck you in. To say "yes" to critical Category II priorities, you have to learn to say "no" to other activities, sometimes apparently urgent things. We expect kids to "just say no to drugs;" as adults, we are equally capable of just saying "no" to the time-wasters.

Time-Wasters

Please turn to Structured Exercise 5–3 and complete it before reading further.

Now compare your list with those that are most commonly cited (in rank order):

1. Telephone interruptions
2. Drop-in visitors
3. Meetings (scheduled and unscheduled)
4. Crisis
5. Lack of objectives
6. Cluttered desk and personal disorganization
7. Ineffective delegation of responsibilities and too much involvement in routines and details
8. Too much work attempted at once and unrealistic time estimates
9. Lack of or unclear communications or instructions
10. Inadequate, inaccurate, or delayed information
11. Indecision and procrastination
12. Confused responsibility and authority
13. Inability to say "no"
14. Tasks left unfinished
15. Lack of self-discipline

I believe that the last point (lack of self-discipline) is the principal villain and essentially allows the other 14 wasters to surface and bug us.

Structured Exercise 5–3

The major contributors to wasting my time at work are as follows:

1. _____
2. _____
3. _____
4. _____
5. _____
6. _____
7. _____
8. _____
9. _____
10. _____

As a group, compare the time-wasters. Look for similarities. Discuss what might be done to lessen their adverse impact on you and others in the group.

ON BECOMING A CATEGORY II POLICE SUPERVISOR

The objective of a Category II supervisor is to manage his life effectively—from a center of sound principles, from a knowledge of his overall (career and personal) mission, with a focus on the "critical" as well as the "fast," and within the framework of maintaining a balance between increasing his actual production and increasing his capability for producing.

Category II organizing requires you to:

- Produce an individual mission statement
- Identify your roles
- Select your goals
- Use weekly scheduling
- Take action and be flexible

Your Mission Statement

First of all, return to Responsibility One and write down on a separate sheet of paper the top six or seven values that you identified at that point. Using those values, create a one-page mission statement for yourself. (It is likely this will take three or four drafts before you are pleased with it.)

I'll try to help you by presenting a hypothetical: Phillip Clark, police sergeant, age 27, is married with two children. Clark's core values were, in rank order, 1) integrity, 2) spouse, 3) children, 4) parents, 5) police work, 6) house, 7) financial security, and 8) physical and mental health. Here is what he might have written.

MISSION STATEMENT
PHILLIP D. CLARK
AGE TWENTY-SEVEN

My mission in life is to demonstrate integrity consistently in myself and with others as follows:

- I will love and care for my wife, being certain that she is receiving top-priority time.
- I will serve as an example of responsible citizenship for my children. They will be daily recipients of my love and help.
- (and so forth)

All right, once you've finished your mission statement you're ready to move to identifying your various roles in life.

Your Roles

The first step is to record your main roles. Write down what immediately comes to mind. You have a role as an individual. You may want to list one or more roles as a family member—husband or wife, mother or father, son or daughter, member of the extended family of grandparents, aunts, uncles, and cousins. You certainly want to list a few roles in your police job, indicating different areas in which you wish to invest time and energy on a regular basis. You may have roles in church or community affairs. (Your mission statement will coach you on what they are.)

You don't need to worry about defining the roles in a way that you will live with forever—just preview the week and write down the areas where you see yourself spending time during the next seven days. For example, our Sergeant Clark might list the following seven roles:

1. Husband
2. Father
3. Son and brother
4. Police sergeant—human relations
5. Police sergeant—production
6. Self-growth—mental and physical
7. Investor

Note how Clark's values, mission statement, and roles are integrated, systematic, and indeed logically compelling. Complete this step for yourself now, and then proceed to the next.

Your Goals

It's late Sunday afternoon, and Sergeant Clark has set aside 30 minutes for managing himself during the ensuing week. Clark lists the following:

Role	Goals
Husband	Discuss vacation plans; review life insurance; schedule dinner and a movie; ask about her job.
Father	Discuss schoolwork; play one group game; play one individual game; develop a new sport.
Son and brother	Phone parents; send photographs of family; write sister.
Police sergeant—human relations	Complete performance evaluations; counsel Officer Mead; meet with each officer for coffee (15 minutes each).
Police sergeant—production	Analyze called-for services; prepare a problem-oriented approach to a major need; assess assigned equipment.
Self-growth—mental and physical	Read assigned textbook chapters; read *Time* and and 50 pages in fiction book; exercise five times for 50 minutes; read national newspaper daily.
Investor	Paint interior of small bathroom (first coat); read *Money* magazine; assess CDs.

You're probably wondering how in the world Clark is going to accomplish all of the preceding goals. At this point it is straightforward, and all he has to do is schedule. It is now your turn to specify your goals for the next week. Stop here and do so.

Your Schedule

Now you can look at the week ahead with your goals in mind and schedule time to achieve them. For example, if your goal is to telephone your parents, you may want to set aside a 15-minute block of time on Sunday to do it. Sunday is often the ideal time to plan your weekly organizing.

If you set a goal to become physically fit through exercise, you may want to set aside an hour three or four days during the week, or possibly every day during the week, to accomplish that goal. There are some goals that you may be able to accomplish only during work hours or some that you can do only on Saturday when your children are home. Do you now see some of the advantages of organizing the week instead of the day? Having identified roles and set goals, you can translate each goal to a specific day of the week, either as a priority item or, even better, as a specific appointment.

Let's return to our Sergeant Clark to illustrate what must be done at this juncture. To begin with, he has to 1) divide up the goals on a per-day basis and 2) at the same time assign them a priority. We'll cover Monday and Tuesday as examples of what you'll soon be doing:

	Monday	Tuesday
Priorities	*Complete performance evaluations*	*Meet with officers*
	Meet with officers	Assess equipment
	Analyze called-for services	Counsel Mead
	Read assigned text	Read assigned text
	Exercise fifty minutes	Exercise fifty minutes
	Schoolwork	College class
Time	*Activity*	*Activity*
0500–0600	Awaken 0530	Awaken 0530
0600–0700	Jog	Drive to work
0700–0800	Drive to work	Lift weights
	Audio tape on current affairs	
0800–0900	Briefings/roll call	Briefings/roll call
0900–1000	Meeting with officers	Meeting with officers
1000–1100	Performance evaluations	Meeting with officers
1100–1200	Performance evaluations	Review reports
1200–1300	Lunch/read text	Lunch/read text
1300–1400	Analyze called-for services	Assess equipment
1400–1500	Field supervision	Counsel Mead
1500–1600	Field supervision	Field supervision
1600–1700	Report review	Report review
1700–1800	Drive home	Drive to college/dinner
1800–1900	Dinner	College course
1900–2000	Review schoolwork	College course
2000–2100	Games with children	College course
2100–2200	Alone time with wife	Drive home/wife

Structured Exercise 5–4

Take a few moments and concentrate on the key tasks that make up your job. If with co-workers, compare the results of your analyses.

The following Job-Time Analysis Form is provided to help you assess the specific areas of time management in which you need improvement. List the individual tasks you perform on the job, and complete each column for each task.

Job task	What percentage of my time does it consume?	What is its priority (high, medium, or low)?	Do I like or dislike performing it?	Can I delegate it?	Is it discretionary or nondiscretionary?

After completing the Job-Time Analysis Form, review it for accuracy. Showing the analysis to colleagues at work and learning their opinion might be helpful in this respect. After ensuring the accuracy of the completed analysis, answer each of the following questions:

1. What unnecessary tasks am I performing?
2. On which tasks am I spending too much time?
3. On which tasks am I spending too little time?
4. What tasks am I performing that could be performed better by others?
5. What specific changes do I plan to make in the way I manage my time?

It's time for us to integrate another step with the preceding ones. Turn to Structured Exercise 5–5 and fill in the blanks. (Remember to prioritize your goals before scheduling the specific activities.) For future time management planning, you're welcome to copy and use the form or design one of your own. Obviously, the time frames will vary according to night- or early morning-shift work. One more reminder: keep the Category II activities prominent in your goal setting, prioritizing, and scheduling.

Action and Flexibility

With Category II weekly organizing, daily action becomes more of a response to daily adaptations, prioritizing activities and adjusting to emergent circumstances, relationships, and experiences in a systematic way. As mentioned earlier, you can analyze each incoming day and fine-tune your schedule as appropriate. (Your after-work travel home or elsewhere is often a convenient time to review the immediate past and confirm your schedule for tomorrow.) You're now organizing and executing around your goals and priorities. While you actually cannot manage time, you certainly can manage yourself—if you want to.

Structured Exercise 5-5

The WEEKLY WORKSHEET		Week of:	Sunday	Monday	Tuesday	Wednesday	Thursday	Friday	Saturday
Roles	Goals	Weekly Priorities	Today's Priorities						
			Appointments/Commitments			Appointments/Commitments			
			8	8	8	8	8	8	8
			9	9	9	9	9	9	9
			10	10	10	10	10	10	10
			11	11	11	11	11	11	11
			12	12	12	12	12	12	12
			1	1	1	1	1	1	1
			2	2	2	2	2	2	2
			3	3	3	3	3	3	3
			4	4	4	4	4	4	4
			5	5	5	5	5	5	5
			6	6	6	6	6	6	6
			7	7	7	7	7	7	7
			8	8	8	8	8	8	8
			Evening	Evening	Evening	Evening	Evening	Evening	Evening

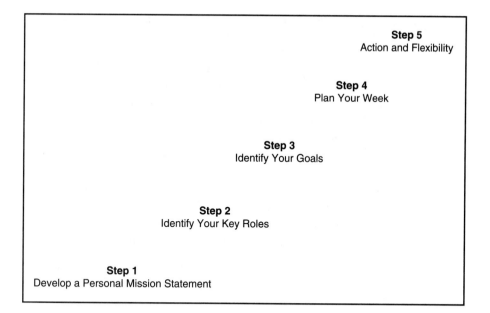

Figure 5–1   Fourth Generation: Five Steps to Effective Management of Priorities

KEY POINTS

Fourth-generation management is devoted to ensuring us that as we manage ourselves, we more effectively supervise others. It is a constant reminder that people are always more important than things. It has been successful because:

- It is value-laden; it encompasses our driving forces.
- It is conscience-focused; it helps us make the correct choices about what comes first, second, and so on.
- We can change our experience with time by changing what we think and feel.
- Time does not exist as an absolute.
- It defines our individual mission, including values and goals that are prioritized.
- It is an alignment of various life roles, allowing us to schedule time accordingly.
- It provides an expanded framework for organizing by scheduling weekly activities.

DISCUSSION

1. If working as a group, divide into subgroups of five to six people, and review your responses to Structured Exercise 5–3. Subsequently, share the contents with one another. Attempt to identify one or two common time-wasters.

2. Earlier you were asked to write down the answers to two questions that I had posed. (See "A Couple of Questions for You.") First, share the responses to question one, and then do the same with the second question. What are some interesting similarities? What are some unusual considerations?

3. Review the existing overloads that individuals in the group are experiencing both at work and on a personal basis. What are some of the tactics for handling or avoiding overloads?

4. What decisions should receive a "fast response"? Conversely, what decisions can and should take more time?

5. Reevaluate the Category II activities that I listed earlier. Expand on that list by adding activities. Next, identify one or more examples of each activity.

6. Share with one another your individual successes in developing and using a fourth-generation time management form.

7. What is meant by subjective time? Have you experienced it? If so, in what way?

TEAM BUILDING

RESPONSIBILITIE°S

TEAM LEADERSHIP

The police supervisor is responsible for cultivating the qualities of a team leader and then applying them in a productive, rewarding, and caring manner.

To lead in the 21st Century, you'll need both competence and character.

—H. Norman Schwarzkopf

Responsibilities One through Five supplied the requisite basics for building a team of employees. Responsibility Six involves team leadership.

Police work of the 2000s will not belong to "supervisors" or those who make the members dance. It will belong to passionate, driven team leaders—those people who not only have enormous amounts of energy, but who also can energize those whom they lead.

Controlling people, stifling them, keeping them in the dark, and wasting their time on trivia and reports are traits I associate with supervising. You can't implant teamwork in people. You have to nurture it and let it grow in them by allowing them to win and then rewarding them when they do. I never associate the word supervisor with passion, and I've never seen a leader without it. Above all else, team leaders are open. They go up, down, and around their agency to reach people. They're informal. They're straight with their team. They're inevitably accessible.

113

Before D-Day, June 6, 1944, General Dwight D. Eisenhower joined the forces of several nations, made up of military personnel with different upbringings and conflicting ideas about fighting a war, and he forged them into a team. His emphasis on teamwork and his never-flagging insistence on working together were the most important reasons for his being selected as "Supreme Commander Allied Expeditionary Force."

TEAM LEADERSHIP AT THE TOP

Since the mid-1980s, police organizations have grown more interested in encouraging high-quality teamwork. Despite the focus on the heroic personality of a police chief or sheriff, these organizations are moving toward being led by a team of managers and supervisors.

It is becoming less frequent that the individual sitting at the top of the pyramid is the sole leader. Rather, we see a group of people with shared responsibilities and clear accountabilities strategizing together, reaching decisions by consensus, coordinating implementation, and generally performing many, if not all, the functions previously performed by a police chief. Through this team leadership at the top, these police agencies are seeking ways of realizing all the talent and intelligence of all the employees.

There are at least two good reasons why the management/supervision team leadership form is on the rise. **First**, the problems our police organizations face today are enormously complex. The most difficult issues that a leadership team faces are often cross-disciplinary or cross-functional. They require a deep expertise in specific areas, complemented by insight into the interrelationships between functions. Few, if any, individuals have the intelligence and breadth to deal with this kind of complexity on their own, yet it must be dealt with. Consequently, major breakthroughs in teamwork are required.

Second, within the past decade there has been a change in the management of police organizations. Managers and supervisors, re-conceiving their own job as setting forth broad visions and strategies, now grant staff much more power to plan and implement. In a police organization led by influence, people are moved and convinced when they see a group of people at the top truly sharing a vision and strategy and modeling it in their behavior. When they don't see that commitment and congruency, their confidence and commitment will be less.

> Creating a competent team of police employees is a new dimension of supervision—and a demanding one. It may be a discipline in its own right. Collective leadership is as different from individual leadership as collective learning is different from individual learning. Mastering team leadership means mastering a larger and more complex learning agenda.

THE POLICE SUPERVISOR AS A LEADER

Police supervisors are comfortable with their role as a leader. When approaching team leadership, however, many revert to their underlying beliefs about control and direction. They agree that leadership can be taught and learned, but team leadership is suspected of being a fleeting fad. Leaders get things done; police employees follow them. Team leaders instill heart, passion, spirit, and vision in the work group.

- Police supervisors-as-leaders reinforce the idea that work accomplishment comes from great individual acts (usually theirs), rather than teamwork.
- Police supervisors-as-leaders want their "subordinates" to rely on them.
- Police supervisors-as-leaders begin to own their power and their successes.
- Police supervisors-as-leaders are expected to choose service over self-interest, but it seems the choice is rarely made.
- Police supervisors-as-leaders attempt to recreate themselves in "their people" so that their beliefs and actions become reproducible.

The current concept of leadership does not leave much room for the concept of team leadership. We need a way to hold on to the initiative and accountability and vision of the team leadership idea, and to abandon the inevitable baggage of superiority and self-centeredness.

THE POLICE SUPERVISOR AS "TEAM LEADER"

The alternative to leadership is team leadership. The latter is not a perfect concept, but an entryway into exploring what fundamental change in our police departments would look like and what strategies are conducive to progress.

Team leadership asks us to be deeply accountable for the outcomes of a work unit without acting to define purpose for others, control others, or take care of others. The current leadership theory is very different. When we train police supervisors or leaders, the topics of defining purpose, maintaining control, and taking care of others are at the center of the curriculum. We were raised to believe that if we were to be accountable, we needed the authority to go with it. How many times have we heard the cry, "How can you hold me accountable without giving me authority?"

Team leadership questions the belief that accountability and power go hand in hand. We can be accountable and give power to (or empower) those closer to police work (i.e., police officers), operating from the belief that in this way police work is better served. Instead of deciding what kind of culture to create and thus defining purpose, team leaders can ask that each member of the work unit decide what the place will become. Team leadership also asks us to forsake care-taking (mentoring is not care-taking), which is an even harder habit to give up. We do not serve other adults when we take responsibility for their well-being. We continue to care, but when we care-take, we treat others, especially those in low-power positions, as if they were not able to provide for themselves. In our working relationships, we have begun to understand the downside of care-taking and the dominance that defining purpose for others can represent. What we have not yet done is to apply these concepts to the structure of how we supervise others.

We are reluctant to let go of the belief that if we are to care for something, we must control it. There needs to be a way for you to be accountable for outcomes of a group of police employees without feeling you must dominate them.

The desire to see team leadership as simply a different form of leadership is to miss the key distinction. When we hold on to the wish for leaders, we are voting for control and accountability at the top. Looking for leadership is some blend of wanting to get on top or stay on top plus liking the idea that someone up there in my police department (my chief/my captain) is responsible for my well-being.

TEAM LEADERSHIP AND EMPOWERMENT

Because it exercises accountability, but centers on service rather than control, team leadership is a means to impact the degree of empowerment each employee feels for the success of the work unit and even the police agency.

> Empowerment has to be felt strongly at every level—from bottom to top—for community-oriented policing to succeed. Team leadership gives us the guidance system for navigating this intersection of supervision, followership, and empowerment.

What is troubling about an idea like team leadership is that even though it is intuitively appealing, it seems removed from the heart of the way we run our police organizations. There needs to be a clear connection between the idea of team leadership and the achievement of measurable results (e.g., crime reduction) for the department. If we do not have a strong reason to initiate significant improvement in our police agencies, no real progress will take place.

AUTHORITY AND POWER

Authority

Once, in a police agency, I noticed that the police chief "managed" and that his assistant chief managed and "led." Briefly, the chief used the authority of his office to gain compliance and provide direction for achieving results. Authority is the "right" to command. The assistant chief had the same right and executed it at times. However, he most often relied on his leadership, or his individual capacity for managing. Although both were successful managers, the assistant chief demonstrated more effectiveness in achieving results than did the chief.

All police supervisors have authority, the right to command. As a police supervisor, your authority originates in your position. Your position grants you the right to reward and sanction the behavior of those who work for you. In other words, all three—position + rewards + sanctions—provide you with authority. And when you exercise your authority, you are attempting to influence the attitudes and behavior of others. If they comply, then your authority is working well.

POSITION.   By its very definition, your position is to command or influence the acts of others. The statement of your duties, your stripes, your salary, your training, and so on attest to the responsibilities of the job.

REWARDS.   Your authority to reward is based on the right to control and administer rewards to others (such as money, promotions, or praise) for compliance with the agency's requests or directives.

SANCTIONS.   Your authority to sanction is based on the right to control and administer punishments to others (such as reprimand or termination) for noncompliance with the agency's requests or directives.

Power

Supervisors, because of the responsibilities of their position, acquire the right or the authority to command. With this right or authority comes influence. Hence, police supervisors are strategically located for moving an agency toward goal attainment. It is the effective supervisor who develops their talent for leading others, and consequently possesses a significantly enhanced influence (authority + power) for achieving results—for achieving results effectively.

Fundamentally, your power is person-based as opposed to position-based. Your power to lead others is derived from your expertise and example. Both combine to attract others to follow you.

EXPERTISE.   Expert power is based on a special ability, skill, expertise, or knowledge exhibited by an individual. For example, a new police sergeant may have some questions regarding the functioning of a piece of equipment. Rather than asking the lieutenant, the sergeant contacts the individual who previously held the sergeant's position for assistance, because of their knowledge of or expertise with the equipment.

EXAMPLE OR REFERENT.   Referent power is based on the attractiveness or the appeal of one person to another. A leader may be admired because of certain characteristics or traits that inspire or attract followers. (Charisma is an example.) Referent power may also be based on a person's connection with another powerful individual. For example, the title of "assistant" has been given to people who work closely with others with titles such as sheriff or police chief. Although the title of assistant to the sheriff may not have reward or coercive (or legitimate) power, other individuals may perceive that this person is acting with the consent of the boss, resulting in their power to influence. The sheriff's assistant is perceived as the sheriff's alter ego. Many will wonder if the assistant is acting for the sheriff or on their own. Rather than taking a chance, one typically opts in favor of the former possibility.

- Power is the capacity to command.
- All police supervisors have it.
- Not all police supervisors use it.
- Hence, only some police supervisors are leaders.

POLICE DEPARTMENT: VOLUNTARY ORGANIZATION

Authority is bottom up! If you really do not want to work for an organization anymore, you can quit. You have that freedom of choice. (There are a few select organizations, such as prisons, where quitting is not an option.)

When you commence working as a police officer, you temporarily loan the department authority over you. If the department abuses it or fouls up in some way, you can merely take it back. As Johnny Paycheck sings, "Take this job and shove it. I ain't workin' here no more." Granted, finding another job may be difficult. The fact remains that you do have a choice.

FORMAL AND INFORMAL TEAM LEADERS

Not all police leaders have sergeant's stripes or lieutenant's or captain's bars. For a number of reasons, there are informal leaders. These people surface in all organizations to fill a one-time or ongoing need. For example, if a particular expertise is required, then the person who possesses it will provide leadership. This could occur if the victim of a crime can communicate only in Spanish. A Spanish-speaking officer thus may temporarily lead in an investigation. Another occurs when the supervisor fails to establish followership because of either inadequate expertise or a poor example. The work group will commonly fill this void by creating an informal leader.

The reasons for an informal leader's emerging determine if it is helpful or harmful to the work group. Informal leaders are a normal phenomenon in an organization. They can be extremely useful to a supervisor if they act in concert with and support of the group's goals.

Leadership is a relationship between two or more people in which one attempts to influence the other(s) toward the attainment of a goal or goals.

The key to the concept of leadership is to look at it as an influence process. It is a process that includes the elements of the power base of the leader and the degree of acceptance of the characteristics, needs, and decision role of the subordinate(s).

COURAGEOUS FOLLOWERSHIP

The term "follower" seems to cause the deepest discomfort. It conjures up images of conformity, weakness, and failure to succeed. Often none of this is the least bit true. The sooner we move beyond these images and get comfortable with the idea of powerful team followers supporting powerful team leaders, the sooner we can fully develop dynamic, self-responsible, mutually supportive relationships in our police agencies.

Rudyard Kipling wrote, "The opposite of courage is not cowardice. It is conformity." It's the courageous followers who openly communicate agreement and disagreement with their bosses. They refuse to engage in groupthink. They are loyal, but not compliant. They strive for unity, but will not submit to uniformity.

If you want to be a courageous follower and if you want the members of your assigned team to be the same, then you must do the following five things:

1. Assume responsibility. Courageous followers assume responsibility for themselves and their police department. They do not view their team leader as paternalistic or wait for the team leader to give them permission to act. Courageous followers discover or create opportunities to fulfill their potential and maximize their value to the agency. The pronoun they most frequently use is "we," and they rarely use "me," "I," or "they." (When "they" is used, it involves praise for the work of others.)

2. Hard work. Courageous followers use the words "I'm going to work," and not "I have to work" or, worse yet, to a co-worker, "Don't work too hard." They assume new or additional responsibilities to unburden the team leader and serve the organization. They stay alert for opportunities in which their strengths supplement the leader's, and assert themselves in these areas. Courageous followers endorse their leader and the tough decisions a leader must make if the police department is to fulfill its mission.

3. Challenge. Courageous followers challenge bad ideas, poor conduct, and dysfunctional procedures. They are willing to stand up, to stand out, and to risk rejection. Courageous followers value their relationship with the team leader, but not at the expense of the overall mission and their own integrity.

4. Champion change. Courageous followers recognize the need for change. They champion it and stay with the team leader and work group while they mutually struggle with the difficulties of real change. They examine their own need to change and do so as appropriate.

5. Separate. Courageous followers know when it is necessary to transfer to another unit or flat out quit the department. They are prepared to withdraw support from and even to disavow or oppose destructive bosses, despite high personal risk.

A Productive Team Leader–Team Follower Relationship

Team followers and team leaders concentrate on the mission of the police department; followers do not concentrate on the leader. A common purpose pursued with decent values is the heart of the healthy leader-follower relationship.

"Follower" is not synonymous with "subordinate." A subordinate reports to an individual of high rank and may in practice be a supporter, an antagonist, or indifferent. A follower shares a common purpose with the leader, believes in what the agency is trying to accomplish, and wants both the leader and the department to succeed.

Like the team leader, the follower is a steward of the resources a police organization can draw on to carry out its work. The resources of a group include its leaders. Thus, a team follower is the leader's cohort every bit as much as a team leader is the follower's cohort.

MANAGING YOUR BOSS

The phrase *managing your boss* sounds unusual, even suspicious. Because of the traditional top-down emphasis in police organizations, it is not obvious why you need to manage relationships upward—unless, of course, you would do so for selfish or political reasons. I am using the term to mean the process of consciously working with your superior to obtain the best possible results for you, your boss, and most importantly the police department.

Misunderstanding the Relationship

Some police sergeants behave as if their bosses were not very dependent on them. They fail to see how much the boss needs their help and cooperation to do his or her job effectively. These people refuse to acknowledge that the boss needs cooperation, dependability, and honesty from them.

Some supervisors see themselves as not very dependent on their bosses. They gloss over how much help and information they need from the boss in order to perform their own jobs well.

A supportive working relationship requires:

- That you have a good understanding of the other person and yourself, especially regarding strengths, weaknesses, work styles, and values
- That you use this information to develop and manage a healthy working relationship—one that is compatible with both persons' work styles and assets, is characterized by mutual expectations, and meets the most critical needs of the other person. (and that is essentially what we have found highly effective supervisors-as-leaders doing)

The Boss's Work Style

At a minimum, you need to appreciate your boss's goals and pressures, strengths and weaknesses, and values. What are your boss's organizational and personal objectives, and what are the pressures on him, especially those from his boss and others at his level? What are your boss's long suits and blind spots? What is the preferred style of working? Does he or she like to get information through memos, formal meetings, or phone calls? Does your boss thrive on conflict or try to minimize it?

Without this information, a police supervisor is flying blind when dealing with the boss, and unnecessary conflicts, misunderstandings, and problems are inevitable.

Your Work Style

The boss is only one half of the relationship. You are the other half, as well as the part over which you have more direct control. Developing an effective working relationship requires, then, that you know your own needs, strengths and weaknesses, personal style, and values.

A Compatible Work Style

With a clear understanding of both your boss and yourself, you can—usually—establish a way of working together that fits both of you, that is characterized by unambiguous mutual expectations, and that helps both of you to be more productive and effective. Above all else, a good working relationship with a boss accommodates differences in work style. Work style differences include the boss's preferred way of: 1) receiving information; 2) making decisions; 3) degree/type of expectation; 4) amount of information required; and 5) willingness to delegate.

Who's Responsible?

No doubt, some police supervisors will resent that on top of all their other duties, they also need to take time and energy to manage their relationships with their bosses. Such supervisors fail to realize the importance of this activity and how it can simplify their jobs by eliminating potentially severe problems.

> Supervisors-as-team-leaders recognize that this part of their work is legitimate. Seeing themselves as ultimately responsible for what they achieve in a police organization, they know they need to establish and manage relationships with everyone on whom they are dependent, and that includes the boss.

LOYALTY OF A TEAM FOLLOWER

Team leaders and team followers need to find a mutual place for their loyalty that transcends their relationship, yet bonds them in a framework of trust. This is the importance of the contemporary emphasis on vision, values, and mission statements: Well formulated, these define the loyalty that leaders and followers pledge to those who have a stake in the group. (See Responsibility Three.)

The values statement evokes a focused loyalty—to fairness, to quality, to honesty, to service, to a common purpose. Focused loyalty to worthy values avoids the pitfalls of unlimited loyalty. Both team leaders and team followers enter into a contract to pursue the common purpose within the context of their values. The loyalty of each is to achieving the purpose and to helping each other stay true to that purpose.

Structured Exercise 6–1

A team leader is by definition a highly adaptive person, open to change and free from conditioned responses. If you want to see whether you have learned the skills that make someone adaptable (e.g., a team leader), answer the following questions as they apply to you, assigning the following points:

Almost never applies	0 points
Sometimes applies	1 point
Usually applies	2 points
Almost always applies	3 points

1. When I am first confronted with a problem and have no idea how it can be solved, I take the attitude that the right answer will emerge.
2. Events in my life happen with their own right timing.
3. I feel optimistic about my future.
4. When someone rejects me, I feel hurt, but I accept that the decision was theirs to make.
5. I feel the loss of family and friends who have died, but the grief resolves itself and I move on—I don't try to bring back what cannot be brought back.
6. I feel committed to ideals larger than myself.
7. When I'm arguing with someone, I defend my position, but I also find it easy to acknowledge the rightness in the other side.
8. I vote the person, not the party.
9. I donate time to worthwhile causes, even if they are unpopular.
10. I am considered a good listener. I don't interrupt others when they talk.
11. If someone has a lot of emotion at stake in something, I will hear them out without expressing my views.
12. Given a choice between a high-salaried job that is fairly boring and a job I like doing at half the pay, I'll take the job I love to do.
13. My style of supervising other people is to allow them to do what they want, rather than try to control them. I interfere as little as possible.
14. I find it easy to trust others.

15. I am not prone to worry; the ups and downs of difficult situations affect me less than most other people.

16. In a competitive situation, I am a good loser—I will say, "Good game," not "I wasn't at my best."

17. Being right in every situation isn't all that important to me.

18. I feel comfortable playing games and laughing.

19. I don't think about my moods very much.

20. I can easily feel what someone else is feeling.

21. Quiet people make me feel comfortable. Nervous people don't make me nervous.

Total score: _____

Evaluating Your Score

50 POINTS OR OVER.   You are an exceptionally adaptable person. Others seek you for guidance. You place a high priority on your ability to remain comfortable under pressure. You pride yourself on being able to resolve conflicts well.

30–49 POINTS.   You are reasonably adaptable to everyday challenges. You are the kind of person whom others consider easygoing, but you are likely to have more worries and regrets. Conflicts upset you, and you tend to fall under the influence of people with emotions stronger than yours.

20–29 POINTS.   You have definite ideas of right and wrong behavior and put a high priority on defending your point of view. You are likely to be well organized and decidedly goal-oriented. If you find yourself in a situation of conflict or competition, you really want to be on the winning side.

UNDER 20 POINTS.   Your sense of "self" needs considerable work. You fear rejection and become upset or critical when others disagree with you. You have your way of doing things and do not like surprises. You are likely to be obsessively orderly, with lots of hidden worry, or else very disorganized, reacting strongly to one external event after another.

The purpose of the findings is not to make anyone feel superior or inferior, but to spur conscious growth. The common denominator of all team leaders is that they actually work, on a daily basis, at having an open mind.

———————

Structured Exercise 6–2
———————

There are several excellent motion pictures that portray leadership characteristics and strategies. The movie "Saving Private Ryan" is one example. Identify a movie that you can borrow or rent. (Be certain the movie depicts an actual leader.) View the movie and analyze it for leadership characteristics. Look for the successes and mistakes that the leader experienced. Record what you see. When the movie is finished, discuss with one another what you saw in the leader's behavior (values, vision, positive self-regard, integrity, etc.).

On Becoming a Team Leader

Team leaders share seven common traits and practices. Whether these traits and practices are genetic or arduously acquired, team leaders:

1. Accentuate the positive
2. Know what's going on
3. Rivet one's attention through vision
4. Create meaning through communication
5. Build trust through positioning
6. Deploy themselves through positive self-regard and trying
7. Master change

Accentuate the Positive

During World War II, General Eisenhower realized that optimism and pessimism are infectious and that they spread more rapidly from the head downward than in any other direction. He learned that a commander's optimism has a most extraordinary effect upon all with whom he comes in contact. He said, "With this clear realization, I firmly determined that my mannerisms and speech in public would always reflect the cheerful certainty of victory—that any pessimism and discouragement I might ever feel would be reserved for my pillow."

Optimism does not mean being foolish about taking on challenges. It means pursuing your adversaries with an abundance of faith and hope in your resources.

Know What's Going On

One of the most difficult tasks for a team leader is to know with great accuracy what is going on within the work unit. Information-gathering mechanisms seem to evolve in ways that result in the top of the system having a limited, incomplete, and even biased understanding of reality. Team leaders develop methods that surface and rectify these mechanisms so that, for example, bad news is as likely to come to their attention as good. Face-to-face, two-way communication is developed deep into the department, and a norm is established of responsibly surfacing and exposing the truth as completely as possible.

Rivet Attention through Vision

Vision grabs. At first, it grabs the team leader, and if effectively projected, it convinces others to get on board. The leader's vision is intended to be magnetic. Winning coaches transmit an unbridled clarity about what they want from their players. If coaches can do it, so can police supervisors—if they want to.

The first thing you do with your vision is convey it to others. Your staff has to know what you see. Second, they must understand it. The understanding may be vague or incomplete, but they have to have at least a fundamental concept of what you're proposing. Third, the people must be convinced that the vision is of paramount importance, even if it initially appears impossible. It excites people and drives them. Fourth, you have to pay close attention to the vision and use it as a transaction between yourself and your followers. It becomes a subtle link that forges you and your followers as one—coach and team, sergeant and officers.

Once the preceding steps have been taken, the team leader must:

- Closely live the enabling vision
- Use it to prioritize (quality first, quantity second, etc.)
- Adapt the vision of changing needs and new opportunities

If you understand your values, the values of your department, and the values of your profession, then visioning is possible for you. You merely allow your imagination and conscience to take charge. Through imagination, you can visualize the uncharted wealth of potential that lies within yourself and others. Through conscience, you can compare your ideas with universal laws or principles, as well as your personal standards.

Create Meaning through Communication

Responsibility Four provides expansive coverage of this strategy. I underscore it here because research has demonstrated that all team leaders master communication. It is inseparable from effective leadership. It isn't just information or facts—it is the context of presentation, the overall meaning.

All police organizations depend on the existence of shared meanings and interpretations of reality, which facilitate coordinated efforts. "Meaning" surpasses what is typically meant by "communication." Meaning has little to do with facts or even knowing. Facts and knowing pertain to technique, tactics, and "knowing how to do things." That is useful and often necessary. But thinking is much closer to what we mean by "meaning" than knowing is. This is not a subtle difference. Thinking prepares one for what ought to be done.

To depend on facts, without thinking, may seem all right, but in the long run, it is dangerous because it lacks direction. The distinctive characteristic of leaders (especially in a volatile police environment) is that the "know-why" occurs before the "know-how." This logic shows, once more, one of the basic differences between leaders and supervisors.

Leadership, by communicating meaning, generates a confederation of learning, and this is what successful police agencies proudly possess. Lack of clarity makes police organizations little more than simple devices for the avoidance of responsibility.

I have conducted more than 2,000 team-building workshops for police and sheriff's departments. (I also have conducted similar workshops for fire departments, city councils, and a variety of business firms.) With rare exception, the number one issue in the workshop is the failure to communicate with one another. Far too often the participants state with detectable anger: "I never got the word." "Everything moves, but there's no feedback." "I've expressed my ideas before, but they could care less." And the worst one is, "I don't know our priorities, let alone our goals."

If our body's arterial system does not touch base with our cells, they'll eventually die. Similarly, if a police organization's communication system does not contact, with meaning, its human resources, the staff may not be dead, but they might as well be.

Build Trust through Positioning

Trust encompasses accountability, predictability, reliability, and faith. To achieve it, there must be a mental or physical act. Something must happen for me to trust you or vice versa. You tell me that you'll be at work on time, and you are—I start the "trust process."

Trusting involves a trust bank account (TBA). You consistently arrive at work on time, and your TBA prospers. You make many daily TBA deposits in a variety of ways. You open new TBAs with people that you meet. Depending on your working relationships, family members, and friends, you may have hundreds of TBAs in existence. You could be trust-rich. Conversely, you could be trust-poor.

It takes a lot of deposits to build a strong TBA with another person. Making a mistake—for example, lying to another person—can wipe out your TBA. It can send you into indefinite, maybe permanent, bankruptcy with the other party. It can also destroy a working relationship, a marriage, a friendship. TBAs take considerable time to build and only one second—in some cases, one word—to dissolve.

Leaders who are trusted make themselves known and make their positions (e.g., values, principles, vision) known. Followers do not stay with shiny ideals and cute words. Only relentless dedication to a position on the part of a police leader will engage trust.

Positioning is a set of actions necessary to implement the vision of a leader. Through establishing the position (by action), the followers are given the chance to trust—trust in the leader and trust in the position; they're synonymous.

For a police organization to foster trust, it first must present a sense of what it is and what it is to do—in other words, a position. The police leader is responsible for seeing to it that the position of the department is known to employees and community members alike. This is not easy because people have different perceptions. The police leader may see the position of the department as X, the employees as Y, and the citizens as Z. If the three positions are contradictory, then trust is hard to achieve.

The greater the agreement on what the position of the department is, the more one is able to trust it. If I know what you stand for, and believe in it, I'll trust your leadership.

Second, positioning needs courageous patience. The leader has to stay with it. With time, he or she starts managing trust. Change may occur, and innovations may be needed; thus, the position must be carefully shifted and then maintained.

Positions must be adjusted as appropriate, to maintain trust. The team leader must recognize when to maintain the steady course or change direction. Trust in the leader's ability to lead depends on their decision to retain or shift a position.

Deploy through Positive Self-Regard

The higher you advance in a police organization, the more interpersonal and relational the working environment is. This deployment of self makes leading a profoundly personal activity. Such a deployment depends on one's positive self-regard. Positive self-regard is a triangle consisting of 1) competency, 2) positive other-regard, and 3) the Wallenda factor.

COMPETENCY.   Positive self-regard is not self-aggrandizement, conceit, or egomania. Essentially, it is confidence in who you are and what you are capable of doing. It is prudent self-esteem and self-respect.

The first step in building positive self-regard is recognizing your strengths and compensating for your weaknesses. The next step involves the constant nurturing of skills. The final step is evaluating the fit between your perceived skills and what the job requires. Being good at your job and knowing why sum up one side of positive self-regard. I label this "competency."

OTHER-REGARD.   Those that have high regard for themselves typically have the same for others. Having positive self-regard is contagious. Potentially everyone can catch it. Positive self-regard creates it in others. It seems to exert its force by generating in others a sense of confidence and high expectations.

Positive self- and other-regard encourage the development of five key people skills:

1. The ability to accept individuals as they are, not as you would like them to be. This ability is fundamental to leading a culturally diverse work force.
2. The capacity to approach people and problems in relation to the present, rather than the past.
3. The ability to deal with those who are close to you with the same active listening ear and courtesy that you give to citizens and casual acquaintances.
4. The ability to trust in another person's dedication and capabilities.
5. The ability to function without constant approval or even support from others.

WALLENDA FACTOR.   Team leaders do not think about failure. In fact, they reject the concept. The closest they identify with it is through words such as "learning experience," "setback," or "delayed success."

Failure to them is like learning to ski. At first, you're destined to fall; with persistence and perspiration, you'll eventually master the art of skiing. It's the same with leadership. Team leaders use their mistakes as a lesson on what not to do as well as what to do next.

Failure and mistakes can open us up to self- or other-criticism, which can erode positive self- and other-regard. The more valid it is, the more bothersome it is to us. The successful leader accepts it, but then twists it into a useful message. Remember, feedback is the breakfast of champions.

Karl Wallenda was one of the premier high wire aerialists. He fell to his death in 1978 while walking a 75-foot-high tightrope. After his fall, Mrs. Wallenda commented that for three straight months before the accident, all he thought about was not falling. He substituted thinking about falling for his past thinking about successfully walking the tightrope.

Karl Wallenda would likely tell the police supervisor to pour his or her energies into success (walking the tightrope) and not failing (falling). To worry places barriers in the path of clear thinking. An absence of clear thinking can cause mistakes for those who possess positive self-regard. An absence of clear thinking can cause failures for those who do not have it.

THREE SIDES OF POSITIVE SELF-REGARD. The three sides combined look like Figure 6–1. Your positive self-regard is a direct derivative of:

- Your competency—you have what it takes and you know it
- Your capacity for instilling competency in others by having high other-regard for them
- Your conviction of an outcome—the expectation of success

For team leadership to occur, there has to be a fusion of competency, capacity, and conviction. It is similar to the archer who builds his prowess to

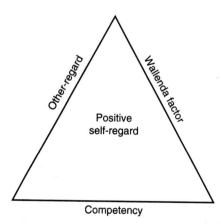

Figure 6–1 Three Sides of Positive Self-Regard

the point where the zeal to hit the center of the target is obliterated and man, bow, arrow, and target become one, united. Positive self-regard magnetically attracts and gradually empowers people to join the police supervisor, the police leader, in a quest for quality services that are good for police departments and for society.

Mastery Change

As a team leader, you must master organizational change—design, structure, and implementation. This must be accomplished through methods that get the entire work unit engaged and committed, both in favor of the shared vision and in a rigorous search for the truth. If you want to create an organization committed to a new way of being and a new set of operational procedures, then the processes that must be employed must foster commitment. Team leaders are superb at anticipating. They get ahead of the learning curve and make an early and easy adjustment to it.

Structured Exercise 6–3

I've described seven critical characteristics or strategies of proven team leaders. What would you add to this list? Which, if any, are unimportant? First of all, create your own list; then along with your colleagues, get consensus on a joint list of strategies.

Two Big Mistakes a Team Leader Can Make

The worst mistake a leader or supervisor can make is **ducking accountability**. If others see the leader attempting to slide away from a bad situation or, worse yet, trying to blame others for it, the TBA is zero. Leadership is down the tubes and is extremely difficult to restore.

A second common trap for even those leaders who have seven characteristics is **taking too much credit**. In fact, a good leader rarely takes credit. We've found that the people who most quickly generate trust, loyalty, excitement, and energy in an organization are those who pass on the credit to the people who have really done the work.

Most good team leaders have strong character and positive self-regard, but they shouldn't let their egos get too big. Your ego needs to be strong enough to handle the kind of anger or abuse you will sometimes incur, and to appreciate contrary feedback. But your ego should not be so big that you lose your associates' respect. Positive self-regard does not preclude being humble.

A Third Big Mistake: Groupthink

Groupthink is a mode of thinking that people engage in when they are deeply involved in a cohesive in-group, when the members' striving for unanimity overrides their motivation to realistically appraise alternative courses of action. It is a clear case of something productive—teamwork—being carried to an extreme and leading to something unproductive—poor-quality decision making.

Groupthink is a shared reality that we create. As a result, the team's decision becomes the sum total of the things its members won't look at. Groupthink is fostered by:

- A team that is highly insulated with limited access to outside feedback
- A stressful decision-making context
- Unreasonable external pressure

Symptoms of Groupthink

There are eight symptoms of groupthink. The more that are present in a work team, the greater the likelihood that the team will succumb to groupthink.

1. *Illusion of invulnerability.* The feeling of power and authority is important to any decision-making team. It gives team members confidence that they will be able to carry through on any decisions reached. However, if the team members come to believe that any decision they reach will, therefore, be successful, then they have fallen prey to an illusion of invulnerability.

2. *Belief in a sacred mandate.* Team members need to believe in the rightness of their decisions. Taken to the extreme, they may defend a decision by pointing to a moralistic code or philosophy "for the good of all." Basically, this relieves them of the responsibility for rationally justifying an action. The protection of the team's self-esteem becomes more important than the accuracy of its judgment.

3. *Rationalization.* In reaching a decision, it is normal and natural to downplay the drawbacks of a chosen course. The problem occurs when legitimate objections exist within the work team, but they are not voiced due to perceived negative reactions to those raising objections to the team position.

4. *Rejection of external groups.* Police teams can fall prey to stereotyping other groups as troublemakers—as enemies. "Don't trust outsiders" is the prevalent attitude in this case.

5. *Self-censorship.* As one of the principles upon which our country was founded, the ability to express oneself without censorship has always been highly prized. The most common form of censorship is that which we commit upon ourselves under the guise of group loyalty, team spirit, or adherence to "departmental policy"—group compliance takes precedence over individual courage.

6. *Direct pressure.* Pressure upon police team members can surface in many forms. The net effect is the same: Team members are conditioned to keep

opposing views to themselves. More, they're urged not to believe in differing views because to do so puts them at odds with the team's integrity. Dissent or argument against the team's presumed agreement is considered counter to the team's interests, even an act of disloyalty.

7. *Mindguards.* In groupthink, a phenomenon may surface to protect us from disturbing thoughts and ideas—a mindguard. Interestingly, mindguards are typically self-appointed and perform their function not within the team, but rather externally from the group decision. Data, facts, and opinions that might bear directly upon the team are deliberately kept out of the purview of the team. Generally, this is done with a variety of justifiable intentions: There is no time, a regular member will "summarize" for the team, the issue is not pertinent, or, saddest of all, the team has already made up its mind.

8. *Illusion of unity.* Rationalizations and psychological pressures have their effect—the team coalesces around a decision. Drawbacks are downplayed; the invincibility of the final course is reinforced. And doubting team members may even feel that they have justifiably put their own fears to rest. More likely, it is simply the sense of relief that an indecision has become a decision.

Avoiding Groupthink

Is teamwork immune to the effects of groupthink? As long as teams are constituted of human beings, prone to all the dynamics and pitfalls of human interaction, and therefore vulnerable, the answer is "no." Fortunately, it is possible to spot the incipient causes of groupthink and thereby reduce a team's chances of falling into it. The police supervisor-as-leader should attempt to . . .

1. *Maintain an open climate.* The police supervisor should practice what is called an open-leadership style—free discussion, nonjudgmental attitudes with an acceptance of divergent thinking—as opposed to a closed-management style, characterized by tightly controlled discussion, highly defensive posturing, and lack of tolerance of opposing thoughts in favor of consensus thinking.

2. *Avoid group isolation.* At times, it is valuable to bring in outsiders to provide critical reaction to the team's assumptions. In this way, the work unit is not isolated with limited data and constrained choices. This is especially helpful when using problem-oriented policing. (See Responsibility Fourteen.)

3. *Assign critical evaluators.* The police supervisor should assign each team member the role of critical evaluator, giving each the duty to question current practices and uncontested team assumptions. By questioning even areas in which a particular team member may not have special expertise, the team members are forced to rethink their assumptions and rationalizations.

4. *Avoid being too directive.* The most important single step a supervisor can take is to avoid being too directive in decision-making. (See Responsibility Eight and the section on micromanaging.) For some, this may mean occasionally

allowing other team members to facilitate a meeting in their presence. In this way, supervisors will lessen undue influence upon their team.

5. *Remember that silence may mean disagreement, not consent.* Individual and organizational values are under siege by blistering technological and social upheaval. It is time to put away the "silence brings consent" notion, which still pervades much of our organizational thinking. Supervisors best assume not that silence means consent, but rather that such silence indicates disagreement with proposed team action. Maintaining an open climate (see above) via an open leadership style can avoid the supervisor's trap of inferring that an employee's silence means agreement.

Groupthink masks itself as teamwork. It is seductive. It is contagious. And it is very dangerous. Here is what the supervisor-as-leader can and should do:

- Understand the significance of groupthink in the team-based decision-making process, and how it can subvert the success of group goals and objectives.
- Realize that groupthink—the striving for agreement leading to faulty decision-making—can occur in any team, no matter how small or how worthy their intentions.
- Recognize the eight symptoms of groupthink and understand that, when more of them are present, it is more likely the team will make an unsuccessful decision.
- Apply the five key strategies for avoiding groupthink:
  - Promote an open climate.
  - Avoid the isolation of the team.
  - Appoint critical evaluators.
  - Avoid being too directive.
  - Remember that silence is not always agreement.

KEY POINTS

- Team leadership is a new dimension of police supervision.
- Leadership and team leadership are not synonymous.
- Authority is the right to supervise, and power is one's capacity to do so.
- Both authority and power seek to influence the behavior of others.
- There are three types of authority: position, sanctions, and rewards. And there are two types of power: expertise and example.
- All police employees are volunteer employees.
- Informal team leadership is a natural phenomenon in an organization.
- Courageous followership requires: 1) assumption of responsibility; 2) hard work; 3) challenge; 4) willingness to change; and 5) withdrawal.
- Without followers, there would be no leaders.

- Successful team leaders demonstrate seven common patterns of behavior. They consistently 1) emphasize the positive, 2) know what's happening, 3) get your attention through a vision they have, 4) create meaning through communication, 5) build trust through positioning, 6) project positive self-regard, and 7) master change.
- The greatest mistakes a leader can make are ducking accountability, assuming too much credit for good work, and engaging in groupthink.

DISCUSSION

1. What's the difference between leadership and team leadership?
2. Discuss authority and power. How do they differ? What is their common bond? If you could only have one, which would you choose?
3. Realizing that you, the police supervisor, are a potential formal team leader, how do you explain the likelihood that there are informal leaders in or around your assigned work unit?
4. What is your reaction to the concept of followership? What are the realities involved? Any concerns?
5. What is meant by "managing your boss?" Have you attempted to do so? If so, what occurred?
6. What is meant by positive self-regard? How does one acquire it? Whom do you know who has this characteristic?
7. Have you witnessed leaders either avoiding accountability or frequently taking credit? If so, discuss what you saw and what occurred as a result of it.
8. What is groupthink? Have you experienced it? If so, what happened? What have you done to avoid it?

MOTIVATION

A police supervisor is responsible for first releasing and then directing an employee's motivation to accomplish the mission of the department.

Things may come to those who wait, but only the things left by those who hustle.

—Abraham Lincoln

In Responsibility Three, we learned how values and vision can be forged into a departmental mission. We further found that strategic thinking serves as a necessary catalyst. Responsibility Seven casts a vision (mission) statement into motivational terms. It causes people to want to work hard for all the right reasons.

Motivating others starts and stops with you. If you're not motivated to do a good job, then those working for you won't be either.

Imagine a police organization full of people who come to work enthusiastically, knowing that they will grow and flourish, and who are intent on fulfilling the vision and mission of the department. There's an ease, grace, and effortlessness about the way they get things done. Work flows seamlessly among teams and functions. Employees take pleasure and pride in every aspect of the enterprise— for example, in the way they can talk openly, reflect on each other's opinions, and have genuine influence on the decisions being made about what they do. That's a lot of energy walking in each day, accomplishing an ever-increasing amount of work, and having fun along the way.

Is this scenario energizing or frightening? If you don't want police employees to bring this much passion, caring, and focus to their work, then don't practice the recommendations that follow. You will find that they reject the assumption that workers are motivated primarily by money, recognition, and fear. Instead, you must assume that in the right atmosphere people will contribute and make commitments because they want to learn, to do good work for its own sake, and to be recognized as people.

As a supervisor-as-leader, you are responsible for motivating your staff to accomplish the mission of your agency. There is no activity more important than worker motivation. A cursory look at any police agency shows that some personnel work harder than others. An individual with outstanding abilities may consistently be outperformed by someone with obviously inferior talents. Why do officers exert different levels of effort in different activities? Why do some employees appear to be "highly motivated," while others do not? These are some of the issues I will address in this chapter.

WHY HAVE MOTIVATED WORKERS?

Why? The obvious answers to this vital question are:

- Job performance
- Job satisfaction

A highly motivated worker is more likely to be a top performer. Further, a highly motivated worker is likely to experience good job satisfaction, which spells good morale.

From the individual's standpoint, being motivated is the key to a productive and satisfying job. Work consumes a sizable portion of our waking hours. If this time is to be meaningful and to contribute toward the development of a healthy personality, the individual must be willing to devote effort toward a purpose, a mission.

Because of the ever-tightening constraints that are placed on police departments by unions, courts, and legislative bodies, agencies must find ways to improve their efficiency and effectiveness in the community. Much of the organizational slack that was tolerated in the past has diminished, requiring that all resources, especially human resources, be utilized to their maximum.

HOW DOES MOTIVATION START?

It starts with you! Clearly, if you are not motivated to do a good job, then those around you will likely feel the same. It starts, and it stops, with you.

When I encounter unmotivated police employees, inevitably I see an unmotivated supervisor. I hope for your sake and the sake of those who work for you and your department that you are motivated to make a difference in your life and the lives of others. It takes a lot of energy and enthusiasm. It's worth it; everyone benefits.

WHAT IS WORKER MOTIVATION?

Worker motivation can be defined as the psychological forces within a person that determine:

- The direction of a person's behavior in an organization
- A person's level of effort
- A person's level of persistence in the face of obstacles

See Table 7–1 for further explanation of these three cornerstones of worker behavior.

THE DISTINCTION BETWEEN MOTIVATION AND PERFORMANCE

Because motivation determines what employees do and how hard and diligently they do it, you might think that a worker's motivation to do a job is the same as the worker's job performance. In fact, motivation and performance, though often confused by workers and supervisors alike, are two distinct

Table 7–1   ELEMENTS OF WORKER MOTIVATION

Element	Definition	Example
Direction of behavior	Which behavior does an employee choose to perform in a police organization?	Does a police officer take the time and effort to convince skeptical superiors of the need to change the specifications for a new patrol plan?
Level of effort	How hard does an employee work to perform a chosen behavior?	Does an officer prepare a report outlining problems with the original plan, or does the officer casually mention the issue when when he or she bumps into a supervisor in the hall?
Level of persistence	When faced with obstacles, confusion, and conflicts, how hard does an employee keep trying to perform a chosen behavior successfully?	When a supervisor disagrees with an officer and indicates that a change in the patrol plan is a waste of time, does the officer persist in trying to get the change implemented or give up despite his or her strong belief in the need for a change?

aspects of behavior in an organization. Performance is an evaluation of the results of a person's behavior. It involves determining how well or how poorly a person has accomplished a task or done a job. Motivation is only one factor among many that contribute to a worker's job performance.

One is apt to expect a highly motivated dispatcher to perform better than one who is poorly motivated. This may not be the case, however. There are intervening influences, such as an innate work ethic or lack of one, amount of training, availability of resources, working conditions, a motivated or unmotivated supervisor, a slave-driver boss, and more.

> Because motivation is only one of several factors that can affect performance, a high level of motivation does not always result in a high level of performance. Conversely, high performance does not necessarily imply that motivation is high: workers with low motivation may perform at a high level if they have a great deal of ability.

Supervisors have to be careful not to automatically attribute low performance to a lack of motivation, or high performance to high motivation. If they incorrectly assume that low performance stems from low motivation, supervisors may overlook the real cause of a performance problem (such as inadequate training or a lack of resources) and fail to take appropriate actions to rectify the situation so that workers can perform at a high level. Similarly, if police supervisors assume that workers who perform at a high level are highly motivated, they may inadvertently fail to take advantage of the talents of exceptionally capable workers. If workers perform at a high level when their motivation levels are low, they may be capable of making exceptional contributions to the department if supervisors devote their efforts to boosting the workers' motivation.

It ain't what you don't know that gets you into trouble.
It's what you know that ain't so.

—Will Rogers

Structured Exercise 7–1

Think for a few moments about past or present jobs you've had. Which ones do you believe you were the most and least motivated to perform? Now the crucial question—why? Further, have you worked hard and done good work, but with little or no motivation to do so? Are you doing that now? Alternatively, have you done, or are you doing, very little work, but with a lot of motivation? In both instances—why? Share this information with your teammates. Probe for similarities and uniqueness in your discussion. What did you discover?

————●—●—————

INTRINSIC AND EXTRINSIC MOTIVATION

Another distinction important to a discussion of motivation is the difference between the intrinsic and extrinsic sources of worker motivation. Intrinsically motivated worker behavior is behavior that is performed for its own sake; the source of motivation is actually a deeply personal satisfaction in performing the behavior. Police officers who are intrinsically motivated often remark that their work gives them a sense of accomplishment and that they feel they are doing something worthwhile.

Extrinsically motivated worker behavior is behavior that is performed to gain material or social rewards or to avoid punishment. The behavior is performed not for its own sake, but rather for its consequences. Examples of extrinsic rewards include pay, praise, and status. Both extrinsic and intrinsic rewards either promote or detract from a motivating job climate.

Intrinsic and extrinsic rewards can be likewise referred to as values (Responsibility One). Hence, if an employee is primarily extrinsically oriented, he or she will respond more quickly to salary, benefits, power and status, and job security. The job per se is not a source of motivation. The person with an intrinsic bent will relate to completing particular assignments, being of service to others, feeling they are achieving to their full potential, and making a difference. In this case, the job itself is a motivator. The majority of us seek to attain both intrinsic and extrinsic rewards from our work. Typically, however, we tend to emphasize one set over the other.

Structured Exercise 7–2

————●—●—————

The purpose of this exercise is to help you be more perceptive and analytical about various kinds of rewards sought by police employees.

To start, set up groups of six to eight for the 45-minute exercise. The groups should be separated from each other and asked to converse only with members of their own group.

The following instrument presents a list of 12 rewards/values that relate to most jobs in police organizations. Two specific job levels are identified: 1) supervisors and 2) first-line employees.

1. Individually, group members should rank order the 12 factors on the basis of their influences on motivating supervisors and line employees, from 1 (most influential) to 12 (least influential). No ties. The individual group

members should provide two rank orders: a) as they believe supervisors would respond to these factors and b) as they believe line employees would respond to these factors.

2. As a group, repeat the instructions presented in Step 1.
3. The group ranking should be displayed, and a spokesperson should discuss the rationale for the group decision and how much variation existed in individual ranks.
4. A final combined ranking for the entire class should be developed. Provide a brief rationale for each one of the twelve factors.

Factor	Supervisors	Employees
1. *Recognition.* Receiving recognition from peers, supervisor, or subordinates for your good work performance.		
2. *Sense of achievement.* Experiencing the feelings associated with successfully completing a job, finding solutions to different problems, or seeing the results of one's work.		
3. *Advancement.* Having the opportunity for advancement or promotion based on one's ability.		
4. *Status.* Being accorded various position-based benefits, such as your own nicely appointed office, selected parking place, or other prestige element.		
5. *Pay.* Receiving a wage that not only covers normal living expenses, but also provides additional funds for certain luxury items.		
6. *Supervision.* Working for a supervisor who both is competent in doing his or her job and looks out for the welfare of subordinates.		
7. *Job itself.* Having a job that is interesting and challenging and provides for substantial variety and autonomy.		
8. *Job security.* Feeling good about your security within the department.		
9. *Co-workers.* Working with co-workers who are friendly and helpful.		
10. *Personal development.* Being given the opportunity in your job to develop and refine new skills and abilities.		
11. *Fringe benefits.* Having a substantial fringe benefit package covering such aspects as personal protection.		
12. *Working conditions.* Having safe and attractive conditions for doing your work.		

THEORIES OF WORKER MOTIVATION: WHY EMPLOYEES DO WHAT THEY DO

There is nothing so practical as a good theory.

—*Kurt Levin*

From the great volume of theories and research on human motivation, I will very briefly cover two schools of thought about why we do what we do at work. Space does not permit otherwise. Please keep in mind as you progress through this subject matter that each theory is substantiated or refuted by literally several thousands of pages of theory, discourse, and scientific research. The two schools can be categorized as 1) needs and 2) process.

All of the theories concerning worker motivation are complementary— that is, each furnishes a slightly different insight into the various spectrums of job motivation. There are still more questions than answers about what motivates us. Nevertheless, what little we have confirmed is very helpful in making employees better performers.

Needs Theories

The four needs theories that I will describe concentrate on a worker's requirements for survival and well-being. Basically, what's really vital to us will cause us to pursue it.

MASLOW'S HIERARCHY OF NEEDS.   The most widely accepted needs classification scheme was proposed by psychologist Abraham Maslow nearly 50 years ago. His list of five needs is conveniently short, yet covers most of the dimensions that psychologists have found to be essential. (See Table 7–2.)

Maslow separated the five needs into higher- and lower-order needs. Physiological and safety needs were described as lower-order needs and love, esteem, and self-actualization as higher-order needs. As each of these needs becomes substantially satisfied, the next need becomes dominant. In essence, the individual moves up the hierarchy. From the standpoint of motivation, the theory would say that, although no need is ever fully gratified, a substantially satisfied need no longer motivates.

ALDERFER'S ERG THEORY.   Clayton Alderfer's existence-relatedness-growth (ERG) theory is also a needs theory of work motivation. Alderfer's theory builds on some of Maslow's thinking, but reduces the number of universal needs from five to three and is more flexible in terms of movement between levels. Like Maslow, Alderfer proposes that needs can be arranged in a hierarchy. The three types of needs in Alderfer's theory are described in Table 7–3.

Whereas Maslow assumes that lower-level needs **must** be satisfied before a higher-level need is a motivator, Alderfer lifts this restriction. According to his theory, a higher-level need can be a motivator even if a lower-level need is not fully satisfied, and needs at more than one level can be motivators at any

Table 7–2   Maslow's Hierarchy of Needs

	Need Level	Description
Highest- Level Needs	Self-actualization needs	The need to realize one's full potential as a human being
	Esteem needs	The need to feel good about oneself and one's capabilities, to be respected by others, and to receive recognition and appreciation
	Belongingness needs	The need for social interaction, friendship, affection, and love
	Safety needs	The need for security, stability, and a safe environment
Lowest- Level Needs (most basic or compelling)	Physiological needs	The basic needs for such things as food, water, and shelter that must be met in order for an individual to survive

time. Alderfer agrees with Maslow that as lower-level needs are satisfied, a worker becomes motivated to satisfy higher-level needs. But Alderfer breaks with Maslow on the consequences of need frustration. Maslow says that once a lower-level need is satisfied, it is no longer a source of motivation. Alderfer proposes that when an individual is motivated to satisfy a higher-level need, but has difficulty doing so, the person's motivation to satisfy lower-level needs will increase.

Douglas McClelland's Achievement, Power, and Affiliation Theory. The major difference between this theory and those preceding is the need for power. (See Table 7–4.)

Herzberg's Motivation–Hygiene Theory. Frederick Herzberg's research led him to conclude that the opposite of satisfaction is not dissatisfaction, as was traditionally believed. Removing dissatisfying characteristics from a job

Table 7–3   Alderfer's ERG Theory

	Need Level	Description
Highest- Level Needs	Growth needs	The need for self-development and creative and productive work
	Relatedness needs	The need to have good interpersonal relations, to share thoughts and feelings, and to have open two-way communication
	Existence needs	The basic needs for human survival, such as the needs for food, water, clothing, shelter, and a secure, safe
Lowest- Level Needs		environment

Table 7–4 McClelland's Achievement, Power, and Affiliation Theory

	Need Level	Description
Highest- Level Needs	Achievement needs	The drive to excel, to achieve in relation to a set of standards, to strive to succeed
	Power needs	The need to make others behave in a way that they would not have behaved otherwise
Lowest- Level Needs	Affiliation needs	The desire for friendly and close interpersonal relationships

does not necessarily make the job satisfying. Hygiene factors in the workplace provide the necessary foundation for the motivator factors to function because they bring motivation to a "zero point" by preventing negative behavior. By themselves, hygiene factors do not motivate individuals to better performance. The motivators, or satisfiers, are higher-level needs. These are the job-content factors that motivate people to perform. According to Herzberg, only such aspects as a challenging job, recognition for doing a good job, and opportunities for advancement, personal growth, and development will provide improved worker performance (see Table 7–5).

RESEARCH FINDINGS AND APPLICATIONS. Of the four needs theories covered, Maslow's is the most widely known. However, it and the three others have tended not to receive support from scientific research. The "power need" in McClelland's work has attained scientific merit, and Herzberg's theory stands

Table 7–5 Herzberg's Motivation–Hygiene Theory

	Need Source	Description
Motivating Needs	Intrinsic (potential satisfiers)	Achievement Work itself Empowerment Responsibility Advancement Personal growth and development
	Extrinsic (potential dissatisfiers)	Job security Salary Working conditions Status Company policies Quality of technical supervision Quality of interpersonal relations among peers, supervisors, and subordinates
Hygiene Needs		Fringe benefits

up reasonably well. Even though the theories have not achieved high validity when studied, police supervisors can still apply some valuable lessons, thanks to Maslow and his colleagues. Consider the following:

- Do not assume that all police employees are motivated by the same needs or values. (See again Responsibility One).
- To determine what will motivate any given worker, determine what needs that individual is trying to satisfy on the job.
- Make sure you have the authority and power to administer or withhold consequences that will satisfy a person's needs.
- Design job situations so that the officers and civilians can satisfy their needs by engaging in behaviors that enable the department to achieve its mission.

Process Theories

In this section, three process theories of motivation are explained: expectancy, equity, and procedural justice.

EXPECTANCY THEORY.   This theory was originally conceived by Victor Vroom and assumes that employees are motivated to receive positive outcomes. Presently, it is the most accepted theory on how we decide which behavior to perform and how much effort to exert. (Needs theories concentrate on what motivates us.)

In order for a police employee to be motivated to perform desired actions and to perform them at a high level, the following conditions are necessary:

- *Valence must be high:* The worker desires outcomes the organization has to offer.
- *Instrumentality must be high:* The worker perceives that they must perform desired actions at a high level to obtain these outcomes.
- *Expectancy must be high:* The worker thinks that trying hard will lead to performance at a high level.

If just one of these three factors—valence, instrumentality, or expectancy—is zero, motivation will be zero. High performance in a police organization depends on what a worker does and how hard they do it. According to expectancy theory, in trying to decide what to do and how hard to do it, police employees ask themselves questions such as these:

- Will I be able to obtain outcomes I desire? (In expectancy theory terms: Is the valence of outcomes that the police agency provides high?)
- Do I need to perform at a high level to obtain these outcomes? (In expectancy theory terms: Is high performance instrumental in obtaining outcomes?)
- If I try hard, will I be able to perform at a high level? (In expectancy theory terms: Is expectancy high?)

Research findings and applications. Expectancy theory is a popular theory of motivation and has received extensive attention from researchers. Some studies support the theory and others do not, but by and large, the theory has been supported. A supervisor should apply its precepts as follows:

- Determine what outcomes your employees desire. More specifically, identify outcomes that have a high positive valence (value) for your crew in order to motivate them to perform at a high level. Clearly communicate to the group what behaviors or performance levels must be obtained for them to receive the valent outcomes.
- Once you have identified desired outcomes, make sure that you have control over them and can give them to employees or take them away when warranted.
- Let your staff know that obtaining their desired outcomes depends on their performing at a high level (raise instrumentalities). Administer the highly valent outcomes only when they perform at a high level (or engage in desired organizational behaviors).
- Do whatever you can to encourage workers to have high expectancies: Express confidence in their abilities, let them know that others like themselves have been able to perform at a high level, and give them guidance in terms of how to perform at a high level (for example, by being better organized, setting priorities, or managing time better).
- Periodically assess workers' beliefs concerning expectancies and instrumentalities and their valences for different outcomes by asking them directly or administering a survey.

EQUITY THEORY.   Equity theory states that if one perceives a discrepancy between the amount of rewards received and one's efforts, one is motivated to reduce efforts; furthermore, the greater the discrepancy is, the more one is motivated to reduce efforts. Discrepancy refers to the perceived difference that may exist between two or more people.

J. Stacy Adams has been associated with the initial development and testing of equity theory. He defined a discrepancy, or inequity, as existing whenever a person perceives that the ratio of his or her job outcomes to job inputs is unequal in comparison with a reference person's ratio of job outcomes to job inputs. The reference person may be someone in an individual's group, in another group, or outside the organization. In equity theory, inputs are aspects such as efforts, skills, education, and task performance that one brings to or puts into a job. Outcomes are those rewards that result from task accomplishment, such as pay, promotion, recognition, achievement, and status.

Equity theory provides the following for police supervisors to consider:

Research findings and applications. The research to date tends to confirm the major ideas in equity theory. Consequently, a supervisor should apply equity theory as follows:

- Because inputs (including effort and behaviors) are likely to vary among police employees, outcomes should also vary. Do not give all workers at a given level the same level of outcomes (such as performance ratings) unless their inputs are identical.

- Distribute outcomes to workers based on their inputs to their jobs and the organization.
- Because it is the perception of equity or inequity that drives motivation, frequently monitor and assess workers' perceptions about relevant outcomes and inputs, and about their own standing on these outcomes and inputs. Then correct inaccurate perceptions by presenting the facts.
- Realize that failure to recognize above-average levels of input (especially performance) has major motivational implications. It might decrease performance.

PROCEDURAL JUSTICE THEORY.   Equity theory focuses on the fair distribution of outcomes; hence, it is often called a theory of distributive justice. As another dimension of fairness in organizations, procedural justice is also crucial for understanding worker motivation. Procedural justice theory, a fairly new approach to motivation, is concerned with the perceived fairness of procedures used to make decisions about the distribution of outcomes. (It is not concerned with the actual distribution of outcomes.) Procedural decisions pertain to how performance levels are evaluated, how grievances or disputes are handled, and how outcomes (such as raises) are distributed among employees. In procedural justice theory, as in equity theory, workers' perceptions are key.

Procedural justice theory holds that workers are going to be more motivated to perform at a high level when they perceive the procedures used to make decisions about the distribution of outcomes as fair. Police employees will be more motivated, for example, if they think that their performance will be accurately assessed. Conversely, if they think that their performance will not be assessed accurately because the police supervisor is not aware of their contributions to the organization, or because the supervisor lets personal feelings affect performance appraisals, they will not be as strongly motivated to perform at a high level. Procedural justice theory seeks to explain what causes workers to perceive procedures as fair or unfair and what the consequences of these perceptions are.

Research findings and applications. Although a lot of work still needs to be done in the area of procedural justice, it nevertheless appears to be of consequence when attempting to understand motivation in organizations.

A police supervisor should:

- Be candid. No matter how unpleasant it may be, diplomatically inform the person or group of the reasons for a decision.
- Encourage the employees to contribute their thoughts about the decision-making process.
- Explain how a performance rating was derived.
- Justify the ethical basis for your decisions and solicit input on how it is perceived.

QUESTIONS AND ANSWERS

Being able to ask the right questions means that the police supervisor has advanced two-thirds of the distance toward answering the question of worker motivation—either for a group of workers or for an individual employee. Together the theories that we've explored afford us a series of questions for the supervisor to ask of himself or herself and others. (As mentioned earlier, the theories are complementary—each one provides different but relevant perspectives and questions.) A prudent assessment of the responses enables the supervisor to formulate strategy for motivating employees. (See Table 7–6.)

Structured Exercise 7–3

OBJECTIVE.   Your objective is to gain experience in confronting the challenges of 1) maintaining high levels of motivation when resources are shrinking and 2) developing an effective motivation program.

PROCEDURE.   The class divides into groups of six to eight people, and each group appoints one member as spokesperson, to present the group's recommendations to the whole class. Here is the scenario:

Each group plays the role of a team of police supervisors in a police department that has recently downsized. Now that the layoff is complete, police management is trying to devise a program to motivate the remaining police employees.

As a result of the downsizing, the workloads of most employees have been increased by about 30 percent. In addition, resources are tight. A very limited amount of money is available for things such as pay raises and benefits. Nevertheless, management thinks that the agency has real potential and that its fortunes will turn around if employees can be motivated to perform at a high level, be innovative, and work together.

Table 7–6   QUESTIONS POSED BY THE THEORIES OF MOTIVATION

Needs theories	What outcomes are individuals motivated to obtain in the workplace?
Expectancy theory	Do individuals believe that their inputs will result in a given level of performance?
	Do individuals believe that performance at this level will lead to obtaining outcomes they desire?
Equity theory	Are outcomes perceived as being at an appropriate level in comparison to inputs?
Procedural justice theory	Are the procedures used to assess inputs and performance and to distribute outcomes perceived as fair?

Your group of supervisors has been asked by management to answer the following questions:

1. What specific steps will you take to develop a motivation program based on the knowledge of motivation you have gained from this chapter?
2. What key features will your motivation program include?
3. What will you do if the program you develop and implement does not seem to be working—if motivation not only does not increase, but also sinks to an all-time low?

When your group has completed those activities, the spokesperson will present the group's plans and proposed actions to the whole class.

JOB SATISFACTION

When we measure individual job satisfaction and combine the results, it adds up to group morale. Low job satisfaction or low morale typically produces poor work performance.

A number of causal factors from the earlier theories of motivation have been grouped into four categories, as shown in Table 7–7.

Structured Exercise 7–4

On an individual basis, complete the following questionnaire. Add up your scores when finished and compare them to the ending scale. As either a work

Table 7–7 PRIMARY CAUSAL FACTORS INFLUENCING JOB SATISFACTION

Organization-wide factors	*Job-content factors*
Pay system	Training
Promotional opportunities	Job scope
Departmental policies and procedures	Role clarity and conflict
Organization structure	Challenge and opportunities
Communications	
Immediate work-environment factors	*Personal factors*
Supervisory style	Age
Participation in decision making	Tenure
Work-group size	Personality
Co-worker relations	Past experiences
Working conditions	Health
Recognition	
Trust	

group or a class, compare your scores and calculate an arithmetic mean and top to bottom ranges. Do you see any patterns or unusual findings? Discuss what can be done to elevate your job satisfaction. (Keep in mind that the group score equals morale.)

1. How satisfied are you with the sort of work you are doing?

1	2	3	4	5
Very dissatisfied				**Very satisfied**

2. What value do you think the community puts on your service?

1	2	3	4	5
None				**Very great**

3. In your daily work, how free are you to make decisions and act on them?

1	2	3	4	5
Not at all				**Very free**

4. How much recognition does your supervisor show for a job well done?

1	2	3	4	5
None				**Great deal**

5. How satisfied are you with the type of leadership you have been getting from your supervisor?

1	2	3	4	5
Very dissatisfied				**Very satisfied**

6. To what extent do you get to participate in the supervisory decisions that affect your job?

1	2	3	4	5
None				**Great deal**

7. How closely do you feel you are observed by your supervisor?

1	2	3	4	5
Too closely				**About right**

8. Are you satisfied with the department as it now stands?

1	2	3	4	5
Very dissatisfied				**Very satisfied**

9. How satisfied are you with your prestige within the city government?

1	2	3	4	5
Very dissatisfied				**Very satisfied**

10. How satisfied are you with your chances of being promoted to a better position?

1	2	3	4	5
Very dissatisfied				**Very satisfied**

11. How satisfied are you with your present salary?

1	2	3	4	5
Very dissatisfied				**Very satisfied**

12. How satisfied are you with your status in the community?

1   2   3   4   5

Very dissatisfied   **Very satisfied**

13. Would you advise a friend to join this department?

1   2   3   4   5

No   **Yes**

14. Do you receive a feeling of accomplishment from the work you are doing?

1   2   3   4   5

No   **Yes**

15. Rate the amount of pressure you feel in meeting the work demands of your job.

1   2   3   4   5

Great deal   **None**

The higher the total score, the greater your job satisfaction. A general rule of thumb is:

55   Very high

50–54   High

45–49   Above average

40–44   Average

35–39   Below average

15–34   Take this job and shove it

THE INCREASING IMPORTANCE OF RECOGNITION AND REWARDS

Few supervisory practices are firmly founded on the concept that positive reinforcement—rewarding behavior you want repeated—works. But in today's police culture, rewards and recognition have become more important than ever for several reasons:

- Supervisors have fewer ways to influence police employees and modify their behavior. Coercion is no longer an option; supervisors increasingly must serve as mentors to influence, rather than compel, desired behavior.
- Employees are being asked to do more. To support empowerment, supervisors must create job environments that are both positive and reinforcing.
- Demographics predict that fewer workers will be available in the post-Generation X timeframe. This emerging pool of employees has different values and expects work to be both purposeful and motivating.

- With tight budgets, rewards and recognition provide a genuine and low-cost way of encouraging higher levels of performance from employees.

A primary reason why most supervisors do not more frequently reward and recognize police employees is that they think they lack the time and creativity to come up with ways to do it. No longer can police supervisors reject the power and practicality of praising. No longer can they fail to recognize a deserving employee because they couldn't think of something to do to show their appreciation. No longer will police employees accept being ignored or getting feedback only once a year (if at all) during a performance review. No longer will using praise, recognition, and rewards be optional in successfully leading people.

Guidelines

The guidelines for effectively recognizing and rewarding police employees are simple:

1. *Be sincere.* Phony attempts to recognize and reward others will be quickly detected. If not genuine, people will see through you. You'll lose credibility. Your trust bank account with these individuals will show a zero balance. If you are sincere and adhere to the following principles, you'll become an even more efficient police supervisor and effective organizational leader.

2. *Fit the reward to the employee.* Start with the individual's personal interest: Reward him or her in ways he or she truly finds rewarding. Such rewards may be personal or official, informal or formal, public or private. The main objective is to ensure that the reward is valued by the person.

3. *Customize the reward to the accomplishment.* Successful reinforcement should be designed to take into account the significance of the accomplishment. An employee who completes a two-year project should be rewarded in a more substantial way than one who does a favor for you. The reward should be an outcome of the amount of time you have to plan and award it.

4. *Make rewards timely and specific.* A reward must be given as soon as possible after the achievement. A reward that comes weeks or months later does little to motivate a police employee to repeat his or her actions. You should always say why the reward is being given—that is, provide a reason for the achievement.

5. *Be accountable.* Hold yourself accountable for identifying police employees; your department should avoid using blanket or "silver bullet" approaches to motivation. "Jelly bean" motivation—giving the same reward to every member of the organization—not only does not inspire employees to excel, but also may actually damage performance, as top achievers see no acknowledgment of the job they have done. An exception to this principle is based on team performance. Much like

Super Bowl champions, all members of the victorious team receive a winner's ring.

6. *Ask.* The ideas in the remainder of this section will be most effective if they are tailored to the individual preferences of the people being recognized. Thus, the way to begin is by asking your staff how you can best show appreciation when they have done a good job.

7. *Rewards are multi-directional.* Many of us mistakenly think that recognition is always downward. Your boss commends you, and you express appreciation to your staff. This is nonsense. Recognition and rewards should move like communication—downward, upward, and horizontally. Sergeants should recognize the good work of their peers. Further, sergeants should be complimenting their bosses. This may sound servile, but bosses possess the same needs and interests. If they do a really good job, let them know it. They'll probably be motivated to become ever-better police managers.

No-Cost Recognition

Some of the best types of recognition cost nothing at all. A sincere word of thanks from the right person at the right time can mean more to an employee than a raise, a formal award, or a whole wall of certificates or plaques. Part of the power of such rewards comes from the knowledge that someone took the time to notice the achievement, seek out the employee responsible, and personally deliver praise in a timely manner.

The no-cost recognition is limited only by your imagination. Here are a few examples:

- Tell your staff up front that you are going to let them know how they are doing.
- A good way to personalize any reinforcement is to use the person's first name when delivering the comment. Tell them why the behavior or result is important to you.
- Greet all employees by name.
- When discussing an employee's or a group's ideas with other people, peers, or police management, make sure you give credit.
- Arrange for the police employee to have lunch with the captain or chief.
- Have lunch or coffee with a police employee or a group of employees you don't normally see.
- Make certain that, in addition to your recognition of the employee, the chief or commander telephones the person.
- Ask the person which training program they would find most useful, and then see to it that he or she attends it.
- Similarly, ask employees what assignment they are most interested in, and help them get it.
- Recognize (and thank) people who recognize others. Be sure it's clear that making everyone a hero is an important principle in your work unit.

- A great motivational act that you can do for another is to listen.
- Send information about an accomplishment to a police association publication and the individual's hometown newspaper. Get your employees' pictures in the department's annual report.
- When a team of police employees achieves, the entire team needs to be recognized. If only one officer or the highest performer of a group is recognized, the group is apt to lose motivation.
- Have the person attend a command staff meeting.

Karen Green, a Los Angeles lieutenant for 20 years, has been responsible for publishing the monthly STAR NEWS Magazine. She and her staff **volunteer** their time, which is considerable. Her small crew twice won the Publication of the Decade (in 1980 and 1990), awarded by the Washington Crime New Services. She and her team celebrate annually with gag gifts and cartooning by a friend. Everyone is recognized. The recently elected sheriff, who knew of her motivation and successes, walked into her office and said, "Karen, I appreciate your good work, and I admire you for your contributions to our Department. I can assure you that your efforts will be rewarded." She told me that the "thank you" alone will be forever cherished. Recognition is so easy to do and so inexpensive to distribute that there is simply no excuse for not doing it.

Structured Exercise 7–5

In a group setting, brainstorm at least 20 additional no-cost recognition items. In your opinion, what are the top five items?

RETENTION

Some police personnel decide not to transfer to another agency although the salary and/or benefits are better. Others decide not to retire although their pension may be 80% or more of their salary. Why? When asked, the frequent response is, "I'm having too much fun."

> New studies show that employees rate having a nice, caring boss more highly than they value money or benefits. How long an employee remains with an organization, and how productive they are, is directly determined by the relationship with an immediate supervisor.

Police agencies are in dire need of experienced and hardworking person-nel. Alternatively, the enticement of improved retirement benefits is compelling. There are now retirement programs that vest at 90-plus percent—meaning the employee is working for 10% of his salary. There are other pro-grams that vest at 3% at age 50 (25 years of employment $\times$ 3% = 75% of salary; 30 years = 90%).

More and more agencies are recognizing that the need to motivate people to stay is as important (in some cases, more important) as motivating them to join the department. The supervisor-as-leader is in a pivotal position to **recruit, get the best out of, and retain police employees**.

Don't Be a Damn Fool

A frustrated and depressed police sergeant told me that "for six months I've attempted to motivate an officer. I've done everything I can think of, and he doesn't respond. What should I do?" I immediately thought of the comedian W. C. Fields, who said . . .

> If at first you do not succeed, try and try again. Then if you do not succeed, give up; don't be a damn fool about it.

I realize that there are some people who enjoy being miserable and thrive on making others the same. No matter how hard you try, they will persist in accentuating the negative. They'll gleefully point out every mistake made. They'll ignore and even ridicule all of the positive events and fun associated with police work. They're likely burned out, burned up, or rusted out. And they do not, will not, or cannot change—no matter how hard anyone tries.

When confronted with the person who is always substandard in perform-ance and a chronic naysayer, then face it; leadership is not the answer.

Key Points

- Supervisors are responsible for motivating their staff to accomplish the mis-sion for the department.
- The reasons for having motivated workers are improved job performance and high job satisfaction.
- Motivating others starts with you.
- Motivation and performance are not identical.
- Motivators can be intrinsic and/or extrinsic.
- There are several theories on human motivation. Basically, they can be cat-egorized as either needs or process.

- Individuals' job satisfaction measures, once combined, depict group morale.
- No longer can supervisors avoid the power and practicality of recognizing and rewarding their staff.
- The first and most critical requirement when praising people is sincerity.
- Retaining police employees depends on the ability of the supervisor-as-leader to motivate them to stay with the agency.
- While everyone is capable of benefiting from being motivated to achieve the department's mission, there are usually a few who resist doing so.

DISCUSSION

1. Why might a person with a very high level of motivation perform poorly?
2. Why might a person with a very low level of motivation be a top performer?
3. What are the distinguishing features of the needs theories?
4. Similarly, what are the unique aspects of the process theories?
5. What are the important differences between the two schools of motivational thinking? Are there any points of agreement?
6. How do one's motivation and job satisfaction relate to one another?
7. Attempt to expand the list of causes of job satisfaction.
8. Also, try to increase the list of consequences of poor job satisfaction.

EMPOWERMENT

The police supervisor is responsible for creating a partnership with his or her work team that is centered in empowerment and results in enhanced commitment, better decisions, and good police work.

The best executive is the one who has enough sense to pick good people to do what he wants done, and self-restraint enough to keep from meddling with them while they do it.

—Theodore Roosevelt

Responsibility Eight is a logical extension of Responsibility Seven—motivation. An empowered employee is typically a motivated one. Additionally, empowered employees take on the role of leader, which was discussed in Responsibility Six. Training for empowerment is essential, and this is the subject of Responsibility Nine.

The supervisory word of the moment is empowerment. It is alleged to be the cure-all for job dissatisfaction, low morale, employee inefficiency, poor performance, and risk avoidance. Everyone seems to be hailing its virtues and scorning any detractors. But just granting power, without some method of replacing the discipline and order that come out of a command-and-control bureaucracy, produces chaos. We have to learn how to disperse power so self-discipline can largely replace imposed discipline. That immerses us in the area of culture: replacing the bureaucracy with aspirations, values, and visions.

Empowerment embodies the belief that the answer to the latest crisis lies within each of us and therefore we all buckle up for adventure. Empowerment bets that people at our own level or below will best know how to organize,

155

serve customers, and get it right the first time. We know that a democracy is a political system designed not for efficiency but as a hedge against the abuse of power. Empowerment is our willingness to bring this value into the workplace. Empowerment enables us to claim our autonomy and commits us to making the organization work well, with or without the sponsorship of those above us. This requires a belief that our safety and our freedom are in our own hands. No easy task.

Empowerment works! The advantages far exceed any downside. My concern is for those who seek to wave a magic wand and "bang"—it happens. My hope is for those sworn and civilian supervisors who choose to nurture and carefully unleash the full potential of their staff.

> If you want community-oriented policing (COP), then you must empower your staff. Without their empowerment, COP will be a great success on paper and an embarrassing failure in reality.

There are several other benefits associated with empowerment. Before discussing them, it is best to disclose some of the issues and pitfalls that could jump up and surprise you when empowering others.

WE DON'T ACT ON WHAT WE KNOW

What is beguiling about our situation is that we already know a lot about service and about empowerment. The books have been written, the experiments have been conducted, and the results are in. We know, intellectually and empirically, that empowerment is a leadership strategy for creating high-performance workplaces. Virtually every police organization showcases the success it has had with empowerment, quality improvement efforts, community-efficient operations, and superior customer service.

What's the Problem?

So what's the problem? The problem is that despite this load of knowledge and evidence, there has been disturbingly little fundamental change in the way police departments manage themselves. Few organizations are working hard to introduce tools and methods to actually help people to make more intelligent decisions, especially decisions that improve system-wide performance. This likely will result in organizations that decentralize authority for a while, find that many poor and uncoordinated decisions result, and then abandon the "empowerment" fad and re-centralize. This, of course, is precisely what many of the newly "empowered" workers, cynical from past management fads, fear. Even the organizations that are out telling their stories about COP and empowered police personnel have enormous difficulty in capitalizing on their experience. This overall problem is comprised of the following barriers:

1. *Being unwilling to really open up.* What remains untouched is the belief that power, purpose, and decision-making can reside at the top and the police organization can still learn how to better serve its customers via COP. When an innovative program such as COP challenges this fundamental belief about how to govern, one of two things usually occurs. Either police management rejects it and it is power and decision-making as usual, or an effort is made to drive new programs across the bottom layers of the department.

> In essence, empowerment is enabling decision-making in others. Since empowerment is cutting-edge stuff today, most police managers and supervisors are espousing its magic. But, in fact, they are averse to really opening up and sharing their decision-making authority.

2. *Ducking.* When you empower your staff, you share with them successes and failures. Everyone is in the same boat. You can't sign on only for the victories and duck the failures. There are some people that do not want to be empowered! They do not, or cannot, make the commitment to be held accountable. They prefer to gripe about decisions and, when asked for theirs, respond with "Whatever you say. You're the boss."

3. *Not believing.* Empowerment necessitates a strong belief in the integrity of the employees' work ethic. If a supervisor does not truly believe that the staff want to do a good job and enjoy their work, then empowering them is impractical.

4. *Risking.* Empowering others is stressful when you lack faith in their ability to make the right decision. Whether unprepared, unskilled, or un-analytical, it matters not. A supervisor would be foolish to chance a set of no-brainer decisions in order to be recognized as an empowerer. Taking a risk and being a fool are not synonymous.

5. *Misunderstanding.* A few moments ago you read that "empowerment is enabling decision-making in others." Those being empowered could erroneously assume that they own the ultimate decision, that the supervisor abdicated the rights and responsibilities of their rank. Empowerment is not giving away the decision; it is permitting those who are affected by it to input their ideas and aspirations. While empowerment is akin to a partnership, the supervisor is the senior partner. The senior partner retains the final authority for saying "yes" or "no." Some see empowerment as a vote on what to do, when it is a voice on what to do. Those who consider empowerment as the "majority rules" will experience frustration and confusion. Those who accept empowerment as a vehicle for expressing, even arguing, one's point of view will be grateful for the opportunity and supportive of the final decision. The final decision can be the result of collective thinking. The accountability for its results sticks with the supervisor.

6. *Using an "all or none" approach.* The "all or none" approach to empower-ment can be mistakenly adopted by a police supervisor. Behind such thinking is equal treatment. While well intentioned, the underlying reasoning is faulty. For example, if a supervisor has a staff of six people and five are ready and willing to share in decisions that affect them, while one is not, such a supervisor decides there is no empowerment. Thus, all experience equal treatment—all or none. If equality really counted, then all of us should have the same salary, same rewards, and so on. What really counts is being fair with everyone. Clearly, it is fair to empower those who are ready, while denying those who are incapable of handling expanded decision-making authority.

7. *Focusing.* The core focus of COP is a police-customer partnership. This partnership seeks to empower members of the public in making decisions about the quantity and quality of police services they experience. Empowering the citizenry without empowering the staff is not only ridicu-lous and confusing, but also counterproductive. An empowered public, combined with an empowered police, spells "COP"—real COP!

EM-POWER-MENT

Many of us approach some of our most vital ideas and emotions as if they were finite—limited. For example, there is only so much beauty to go around. Fair-ness can be counted up to 100 percent. Love is like a pie; there are only so many pieces to serve. Loyalty, trust, integrity, and power can be thought of in the same terms. In fact, all of these values are unlimited in mind and deed.

Some would agree, as I do, that the more you give away, the more you're likely to possess. Rodgers and Hammerstein wrote in a lyric, "A bell is not a bell till it's rung, a song is not a song till it's sung, and love is not love until you give it away." Similarly, power is not power until you give it away.

It stands to reason that the police supervisor who opts to give a share of their power to others automatically expands their sphere of influence. Basically, the supervisor has empowered others and is in turn in a much better position to accomplish their assigned tasks.

By now, you may see the link between empowerment and delegation. Delegation means sharing power, sharing power leads to empowerment, and empowerment means that employees experience ownership of their jobs. In essence, they are given the opportunity to become 100 percent responsible.

Next, we'll cover delegation in detail and then, later on, its partner in empowering others—participation. Remember the following simple but proven formula:

Delegation + Participation = Empowerment

Structured Exercise 8–1

INSTRUCTIONS. Twenty-seven statements follow. They are statements about your job environment. If you feel the statement is true or mostly true of your job environment, mark it T. Conversely, if you believe the statement is false or mostly false, mark it F.

1. The work is really challenging.
2. Few employees have any important responsibilities.
3. Doing things in a different way is valued.
4. There's not much group spirit.
5. There is a fresh, novel atmosphere about the place.
6. Employees have a great deal of freedom to do as they like.
7. New and different ideas are always being tried out.
8. A lot of people seem to be just putting in time.
9. This place would be one of the first to try out a new idea.
10. Employees are encouraged to make their own decisions.
11. People seem to take pride in the organization.
12. People can use their own initiative to do things.
13. People put quite a lot of effort into what they do.
14. Variety and change are not particularly important.
15. The same methods have been used for quite a long time.
16. Supervisors encourage employees to rely on themselves when a problem arises.
17. Few people ever volunteer.
18. Employees generally do not try to be unique and different.
19. It is quite a lively place.
20. Employees are encouraged to learn things even if they are not directly related to the job.
21. It's hard to get people to do their work.
22. New approaches to things are rarely tried.
23. The work is usually very interesting.
24. Things tend to stay just about the same.
25. Supervisors meet with employees regularly to discuss their future work goals.
26. Things always seem to be changing.
27. Employees function fairly independently of supervisors.

Scoring. This awareness consists of three dimensions: involvement, independence, and innovation (I^3). We believe that a high I^3 score for you means high empowerment. The lower the I^3 score, the greater the likelihood that you're not experiencing much, if any, empowerment at work.

> Give yourself one point if you've marked these statements as follows: 1 = T; 4 = F; 8 = F; 11 = T; 13 = T; 17 = F; 19 = T; 21 = F; and 23 = T. Your score for involvement is _____.
>
> Give yourself one point if you've marked these statements as follows: 2 = F; 6 = T; 10 = T; 12 = T; 16 = T; 18 = F; 20 = T; 25 = T; and 27 = T. Your score for independence is _____.
>
> Give yourself one point if you've marked these statements as follows: 3 = T; 5 = T; 7 = T; 9 = T; 14 = F; 15 = F; 22 = F; 24 = F; and 26 = T. Your score for innovation is _____.

If your score is 0 to 3, that particular dimension is very low; 4 to 5 is below average; 6 is average; 7 is above average; 8 is well above average; and 9 is very high.

Obviously, I'm hoping that you are looking at scores from 6 on up. An understanding of your job environment can help you deal with both the positive and the negative aspects of your work. This information may help you in improving the various aspects of empowerment.

DELEGATION

Delegation of responsibility has been a central topic in supervisory and management texts through the ages. But today's demands on police employees to initiate far-reaching actions and think creatively propel the subject toward the top of the list.

Delegation frees up the police organization to work faster and with less traditional hierarchy (e.g., strict adherence to chain of command, rules and regulations for everything, established routines). Much more delegation is required now than ever before in meeting the challenges of police work.

Yes, But . . .

A very bright trainer once commented, "When you delegate you are always delegating one thing for certain—uncertainty!" In other words, will the person who now possesses the responsibility come through? Will the empowered individual perform the task, and if so, will it be done correctly?

The media are quick to expose police corruption. It makes exciting news. In many instances, a newspaper article will implicitly point out that someone or a group of officers failed to execute their duties correctly or faithfully. The officers may have been delegated certain responsibilities and either accidentally or willfully violated the trust placed in them.

Is it any wonder that many police supervisors are fearful of delegating? After all, when something goes sideways, they're accountable. They must answer for their decision to delegate. At the same time, how would police work ever get done if delegation did not occur? The "yes, but . . . " syndrome is often voiced like this: "Yes, but if I delegate this task, it may not get done, or at least done to my satisfaction." This leads us to not really let go.

Really Letting Go

> The plain fact is that nine out of 10 police supervisors are not delegating enough. They think they are. They hand over tasks and pass out assignments routinely. But rarely does the officer really become empowered with true ownership—and its parallel, the sense of being 100 percent responsible.

What goes wrong? First of all, there is a distinction between "letting go" and "really letting go." However, does really letting go mean chaos, confusion, and substandard performance? Perhaps, but not necessarily. Steps can be taken to avoid the pitfalls of delegation, all the while assuring that its advantages are secured for the police agency. Before I review these steps, it's important that we consider the benefits of delegation.

Who Benefits

First of all, many police organizations would cease to function, or at minimum be highly dysfunctional, if delegation did not occur. After all, the chief or the sheriff cannot effectively both administer the department and conduct criminal investigations. Watch commanders cannot effectively supervise their crew if they're responding to police radio calls. The key word here is "effectively." Yes, they can engage in police work if they choose to do so. Unfortunately, there are some police managers and supervisors that just can't let go, let alone really let go.

When we are expected to work with and through people and systems to produce results, we become a supervisor or manager. Many of our other life roles involve working with and through people such as family and friends.

We can (assuming no loss of efficiency) generate one hour of effort and produce one unit of results or police services.

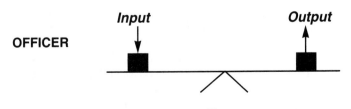

Figure 8–1 Officer

A supervisor, however, can invest one hour of energy and create 10 or 50 or 100 units of services through effective delegation. Police supervision, after all, is shifting the fulcrum over to achieve 1:10 or 1:50 or 1:100. Effective supervision is effective delegation.

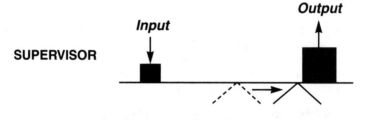

Figure 8–2   Supervisor

There are four parties that benefit from appropriate delegation. First, there is the community—you and me. Empowered police employees are typically more skillful and dedicated. Hence, we get better, less costly services. We in turn are more likely to respect and support our police department.

Second, the organization itself harvests the wealth of brainpower that exists within its ranks. Everyone says, "I'm 100 percent responsible!" Everyone sets his or her sights on excellence.

Third, you benefit as a supervisor because you're:

- Building motivation for getting the job done
- Increasing mutual trust between yourself and your officers
- Enhancing the officers' job skills and knowledge
- Encouraging a feeling of ownership
- Leveraging your power to provide quality police services (most important)

Fourth, your staff benefits by becoming more:

- Motivated to do their work
- Trusting and trustworthy
- Professional
- Competent
- Self-confident
- Capable of producing top-notch police work (most important)

Obviously, everyone stands to benefit from really letting go. Again, far too many of us are unwilling to take the risk; we resort to the "yes, but . . ." tactic. The "yes, but . . . " game that some of us play today cannot be tolerated any longer. Empowerment is the game, and being 100 percent responsible is the price you pay to play it.

Setting the Context

Seven forces must be at work when you delegate. Without them, you're taking a big risk. With them in place and functioning, you are apt to achieve superb performance:

- Those being delegated to must be well trained in doing their job (and it must be ongoing, reliable, and pertinent).
- You should project high standards, which you live by and demand of everyone uniformly—including yourself.
- You should understand the values and needs of each employee.
- From the preceding, establish and maintain a conduit for open and candid communications.
- Known anticipations should exist for those who fulfill their duties—rewards.
- Known anticipations should exist for those who do not fulfill their duties— reprimands.
- There should be feedback systems. The new employee should receive feedback more often because they are earning your trust. The established officer should receive feedback less frequently because they have gained your faith.

Four Types of Delegation

Delegation does not come in one style or shape. There are four ways to delegate: 1) stewardship; 2) gofer; 3) dump; and 4) micro. Only one promotes empowerment—stewardship. The last three either inhibit or prevent empowering employees.

STEWARDSHIP. Stewardship delegation concentrates on results instead of methods. It affords police personnel with a choice of method, but, more important, makes them 100 percent responsible for results. Admittedly, it takes more time in the beginning. But it's time wisely invested. Stewardship delegation moves the production fulcrum way over, thereby increasing your empowerment leverage. This holds for both growth and routine activities.

Stewardship delegation involves commitment regarding expectations in five areas:

1. *Desired results.* Generate a mutual understanding of what needs to be accomplished, focusing on what, not how, and on results, not methods. Spend time. Visualize the needed outcome. Have the officer describe for you how the results will look and when they will be achieved.
2. *Guidelines.* Carefully identify the boundaries within which the person must function. These should be as flexible as possible. If you know of any land mines, be certain to reveal them. In other words, instruct the officer in what not to do, but don't tell him or her what to do. Keep the responsibility for his or her performance with the officer—to do whatever is essential, but within the guidelines.

3. *Resources.* Identify the various resources that the officer can utilize to obtain the preferred outcomes.
4. *Accountability.* Establish minimum standards that will be applied in evaluating the work effort and when violations will occur.
5. *Consequences.* Indicate what will happen, both positive and negative, as an outcome of the evaluation. This involves rewards and reprimands.

Stewardship delegation on occasion may include some highly routine processes. Writing crime reports can become monotonous after a while. Routine work is unavoidable. It happens to all of us. The saving grace is that at least it's our routine and not someone else's. We own it and can even change it within the guidelines.

Stewardship delegation means no nagging on your part. Within the guidelines and standards you set, the other person becomes the boss.

GOFER.   Gofer delegation is highly routine assigned work wherein you go for this, go for that. You're not encouraged to think of the task as being part of your job. Indeed, you're probably not encouraged to think at all.

Gofer delegation is a turnoff for police employees. Ask them—they'll tell you it is. Some may open up and respond with, "Why don't you just do the job yourself? I'm merely an errand boy. I'm not learning anything. I'm not growing."

DUMP.   Delegation dump occurs when you give one of your staff all of your work. Or you assign your work out over all of your crew. Those that engage in the dumping of their work on others are viewed as lazy and incompetent. The delegation dumper rationalizes that he or she is doing a great career service to others. They're learning to do advanced types of tasks. In reality, they are being victimized by a clueless boss who is assigning them excessive work.

MICRO.   Micro-delegation is micro-supervising. The micro-delegators are afraid that if they do not direct you each and every moment, the work won't be done right. They look over your shoulder and constantly meddle in your work. How much does micro-delegation really accomplish? How many people is it possible to supervise when you microdelegate? The answers are, respectively, "not much" and "very few." Those subjected to micro-delegation are often angry, frustrated, and seeking another work unit. In an environment where we must have every good idea from every man and woman in the police organization, we cannot afford management or supervisory styles that suppress and intimidate.

Delegation and Trust

Trust brings out the very best in us. But it takes time and persistence, including constant training and consistent encouragement for people to enhance their competencies. Stewardship delegation changes the nature of the supervisor–police employee relationship. The police officer, civilian dispatcher, or criminal investigator becomes their own boss, governed by a conscience committed to agreed-on, desired outcomes. Such delegation also frees creative forces for conduct that is in harmony with the mission of the department.

Stewardship delegation is the best indicator of effective supervision because it is so fundamental to both professional and personal growth. Stewardship delegation takes time; time to train, time to mentor, time to evaluate—all of which build the trust level to the point that stewardship works.

When an officer is ready for 100 percent responsibility and stewardship, then it is up to the supervisor to really let go. If the supervisor eventually fails to transform the lonership into ownership, then regression to a gofer situation will occur. In essence, the training and growth phase will devolve into one of over-supervision. Skill development will be replaced by ill will.

If an employee proves incapable of functioning under stewardship delegation, then don't do it. If the person is incompetent, a malingerer, a malcontent, then gofer delegation and microsupervising are required along with frequent (daily, if needed) performance appraisals. (See Responsibility Twelve.)

Earlier I described seven contextual forces that must be in place before you can "really let go." They were:

- Training
- High standards
- Values and needs
- Open and candid communications
- Rewards
- Reprimands
- Feedback

There is one more. Without it the above seven forces are meaningless. You must first and foremost trust the person's work ethic. Remember, you're the one accountable for your staff member's work.

How Do I Know?

Are you really letting go? Here is a list of questions that will help you know if you are or not:

- Have you transmitted the overarching vision with clarity? Does the officer, through demonstrated behavior, clearly "buy in"?
- Is the person aware of the level of performance standards?
- Do you trust the person and have you conveyed it?
- Are you known for butting in at the last minute to handle a problem that someone is experiencing with his or her assignment?
- Do you hold your tongue on asking questions about someone's work efforts?
- Have you avoided excessive reporting?
- When the officer stops by, do you avoid giving direct orders or implying that such and such may be a better approach?

Structured Exercise 8–2

——•◦✲◦•——

Make a list of responsibilities you could delegate and the police personnel you could delegate to or train to be responsible in these areas. Determine what is needed to start the process of delegation or training.

——•◦✲◦•——

PARTICIPATION

I have seen on the desks of a couple of police supervisors the epigram "When I want your opinion, I'll give it to you." Unfortunately, I discovered that they weren't kidding. A few years ago a police chief told me, "I'm a great believer in participative management. I'm going to manage, and you'd damn well better participate." How do you feel about working for such a person? Are you working for that person right now? (Are you that type of a supervisor?) What's delegation like in your organization? How about empowerment?

Misconceptions about Participation

> Allowing others to have an opportunity to express their ideas, needs, and hopes about an issue or a pending decision that affects them is what I mean by participation.

I've heard some police supervisors voice irritation with, and resistance to, participation as follows: "We're not running a democratic vote here. I'll make the decision, and they're expected to get with it." In part, I agree. A police organization cannot be effective if the majority rules. Can you imagine a police sergeant, during roll call briefing, asking his officers to vote on whether they want to patrol or stay in the station? The sergeant is being paid to make such decisions.

My proposition is rather simple, but extraordinarily compelling—when a decision is going to affect others, let them have a chance to express their ideas. Do you wonder why people reject an idea, general order, new policy? Often it is because they had no input—"No one asked me!"

Letting others participate in decisions that may affect them does not surrender your authority or responsibility for the ultimate decision. It's yours; you got it when you decided to become a supervisor. You can give it away, but no one can take it away from you. Through the participation of others, you listen, you learn, and then you're likely to make a much more reliable decision.

Why, and Why Not, Allow Others to Participate?

Let me rephrase the preceding heading—why, and why not, encourage others to participate in decisions that will (or might) affect their ability to do their job? Here are some reasons that you will want to review.

The best means for getting a good idea is to generate a lot of ideas:

- It builds others' faith that you really care about their welfare and workfare.
- Others' inclusion in a decision-making process usually increases their commitment to the eventual implementation of the decision.
- Increased commitment often causes increased productivity.
- A sense of teamwork is fostered.
- Teamwork leads to synergy, wherein the mental energy of a few people multiplies into what hundreds are capable of contributing.

Let's now examine some reasons not to encourage your staff to get involved in the decision process:

- Participation takes time—you have to listen to others (eight, nine, or more people).
- You may experience a sense of frustration or insecurity when confronted with ideas that refute yours.
- You may be convinced of the correctness of their approach—the easy route—and thus opt for group consensus.
- Some may accuse you of manipulating or conning them. "The sergeant asked me for my opinion. She then proceeded to do the exact opposite of what I suggested." (This can be corrected by simply providing feedback on the reasons for your decision. It may be so candid as, "My gut told me so.")

The preceding lists of reasons for and against participation are starter lists. Please add to them as you deem appropriate. But if you've decided to empower yourself and those who work for you, then participation is in.

Structured Exercise 8-3

ALPHA II SUGGESTED REGULATIONS SHEET. The following group exercise will help you and your associates to identify the key variables in group dynamics, decision-making, consensus, and conflict resolution. Enjoy your journey to Alpha II.

BACKGROUND. Scientists have discovered that the second planet orbiting Alpha Centauri is almost a duplicate of Earth, except there are no intelligent life forms. A colonization party, including you and your group, has been formed to settle on Alpha II. The 500 members of the colonization party come from many different regions and cultures with many differing customs and mores.

INSTRUCTIONS.   Your group has been asked to recommend a list of the five most important rules from the following list to govern social conduct and relationships both on the space journey and on Alpha II. You need not concern yourself with questions of enforcement; assume that all rules can be enforced.

Rules Recommended by the International Social Control Commission (can be revised)

1. The social control process will be governed by a three-member body representing the police, courts, and corrections.
2. There will be no plea-bargaining in the court system.
3. The Bill of Rights will apply in total on Alpha II.
4. There will be no death penalty.
5. The police will not carry guns.
6. No juvenile, regardless of the offense, will be incarcerated in an institution.
7. The social control mechanism (police, courts, and corrections) will be at the national level of government.
8. All social control personnel will not be under civil service, but will serve at the pleasure of the community.
9. No harmful or addictive drugs will be permitted in Alpha II.
10. There will be no public displays of sexual behavior, but sexually explicit literature will be available privately as desired.
11. No individual will be discriminated against or be judged guilty of any sexual act solely because of his or her sexual preferences.
12. All police officers will possess a bachelor's degree.

Why Is Participation So Effective?

In today's employer-employee relations, few practices have been so successful in developing consensus and attaining common goals as the development of participation by the police supervisor.

- Participation is an amazingly simple way to inspire police employees. And its simplicity lies in the definition of participation: "to share in common with others."
- Sharing, then, is the secret. You must share knowledge and information with others to gain their cooperation. You must share your own experience so that officers will gain from it. You must share the decision-making process itself so that personnel can have impact. And you must share credit for achievement.

Participation or sharing may not be easy for you. However, once you've learned how to share, participation is self-perpetuating. Supervision becomes easier when police employees begin to share responsibility with you. No longer do you alone have to watch for every problem. Employees won't wait for you to say what to do in an emergency. You'll find the officers using their own initiative to keep crime down. So sharing pays off as employees share your decision and their work accomplishments with you.

Three Rules

There are three fundamental rules to abide by. First, recognize that without group support your chance of achievement is slim. Second, your best chance for winning group support is by allowing the forces within the group to comment on a decision with minimum interference from you. But you must not stand by while your "team" strikes off in the wrong direction. You can offer sound coaching by providing facts that might be overlooked and by asking the group to weigh pros and cons of various options. Third, be honest with yourself. Are you using participation to motivate or to manipulate? If it is the former, congratulations. If it is the latter, eventually the officers will discover that they are being conned. When this happens, kiss both your supervisory power and leadership goodbye.

Police supervisors must strive for the antithesis of blind obedience. They need people who have the self-confidence to express opposing views, get all the facts on the table, and respect differing opinions. It's a preferred mode of learning; it's how we form balanced judgments.

ENTITLEMENT IS EMPOWERMENT IN EXCESS

All the recent attention to empowerment has reinforced, unintentionally, our zeal for entitlement (you-owe-it-to-me). Believing that, now empowered, we can do exactly what we want, and get all that we ask for, is simply trying to win at the new game. Doing our own thing is a self-serving act. Line employees can use empowerment as a weapon. In the name of empowerment, I have heard people ask for:

- More pay
- A larger budget
- More people, more empire
- Freedom to pursue strictly personal projects
- Greater recognition and privilege
- Immunity from disappointment from those above
- A risk-free environment

Wrong! That we have been encouraged to find our voice and stand up without getting mistreated does not mean that we are going to get all we ask for, nor can we expect to be protected. Empowerment is a commitment to a dialogue, not an act of concession. It is based on reciprocal commitments. When coming out of a high-control management system, there is a tendency to take advantage of the choice handed us. The following are some ways people exploit their freedom:

- If a decision is made that we don't agree with, we begin to undermine that decision, either actively or passively.
- We do not take responsibility for promises others in our unit have made. The belief that no one else can represent my viewpoint is a subtle form of anarchy.
- In expressing our opinion, we expect immunity from other people's rejection or resentment.

> A sense of being entitled is based on the "you-owe-it-to-me" syndrome. It is a warped sense of duty to one's self. When we think of looking out for our own interests as a duty, it legitimizes a self-absorbed viewpoint that puts personal desires on equal footing with our ethical responsibilities to others, both within and without the workplace.

Entitlement also rests on the belief that something is owed us because of sacrifices we have made. What is hard to accept, though, is that, whatever we think we sacrificed, it was a choice that we made. We have to reclaim what we gave away. No one owes it to us. In fact, the more the police department gives us that we may not have earned, the more entitled we feel. Entitlement is claiming rights that have not been earned.

Choosing Empowerment

The decision to pursue the principles and practice of empowerment is an issue of leadership strategy, but at its core, it is first a matter of individual choice. Managers can create the social architecture and practices to support teamwork and empowerment, but individuals have to make the decision to reclaim their own sovereignty, and this is no small matter either. Finally, training people to be empowered requires team training, and, thus, we now move forward to Responsibility Nine.

KEY POINTS

- Delegation and participation lead to empowerment of personnel.
- A lot is known about the benefits of empowerment, but few supervisors actually practice it.
- When it comes to delegation, there is a significant difference between "letting go" and "**really** letting go."
- Four parties benefit from proper delegation: the community, the department, the supervisor, and the staff.
- There are four ways to delegate: stewardship, gofer, dump, and micro.

- Building a workplace context requires: training; high standards; values and needs; communications; rewards; reprimands; feedback; and most of all **TRUST**.
- It may be necessary to microsupervise a few employees.
- Letting others participate in decisions that are going to affect them does not surrender a supervisor's authority or responsibility for the final decision.
- Teamwork is participative supervision.
- The key to participation is sharing.
- Empowerment, when emphasized excessively, results in an "entitlement mentality."

DISCUSSION

1. What is meant by "really letting go" when one delegates? What are the advantages in doing so? Are there any risks involved?
2. There are eight forces that must be functioning when you delegate. Rank order the eight forces in terms of their importance.
3. When and why is a supervisor justified in using either gofer or micro-delegation, or both?
4. What are the reasons for others to participate in decisions that are going to affect them? What are the reasons not to?
5. What is the key or secret of participation? Why is it effective?
6. What should the supervisor do to avoid—or if it exists, combat—entitlement thinking within the work team?

TEAM TRAINING

The police supervisor is responsible for training a group of independently minded employees with all of their vast diversity and forging them into an interdependent team—one that is united, but not uniform.

Team spirit means you are willing to sacrifice personal considerations for the welfare of all. That defines a team player.

—John Wooden

All of the prior responsibilities (Responsibilities One through Eight) are now fused with mutual trust and team-training in order to facilitate team-based decision-making.

One of a baby's earliest words is "mine." We enter the world totally dependent on others for our very survival. Most of us are encouraged as we grow up to be independent—to be self-sufficient, to be competitive. We place a high value on being independent. But being interdependent is of higher value than being independent.

As we grow and mature, we become increasingly aware that all of nature is interdependent. We realize that an ecological system governs nature, including society and the organizations within it. We further discover that human life also is interdependent.

Let us look at maturity as a continuum:

- Dependence is seeing the world in terms of you—you take care of me; you help me; you're responsible for me.
- Independence is seeing the world in terms of I—I can do it; I am responsible; I can choose.

- Interdependence is the model of we—we can do it; we can cooperate; we are responsible.

> Dependent people need others to get what they want. Independent people can get what they want by their own effort. Interdependent people combine their efforts—form a team—to achieve their goals.

It is the successful supervisor-as-leader who realizes the need for the best thinking, a coordinated effort, and mutual support to be truly effective. Independent supervisors who do not have the maturity to think and act interdependently may be good individual producers, but they won't be good leaders or team players.

Teamwork depends on people who are willing to function as interdependent contributors. For this to occur, they must first trust one another and then be trained to operate as a team. This section centers on the need for interdependence as compared with independence or dependence. In the two sections that follow, we'll cover the important advantages of team performance. We then deal with trust and training, which are the two essential underpinnings for team building. Finally, we will direct our attention to two major hurdles confronted by any endeavor to foster teamwork—cultural diversity and core-cracking. Work groups that are trained in interdependency evolve into teams. This team approach will be the hallmark of the great police departments of the 21st century.

WHY TEAMS?

Although establishing teams frequently involves a lot of training, the effort provides three factors important to group effectiveness:

- Synergy
- Interdependence
- A support base

Synergy

What energy is to the individual, synergy is to groups. The synergy of a group is always potentially greater than the sum of the combined energies of its members. Thus, it is not infrequent in laboratory exercises that a group effort results in a better performance than that achieved by the group's most competent member. If you doubt it, have three people independently make a bed. Then have them make three beds jointly.

Interdependence

Effective teams are made up of highly independent individuals who must combine their separate efforts in order to produce an organizational result. The focus of the team effort is on combining rather than on coordinating resources. Interdependence in today's organizations is a simple reality. Police services are too complex and the respective technologies too specialized for any one individual to master alone.

A Support Base

The police team constructed for alignment has the potential to provide social and emotional support for its members, producing a more satisfying and work-productive environment. It is important to note that, for a group truly to function as a support base, the group norms that emerge for any specific team must originate from within the team itself and not represent a set of "shoulds" from the behavioral sciences or other social institutions. Sometimes, also, it is simply more fun to work with someone else than to work alone!

TEAM-TRAINING

By its very nature, teamwork depends on the effectiveness of the interaction among team members. The concepts of contact, role, and values are elements of effective team interaction. Good contact is based on authenticity among team members. It implies that each individual is aware of their individuality and is willing to state views and ideas clearly and to support the principles of openness and conscious choice. An environment that encourages the open expression of disagreement, as well as agreement, accepts the reality that an individual may like some co-workers more than others. This is legitimate as long as openly stated preferences do not result in discriminatory, unfair, or task-destructive behavior.

All decisions, whether made by individuals or by groups, are based on values. Three specific values seem to identify good working police teams: 1) task effectiveness, 2) dealing in the present, and 3) conflict viewed as an asset.

1. *Task effectiveness.* The well-functioning group of police officers places a high value on task effectiveness, with greater emphasis on doing the right things than on doing things right. This value implies that the team also focuses on the objective, or end result, rather than only on the team's ongoing activity.

2. *Dealing in the present.* The effective team focuses on "right here, right now," an emphasis that allows a flexible response to changing conditions within the team itself and within the larger organization. The team can make more appropriate decisions when it is concentrating on what is happening, rather than on why it is happening.

3. *Conflict viewed as an asset.* Conflict provides two very necessary elements to the effective work group. First, it is the prime source of energy in systems, and, second, it is the major source of creativity. Since conflict is absolutely unavoidable in any case, an effective team's approach to dealing with it is

to use it, rather than to try to resolve, avoid, or suppress it. More potential for ineffectiveness and marginal performance exists in avoiding conflict than in conflict itself. When conflict is seen as an asset, the preferred approach is to deal with it through collaboration, although competition or even compromise is not precluded, when called for by the situation.

Complete the questionnaire in Structured Exercise 9–1 and share the results.

Structured Exercise 9–1

Work-Group-Effectiveness Inventory
Work Group: _____
Date: _____
Circle one number for each statement:

1. I have been speaking frankly here about the things that have been uppermost in my mind.	1	2	3	4	5
2. The other members of this team have been speaking frankly about the things that have been uppermost in their minds.	1	2	3	4	5
3. I have been careful to speak directly and to the point.	1	2	3	4	5
4. The other members of this team have been speaking directly and to the point.	1	2	3	4	5
5. I have been listening carefully to the other members of this team, and I have been paying special attention to those who have expressed strong agreement or disagreement.	1	2	3	4	5
6. The other members of this team have been listening carefully to me and to each other, and they have been paying special attention to strongly expressed views.	1	2	3	4	5

7. I have been asking for and receiving constructive feedback regarding my influence on the team.	1	2	3	4	5
8. I have been providing constructive feedback to those who have requested it—to help them keep track of their influence on me and the other team members.	1	2	3	4	5
9. Our team's operating procedures and organization have been changed rapidly whenever more useful structures or procedures have been discovered.	1	2	3	4	5
10. Everyone on the team has been helping the team keep track of its effectiveness.	1	2	3	4	5
11. Members of this team have been listening carefully to each other, and we have been paying special attention to strongly expressed values.	1	2	3	4	5
12. We have been speaking frankly to each other about the things that have been uppermost in our minds.	1	2	3	4	5
13. We have been speaking directly and to the point.	1	2	3	4	5
14. We have been helping our team keep track of its own effectiveness.	1	2	3	4	5
15. Our team's internal organization and procedures have been adjusted when necessary to keep pace with changing conditions or new requirements.	1	2	3	4	5
16. All members of this team understand the team's goals.	1	2	3	4	5

17. Each member of our team understands how they can contribute to the team's effectiveness in reaching its goals.	1	2	3	4	5
18. Each of us is aware of the potential contributions of the other team members.	1	2	3	4	5
19. We recognize each other's problems and help each other to make a maximum contribution.	1	2	3	4	5
20. As a team, we pay attention to our own decision-making and problem-solving processes.	1	2	3	4	5

Calculate your score, and compare it to those of others. Where are the similarities and differences? What should be done to improve the scores?

⸺⬦⬥⬦⸺

ADVANTAGES

You'll discover that the term "team" means:

T   ogether
E   veryone
A   chieves
M   uch

Despite the potential advantages of creating a shared-responsibility team, many supervisors express strongly negative sentiments about teams, groups, committees, and meetings. They associate teams with delays, endless talk (or false, constrained politeness), avoidance of responsibility, and other unpleasant outcomes. Indeed, too few management teams now function in ways that could produce enthusiasm and encourage emulation.

Suppose, however, that your direct subordinates could function as a team with the following characteristics:

1. *Everyone knows* their own and others' tasks well enough so that nothing falls through the cracks; everyone knows who is, and who should be, doing what.
2. *Trust* is so high that the group does not need to meet on every issue. Each member is confident that no one, including the boss, would act without consultation unless there was a good reason—such as prior general

agreement, special expertise, legitimate time pressures, or unavailability of affected parties. And the person who does act would know that others would back any action.

3. Such a group is not very "groupy" or clingy and does not waste time meeting on trivial issues or limiting those who have taken *individual initiative*.

4. Members who are clearly *more expert* than the others, in certain areas, are given great latitude to make the decisions on those matters.

5. Nevertheless, if issues cross several areas or affect the department as a whole, members seriously *address the issues together*, fight hard and openly for their beliefs, and insist that their concerns be addressed, yet also pay attention to the needs of the department as a whole. Everyone is comfortable wearing at least two hats, one for their area and one for the department.

6. Although skilled at persuasion and willing to fight hard over important differences, members feel no obligation to automatically oppose initiatives from other members or the manager. There is *no competition for competition's sake*. Members enthusiastically support the positions or ideas of others when they happen to agree.

7. Despite members' willingness to fight when necessary, the climate is *pervasively supportive*, encouraging members to ask one another for help, acknowledge their mistakes, share resources (people, information, or equipment), and generally further everybody's performance and learning.

8. The group pays attention to *successful task achievement* and to individual members' learning. Members are not restricted to areas where they have total competence and hence can't acquire new expertise; neither are they so overloaded with learning experiences that group performance seriously suffers.

9. The group has *self-correcting mechanisms*; when things aren't going well, all members are ready to examine the group's processes, discuss what is wrong, and take corrective action. Whatever the problems—overly lengthy meetings, inappropriate agenda items, unclear responsibilities, lack of team effort, overly parochial participation, or even poor leadership practices—the group takes time out to assess its way of operating and to make mid-course corrections. Individual members as well as the manager feel free to raise questions of team performance.

Does this team profile sound too ideal? Is the well-developed team a fantasy projection that will remain frustratingly out of reach in the real world of petty politics, indirection, waffling, and hushed-corridor cabals? It could be, but not necessarily. I've seen police teams achieve this level of alignment. If you want a team effort, develop one. Trust and training are a two-seated vehicle for pursuing teamwork.

Structured Exercise 9–2

Reread the above nine characteristics that, if present in a group of co-workers, will produce teamwork. Think carefully about each characteristic as it might exist within your work group. Circle the proper number and then compare your ratings with other fellow employees. How do you look as a team? Where are your strengths, and where are your deficiencies?

1. **No One Knows**   **Everyone Knows**

    1   2   3   4   5   6   7

2. **Low Trust**   **High Trust**

    1   2   3   4   5   6   7

3. **Group Think**   **Individual Initiative**

    1   2   3   4   5   6   7

4. **Little Expertise**   **A Lot of Expertise**

    1   2   3   4   5   6   7

5. **Issues Are Buried**   **Issues Are Addressed**

    1   2   3   4   5   6   7

6. **Dysfunctional Competition**   **Functional Competition**

    1   2   3   4   5   6   7

7. **No Support**   **Great Support**

    1   2   3   4   5   6   7

8. **No Attention to**   **High Attention to**
   Task Achievement   **to Task Achievement**

    1   2   3   4   5   6   7

9. **External Correcting**   **Self-Correcting**
   Mechanisms   **Mechanisms**

    1   2   3   4   5   6   7

TRUST

In Responsibility Four, I underscored trust by discussing the concept of trust banking accounts (TBAs). Please return to that section now and refresh your memory. What was stated there has clear applications here.

There is no foolproof formula for establishing and maintaining trust in a work group. Nonetheless, here are some steps that have proven valid in funding TBAs:

Believing

Police leaders (managers and supervisors) must have an enduring belief that most people want to do a good job and that it is important for them to enjoy their work. Closely coupled with this is a strong belief that all individuals should be treated with consideration and respect and that their achievements should be recognized. This belief should encourage a work culture where each person in the department counts and every job counts.

Personality

One should not base one's work relationship on another person's personality, chemistry, or enjoyment. He or she may be a fun person, clever, bright, and more. But this doesn't mean you can trust that person. People who rely only on similar tastes, on personalities that mesh, or on the right chemistry, and who ignore character and values, are setting themselves up for great disappointment.

Values—Theirs

Find out what the other person's values are. Have a dialogue with the person and probe his or her values. How important are goodness, honesty, and unselfishness to the person? What, if anything, is more important to the person than personal happiness? Not only are the person's answers to these questions important, but also it is revealing if the person gets annoyed when such issues are raised.

Finally, ask yourself, "If I had to prove to someone who never met my co-worker how decent a person he or she is, what concrete evidence could I submit?"

Behavior

Pay at least as much attention to how the person treats others—especially people from whom they need nothing—as to how the person treats you. Watch, for example, how your co-worker treats a customer.

People generally treat decently those from whom they want something—a better assignment, help, approval, or a special favor. That someone treats you well may, therefore, reveal nothing about character (and may, therefore, not indicate how that individual will treat you later).

Values—Yours

Know your own values (Responsibility One). If you don't have strong values yourself, or if you do but cannot clearly articulate them, the previous suggestions may be useless. How can you inquire or talk about values that you yourself either don't hold or can't identify? Thus, the stronger and more focused your values become, the less likely you are to trust people with poor values.

Having the right values serves a selfish purpose. Those who live by solid, proven values tend to bring such people into teams. And such employees are a great deal less likely to disappoint us as teammates.

In summary, you can best determine whom to trust or not by following these rules:

1. Do not trust co-workers based on personality, chemistry, or enjoyment alone.
2. Find out what the other person's values are. While values are not enough to ensure a good working relationship, they can guide you in terms of whom to trust.
3. Pay careful attention to how the co-worker treats others, especially others from whom he or she needs nothing, and how the co-worker treats you.
4. Know your own values. If you do not have firmly held values and cannot clearly articulate them, the above rules are useless.

TRAINING

It is a paradox that while everyone seems to be in favor of teamwork, there isn't a lot of it around. Trust-building and team-building are synergistic. You push for one and the other responds as well. Hence, if you start training employees as a team, they are likely to trust each other more and function as a team.

Regretfully, the majority of police training is individual-based. One person heads for a problem-oriented policing seminar and another for an ethics course. The majority of police training today at all levels in a department constrains team-building. The more team training, the better the morale and the better the quality of services.

As a trainer (or developer of human resources), you influence an officer's values, attitudes, perceptions, learning, motivation, job satisfaction, stress, and wellness. Furthermore, as a trainer, you sway group dynamics, communications, and followership (your leadership). Likewise, as a trainer, you affect goal-setting, planning, managing by objectives, performance appraisal, discipline, conflict resolution, community relations, labor relations, and one's professional success. Pointedly, then, much of your success or failure as a supervisor hinges on your ability to train—especially teamwork.

Police Supervisor as Trainer

The police supervisor is in a most advantageous position to influence personal and organizational development in a local law-enforcement agency. Hence, my basic premise—the police supervisor has a responsibility to improve the human resources within his or her purview, in line with attaining the goals of the agency.

Many police agencies have established a field training officer (FTO) position. This officer is usually provided with some form of incentive to "coach" a newer officer in the performance of his or her duties while on the job (on-the-job training, or OJT). Agency after agency has found the FTO program most helpful in assisting a new police officer to quickly build proper job attitudes and behavior. Briefly, an FTO program provides close coaching and monitoring of a new officer's demeanor by a senior officer who has received special instruction on doing so. Untrained FTOs can create as much damage as benefit to a department. An FTO program should be used by a police supervisor as one of many training methods for assuring the agency that their assigned staff are peak performers. An FTO program does not eliminate or reduce the supervisor's responsibility for training.

Training Goals

Training has two fundamental goals: to make lasting improvements in the performance of one's organizational role and to develop one's capacity for handling higher levels of responsibility. In other words, training helps a person do her or his job better, while at the same time preparing her or him for more challenging duties. Consequently, training means a change, that is, a change on the part of the individual and the organization. Both are interdependent partners in any process of change. Six key attitudes underscore police training goals today:

1. Motivations attached to skills lead to action. Skills are acquired through practice.
2. Learning is a result of the motivation and capacity of the individual, the norms of the training group, the training methods and the behavior of the trainers, and the general climate of the police organization.
3. Improvement on the job is caused by individual learning, the norms of the working group, and the general climate of the organization. Individual learning, unused, leads to frustration.
4. Training is the responsibility of three partners: the organization, the trainee, and the trainer. It has preparatory, pre-training, and post-training phases.
5. Training is a continuous process and a vehicle for consistently updating the skills of the individual human resources.
6. Training is also a continuous process and a vehicle for consistently improving the capacity of the individual officers to behave as a team.

Structured Exercise 9–3

Learning Needs Questionnaire

DIRECTIONS.   Circle the number that you feel best represents your experience.

I am not well prepared for my job.	1	2	3	4	5	I am fully prepared for my job.
I lack essential skills for my job.	1	2	3	4	5	I have all the essential skills for my job.

I was not carefully introduced to my job.	1	2	3	4	5	I was carefully introduced to my job.
I found it difficult to learn my job.	1	2	3	4	5	I learned my job with minimal difficulty.
I have no opportunities for development.	1	2	3	4	5	I have good opportunities for development.
I have far too little proper training.	1	2	3	4	5	I have sufficient training.
My boss is not concerned about training needs.	1	2	3	4	5	My boss is concerned about training needs.

ESTABLISHING TRAINING OBJECTIVES.   Since any training objective is based on the objectives of the police department, the main question is whether the department's objectives are realistic. Furthermore, is the training input of the program envisaged also realistic? Or is training in danger of being misused? For example, is it too little and too late? All this is to say that:

> The training objectives must support organizational activities, and the training objectives must be realistic.

In order to accomplish these two foundational training principles, the following four questions must be answered:

1. *Is the training needed?* Be certain that a needed change calls for training. What the police organizations needs may not be training, at least not immediately, but lots of detailed operational planning and implementation of plans. Training at this stage would be a disservice if it deprived the organization of skilled people currently needed for action.

2. *Where does it fit?* Define the part that police training can play in the change. What new competencies does the department require, and which of these can be acquired through systematic training? Training strategy determines which goals can reasonably be achieved through a training program and which cannot. And vice versa: The goals determine which training strategy is most appropriate.

3. *How much and who?* The third step is more taxing, and worthy of the most careful consideration; it concerns questions of quantities and levels of police personnel to be trained, and of timing and training as well.

4. *The team?* The final question involves training for teamwork. People who work together should be trained together. The truly effective work groups are trained like any successful sports team. All members know what their jobs consist of, what they should provide to others, and what they can expect of others.

SELECTING TRAINING STRATEGIES.   Any attempt to train—that is, to change— an individual automatically means a freezing-up of relations between people. The freezing-up of relations involves three stages: unfreezing, moving, and refreezing.

Unfreezing is necessary because the police officer (and his or her organ- ization, family, and locality) comes up with habits, values, and practices, the very opposite of a clean slate. To affect them through training, normal habits first have to be questioned and disturbed, or unfrozen.

Training can do this by focusing on needs that police trainees cannot sat- isfy by habitual behavior. The supervisor then introduces other events that allow participants to try new ways of behaving, that is, changing. If the police trainees find the new behavior more useful in meeting the "new" needs, they can then be helped to make it habitual. Each officer thus gains a new set of behavioral patterns, which he or she then freezes.

DELIVERING TRAINING.   As a police supervisor, you are responsible for the delivery of needed training to your personnel. While the style may vary from a stand-up, roll call lecture to ride-along coaching, train you must.

It is not sufficient to make police training supplemental to work; police work must be organized to facilitate training and development. Three factors support this conclusion:

- First, any help in training provided by the police agency is critical because the training demands are ever expanding in local law enforcement.
- Second, we live in an age of revolution in the processes, in the systems, and in the products of public and private organizations.
- Third, in some instances you and the agency may be legally vulnerable if personnel are not trained in certain critical skills.

The training burdens are great. Increasingly, training must be part and parcel of the work itself, and it should be increasingly supplied and directly monitored by the immediate supervisor.

If your department managers are astute, they are rating your performance as a police supervisor, to a major extent, on your ability to deliver timely and useful training to others. Trainers and supervisors are one and the same. Effect- ive trainers and effective supervisors build teams.

EVALUATING YOUR ACCOMPLISHMENTS.   The evaluation of training fre- quently falls prey to becoming a popularity contest and/or merely an instance of entertaining feedback. The key questions are, or should be:

- What, precisely, did you learn?
- Why is it important to you and your agency?

- How do you plan to use it?
- When and where will the new learning be applied?

Asking these pointed questions demands follow-up and feedback on your part. A final critical and, at times, risky question is, "How can I, as your supervisor, improve as a trainer?"

TEAM-BASED DECISION-MAKING

The supervisory responsibilities that precede and follow team-training will be extremely difficult to fulfill if teamwork is not encouraged via team-training. Of all the supervisor's training goals, team-training is the most important and challenging.

> Team-training cultivates team-based decision-making.

Team-based decision-making is not a democratic process. There isn't any vote among your crew on "Should we patrol tonight or stay in the station?" Team-based decision-making is a process wherein everyone is expected to think out and voice their opinions on a subject or an issue. The supervisor retains full accountability for the ultimate decision.

Why consider using a team-based approach for making choices? First, you get more and better ideas. Second, individual commitment to implementing a decision is significantly enhanced. Third, it makes for fast and accurate decision-making when teams are under duress, but must act.

Team-training is neither simple nor easy. It is complex and time-consuming. It depends on your galvanizing a group of independently minded police officers into a mutually supportive crew that is dedicated to getting results. Any rewards or accolades go to the team, not to an individual. A supervisor's ability to lead a team is now a function of the team members' capacity to participate in its leadership.

TRAINING A DIVERSE WORKFORCE

Until the 1950s, American law enforcement primarily consisted of white, male employees representing two to three generations. The few females were relegated to clerical and technical jobs. Hence, police departments were homogeneous in appearance. Obviously, the employees did differ due to their own unique individuality. As compared with today, training diverse workers was relatively simple. That's not the case now.

Defining Diversity

Training a diverse workforce means creating and maintaining a work environment where each person is respected because of his or her differences and all can contribute and be rewarded based on their results.

"Respected because of their differences" means that we need to under-stand, first, that different does not mean less than, and, second, that different approaches and different opinions can be beneficial to making decisions and providing service delivery to a diverse customer base.

"Rewarded on the basis of their results" means that people should be rewarded on the basis of what they do and how they produce, not on the basis of who they know or their race, or their gender, or their age, or their religion, or any other characteristic.

There are four harmful misconceptions of diversity:

MISCONCEPTION 1: TRAINING A DIVERSE WORKFORCE IS A DISGUISE FOR AFFIRMATIVE ACTION PROGRAMS.   Often, in an organization where perceptions and behaviors are not explored carefully, some people express and act out the opinion that the organization's goals for training simply are an attempt to sneak in affirmative action goals and quotas.

MISCONCEPTION 2: TRAINING A DIVERSE WORKFORCE IS CULTURAL DIVERSITY TRAINING.   Some may think that training is simply teaching appropriate behaviors to use when interacting with people of specific races, national ori-gins, mental or physical abilities, sexual orientations, or lifestyles.

Team-training for diversity goes beyond learning to act out a prescribed behavior. For some organizations or work teams, it will mean a basic change in the way people communicate, interact, process information, make decisions, and serve customers. It is not a quick-fix recipe!

MISCONCEPTION 3: TRAINING A DIVERSE WORKFORCE IS SENSITIVITY TRAINING. Team-training is not some touchy-feely training session. Supervising and train-ing are a way for us to understand and appreciate ourselves better so we can understand the factors and situations that motivate our personal beliefs, values, and behaviors. This allows us to accept, then respect, others who may have different beliefs, values, lifestyles, and ways of doing things at work.

MISCONCEPTION 4: TRAINING A DIVERSE WORKFORCE IS AN EFFORT TO MIRROR OUR CUSTOMERS OR CITIZEN BASE.   At times, managers and organiza-tion leaders feel it is important that we mirror, or look like, the customers or citizens we serve. While it may give us some initial comfort, merely having work teams that look like those we serve cannot represent the ultimate goal for achieving success.

When we train effectively, we discover that added personal differences or personal similarities cannot be attributed necessarily to race, gender, or lifestyle. We get better at recognizing the differences, respecting the differences, and expecting the differences to enrich our relationships and contribute to better-quality performance and behavior results.

Everyone Belongs to a Minority Group

The all-male work force is history. Sameness of sex and ethnicity is out, and differences are in.

In sheer numbers, women dominate the information society. Ninety percent of working women are part of the information service sector. Of the people whose job titles fall under the category of "professional"—versus clerical, technical, or laborer—the majority are women. Forty-four percent of adult working women (ages 25 to 64) are college-educated, compared with 20 percent in 1965. Further, six out of 10 joining the work force right now are female.

As the 21st century begins, white men are already less than half of the labor force. By 2010, married couples will no longer be a majority of households. Asians will outnumber Jews by a margin of two-to-one, and Hispanics will lead blacks as the nation's largest minority.

By 2020, immigration will become more important to U.S. population growth than natural increase (the growth that occurs because births outnumber deaths). The population will diversify even more rapidly.

Dangerous Delusions

No other nation is as challenged as the United States in bringing large numbers of highly diverse people together in organizational settings and then expecting our supervisors to build cooperative and happy work teams. Unfortunately, some of us have been deluded by the false hopes or assumptions that follow:

LAWS AND POLICIES.   Legislating and policy-making are not the answers to worker diversity! Granted, we need laws and policies concerning hate crimes, discrimination based on age, sexual harassment, and other such illegal behavior. But they do not ensure anti-racist, -sexist, -sectarian thoughts. The ideal we seek is best approached by encouraging individuals to share and resolve their differences. Team-training works!

POLITICAL CORRECTNESS.   Being politically correct (PC) means suppressing "hate speech," which is loosely defined as anything that any recognized minority or victim group chooses to find offensive. Hence, there is considerable latitude in determining what is or is not PC. For example, we might use the term "female athlete," which is not "in" today ("woman" should be used), and, thus, we're not PC. In my opinion, political correctness is insincere, deceitful, and dysfunctional.

A more honest alternative for genuinely building solid working relationships is being professionally correct (PRO-C). If you are PRO-C, then you are automatically behaving in accordance with ethical standards and common decency. You in turn are being truthful to yourself and others, while simultaneously being sensitive to human feelings. Team-training works!

GIVE ME THE LIST.   Some of us are deluded by assuming that you can get a laundry list of do's and don'ts, and that following that list will help you be PC and avoid blunders. In matters of humor or just ordinary topics of discussion, "you have to shed knee-jerk assumptions." Not every African-American plays basketball. Not everyone with a Latino surname speaks Spanish. Not all Asians are Chinese. For that matter, not all whites come from the ruling class. As a consequence, assume nothing about the person except that he or she has values and you must understand them to be successful in your job as supervisor and leader. Team-training works!

DIVERSITY FOR PROFIT.   There are consultants, lecturers, tests, films: an entire industry has been born to fuel and feed off of the privilege of a lifetime—being who you are.

American civil society, long founded on the notion of "from many, one,"— e pluribus unum—is being deluded into a poisonous floodtide of negation, sectarianism, self-pity, confrontation, vulgarity, and flat-out, old-fashioned hatred.

Almost a hundred years after the last great immigration wave changed the face of American society, vast numbers of Americans—including, sadly, the best-educated—are again being taught to identify themselves with the qualifying adjectives of race, religion, generation, and gender. Our self-identity is shaped not by will, choice, reason, intelligence, and desire, but by membership in groups. We are not individuals, but components of categories. Team-training works!

What Can the Police Supervisor-as-Leader Do?

This is a list of things the supervisor-as-leader can do:

- First, the supervisor-as-leader has to remember and appreciate that each one of us, including themselves, is diverse—we're individuals with unique value systems.
- Second, when one's values are being assaulted, remember that conflict will ensue.
- Third, remember that in many cases, what may be referred to as a diversity problem (e.g., male versus female) is in reality a supervisory problem, such as one caused by status differences (e.g., sworn officers demeaning the work of civilian dispatchers). What may be a work issue may be cleverly masked as a diversity issue and thus made worse by using the wrong approach to it.
- Fourth, remember that the three core values for either avoiding or solving employee diversity problems are caring, trusting, and communications/understanding.
- Fifth, police supervisors will have to be especially adroit in team-training a more diverse work force. I would urge that all supervisors recognize the enormous power that is unleashed by a diverse work force. In my opinion, it is one of this nation's paramount strengths, and this should hold true for its police agencies.
- Finally, remember that team-training a diverse workforce demands a lot of intelligence—**emotional intelligence.**

EMOTIONAL INTELLIGENCE

Emotions have never been completely welcome in our work lives. Most of us have traditionally been conditioned to leave emotions "at home," believing that to be effective, we need to base all our team strategies and decisions only upon cold, logical "intelligence." And yet, as we all know, emotions are a fundamental part of who we are, and of working with others. They can't be left out of the picture. In fact, to do so often guarantees that suppressed emotions will flare, causing increased conflict and affecting climate and morale.

Let us view emotions in a different way altogether, as another kind of "intelligence," beyond reason and logic; an intelligence that—if we could learn to access it—could become nothing short of a touchstone to greater collaboration, a higher level of influence with others, more productivity and effectiveness. The fact is, such an intelligence exists—it's called "emotional intelligence." Unheard of only a decade or so ago, emotional intelligence, or EI, has become something remarkable in the past few years—the centerpiece of mainstream **team-training**.

> As the pace of workplace change increases, and our workplaces make ever-greater demands on our cognitive, emotional, and physical resources, emotional intelligence will continue to emerge—not as something "nice" to have but as an increasingly important set of "must-have" skills.

The good news is that unlike your IQ, **EI is not fixed at birth**. Emotional intelligence can be developed and raised to higher levels. While we all must experience our emotions, we can choose to express or repress them. The goal is to express them intelligently for our advantage and for the benefit of others.

What is EI?

EI is knowing **how** we and others feel, **why** we feel that way, and **what** can be done about it. EI is **our ability to understand and use the power of our emotions** wisely. It's learning the difference between "I think" and "I feel," and hearing the difference when others say it. Just as importantly, EI is learning to **manage our emotions** rather than letting them control us. The thing to remember is that emotions are not good or bad. Emotions are information. By listening to them, we can use our IQ more effectively because we reason better when our feelings are taken into account. They give us valuable information we can't get anywhere else.

Police employees most often screw up because they can't 1) handle change, 2) build a team, and/or 3) cope with interpersonal relations. Those that really screw up believe and act as if feelings do not count. They believe and act on only what can be counted or quantified. Their thinking centers on "what're the numbers," "what's your point," and "only facts matter."

> Eighty-five percent of a leader's abilities deal with EI.

What are the results of higher emotional intelligence on the job? A better work environment, happier and more loyal employees and clients, and a stronger team. EI consists of five essential competencies that build upon each other to raise our level of emotional intelligence. Those five competencies are:

- Self-awareness
- Self-regulation
- Self-motivation
- Empathy
- Effective relationships

Self-Awareness

The centerpiece of EI is one's "self-awareness." Do you understand yourself? Do you comprehend your emotional states? The subjects covered earlier (especially in values and ethics) should assist you in being more aware of who you are, what you stand for, and where and why you are headed. This type of in-service team-training pushes you to tune into your emotions:

- EI supplies you with valid information about your responses to stressful situations.
- EI recognizes that all technical skills have an emotional appendage.

Remember, your EI commences with your self-awareness. (Self-awareness was a significant part of Responsibilities One and Two—Values and Ethics.)

Self-Regulation

This phase of your EI concentrates on your willingness to accept responsibility for your thoughts and deeds. It requires sound reasoning, and the quick rejection of rationalizations. It means reframing stressful events into challenging opportunities. Self-regulation guards against unexpected and unwarranted emotional triggers. (The majority of this book is dedicated to our ownership of responsibility.) Self-regulation is another term for holding oneself accountable.

Self-Motivation

Our motives are laced with our emotions. Our motions or motivations are a direct derivative of our emotions. Our emotions affect our work performance. Emotions can drastically modify our brain chemistry. They can cause us to think, "It's useless, why even try?" or "I can fix it; I'm going to move forward!" As stated earlier, if you're not motivated (directing your emotions), then there is little chance that you'll motivate others into acts of high work performance. (For more thinking on this competency, return to Responsibility Eight—Motivation.)

Empathy

Earlier in Responsibility Four we learned that empathy and sympathy are not identical. Empathy means that we understand the position or feelings of another person. It does not mean that we have to agree—only that we understand. Once we understand, then we can endeavor to be understood. From a mutual under-standing, we arrive at a point of being able to resolve conflicts and solve problems.

Empathy is first of all recognizing and then responding to the emotional needs of others. It is evidenced by human compassion and mutual trust. The best way to get empathy is to give it. It comes as a repayment for our interest in the welfare of others.

Effective Relationships

This, while a mixture of the four others, actually results in even greater rewards to the individual worker, the work team, and the department. Your EI is demonstrated by the effectiveness of your working relationships. It is not about being nice; it is about being honest. It is not about being touchy-feely; it is about being aware of feelings—yours and others. It is not about being emo-tional; it is being smart about your emotions. It is knowing how to motivate yourself and others while keeping your distressing emotions under control.

The higher the degree of emotional smartness in a police agency, the less the need for an emphasis on being "politically correct." High EI abro-gates one's tendency for being politically incorrect, and it all begins with self-awareness.

KEY POINTS

- Teamwork requires interdependent thinking and effort.
- The main purpose for teamwork is, through alignment, to produce synergy within the work group.
- Teamwork can occur only if there is mutual trust and training as a team.
- Trust should be based on knowing the other person's values, as well as your own.
- Team-training is a key responsibility of a police supervisor.
- An FTO program does not diminish or detract from a supervisor's training function.
- Your delivery of training should be subjected to constant evaluation by your boss, yourself, and the trainees.
- The most difficult of all training goals for the supervisor is that of building and maintaining a work team.
- Team-training is the basis of team-based decision-making.
- Team-training is one of the better ways to solve diversity problems.
- Emotional intelligence is the cornerstone for team-training in a diverse workforce.

DISCUSSION

1. Why is an interdependent work group so important? How can interde-pendence avoid the pitfall of "groupthink"?

2. Review the steps mentioned for building trust. Are there steps that should be added? If so, what are they? Can I like you and not trust you? What about the reverse—trust but not like you?

3. In your opinion, what are (in rank order) the major training needs of a police officer today?

4. What is being done in your department or work unit to respect diversity (our individuality), while forging a team effort? What else should be done?

5. Who has the primary responsibility in making a team-based decision—the team leader or the team members?

6. When an individual speaks out against the group consensus in your police organization, what is the probable outcome? Will the individual be rewarded or censured?

7. What is emotional intelligence, and how does it relate to team-training?

VITALITY

The police supervisor is responsible for combating distress and maintaining vitality within the work group.

The height of human wisdom is to bring our tempers down to our circumstances, and to make a calm within, under the weight of the greatest storm without.

—Daniel Defoe

All of the preceding responsibilities, as well as those that follow, encompass change, and change is stress-laden. Incoming stress can be converted into human vitality.

Victor Frankl was a Jewish psychiatrist imprisoned in the death camps of Nazi Germany, where he directly experienced the living hell of the Holocaust. Except for his sister, his entire family died. He suffered torture and the daily uncertainty of being sent to the gas ovens (the ultimate in distress).

One day, naked and alone in a small room, he became aware that his Nazi captors could not take away his freedom or power to choose, within himself, how all of the threats, punishment, and injustices were going to affect him.

Using his disciplined mind and applying mainly his memory and imagination, he exercised his freedom of choice until he actually had more freedom than his captors. He survived the death camps, and he wrote and lectured about his experiences for many years thereafter.

Why this story? Every day we have many choices facing us. One option is to use stress or incoming demands for change as a positive force for vitality.

STRESS AND VITALITY

Stress is an everyday fact of life. You can't avoid it! **Stress is any change that you must adapt to, ranging from the negative extreme of actual physical danger to the exhilaration of falling in love or achieving some long-desired success.** And in between, day-to-day living confronts even the most well-managed life with a continuous stream of potentially stressful experiences. All stress is not bad. In fact, stress is not only desirable, but also essential to life. Whether the stress you experience is the result of major life changes or the cumulative effect of minor everyday worries, it is how you respond to these experiences that determines the impact stress will have on you.

> A recent poll reported that adults experience stress in their daily lives: frequently—42%; sometimes—38%; rarely—18%; never—2%.

Stress is a given; the only way to eliminate it is to die. If mismanaged or ignored, it can cause us a great deal of harm. Stress can become distress. But if recognized and managed, stress can produce wellness. Similar to Victor Frankl, you have a choice. When a change occurs, will you handle it as something distressful or an opportunity for wellness?

We will first cover some general information about stress. Next, you'll explore your stress levels. Finally, we will consider personal mastery, your wellness, and vitality as a supervisor. Keep in mind as you proceed that:

> - Stress is a demand on us to change.
> - How we handle stress determines if it is harmful (distress) or helpful (vitality).

FIGHT OR FLIGHT RESPONSE

The groundwork for the modern meaning of "stress" was laid by Walter B. Cannon, a physiologist at Harvard around the turn of the last century. He was the first to describe the "fight or flight response" as a series of biochemical changes that prepares you to deal with threats or danger. Primitive man needed quick bursts of energy to fight or flee such predators as a sabertooth tiger. These days, when social custom prevents you from fighting or running away, this "emergency response" is rarely useful.

What Happens to Our Body

Hans Selye, the first major researcher on stress, was able to trace exactly what happens in your body during the fight or flight response. He found that any problem, imagined or real, can cause the cerebral cortex (the thinking part of the brain) to send an alarm to the hypothalamus (the main switch for the stress response, located in the midbrain). The hypothalamus then stimulates the sympathetic nervous system to make a series of changes in your body. Your heart rate, breathing rate, muscle tension, metabolism, and blood pressure all increase. Your hands and feet get cold as blood is directed away from your extremities and digestive system into the larger muscles that can help you fight or run. You experience butterflies in your stomach. Your diaphragm and anus lock. Your pupils dilate to sharpen your vision, and your hearing becomes more acute.

While all of this is going on, something else happens that can have long-term negative effects if left unchecked. Your adrenal glands start to secret corticoids (adrenaline, epinephrine, and norepinephrine), which inhibit digestion, reproduction, growth, tissue repair, and the responses of your immune and inflammatory systems. In other words, some very important functions that keep your body healthy begin to shut down.

The Relaxation Response

The same mechanism that turned the stress response on can turn it off. This is called the relaxation response. As soon as you decide that a situation is no longer dangerous, your brain stops sending emergency signals to your brain stem, which in turn ceases to send panic messages to your nervous system. Three minutes after you shut off the danger signals, the fight or flight response burns out. Your metabolism, heart rate, breathing rate, muscle tension, and blood pressure all return to their normal levels. You can use your mind to change your physiology for the better, improving your health and perhaps reducing your need for medication. This is the "relaxation response," which refers to a natural restorative process.

In Summary

The response to stress involves a threefold mechanism, consisting of 1) the direct effect of the stressor on the body, 2) internal responses that stimulate tissue defense or help to destroy damaging substances, and 3) internal responses that cause tissue surrender by inhibiting unnecessary or excessive defense. Resistance and adaptation depend on a proper balance of these three factors. Specific steps to protect yourself and your personnel are covered later in the section on "wellness." But for now, realize that the most standard medical textbooks attribute anywhere from 50 to 80 percent of all disease to psychosomatic or stress-related origins. And stress-related psychological and physiological disorders have become the major social and health problem in the last decade. Stress-induced disorders have long since replaced epidemics of infectious disease as the major medical problem of the 21st century infotech nations.

STRESS AND INTEGRITY

> Stress may be as much a question of a compromise of values as it is a matter of time pressure and fear of failure.

When we are tempted to compromise our values, we are tampering with our integrity. When we succumb to such temptation and do something we really don't believe in doing to attain a goal, one of two very stressful things occurs: Either we gain the prize and realize it wasn't worth it, or we end up with neither the prize nor our integrity. One person put it this way—even if you end up winning the rat race, you're still a rat. And this is highly stressful.

A police supervisor's vitality and wellness depend on maintaining one's integrity. Integrity means being whole, unbroken, undivided. It describes a person who has successfully united the different parts of their character. A person with integrity has no difficulty solving ongoing internal battles. This person is at peace with themselves. Stressful events are easily and quickly dispatched because of a character that is centered in integrity. Character counts, but it only counts when based on integrity. Vitality and values are positive teammates; we need them in our quest for the person and supervisor we want to be. Conversely, moral compromise and its partner—debilitating distress—are cleverly programmed to attack our character and destroy our number one value: integrity.

> No matter how competent a supervisor is, one without integrity is doomed to failure. As many of us have discovered, failure is very distressful.

Structured Exercise 10–1

When faced with a potential compromise of your integrity, try using the Three-Minute Temptation Buster. Find a quiet and private spot, take off your watch, and sit down. Focus on your integrity and what you stand for. In less than three minutes the temptation will have vanished.

RESPONSIBILITY OF THE POLICE SUPERVISOR-AS-LEADER

The responsibility of the police supervisor-as-leader is to understand and effectively deal with the individual and organizational implications of maintaining one's vitality.

Individual Implications

There is a "stress fad," or syndrome, in police organizations today. Granted, police work is a stressful occupation. But so are many others. I can assure you that the business supervisor, fire captain, supervising nurse, construction supervisor, and so on experience stress in their daily activities. What counts is that the supervisor 1) knows when stress has become too much or too little and 2) maintains a stress-reduction or wellness program. This applies to both the supervisor and their assigned personnel.

Police supervision is largely a constant process of adaptation to the "spice of life" that is change. The prescription for health and happiness is 1) to successfully adapt to ever-changing circumstances and 2) to remember that the penalties for failure to adjust to change are illness (physical and mental) and unhappiness. Interestingly, the very same stressful event or level of stress that may make a person ill can be a motivating experience for someone else. It is through the general adaptation syndrome (GAS) that the various internal organs, especially the endocrine glands and the nervous system, help one 1) adapt to the constant changes that occur in and around one, and 2) navigate a reasonably steady course toward whatever one considers a meaningful purpose.

As a supervisor-as-leader, remember that your vitality depends on how well you cope with stress:

- Stress in daily life is natural, pervasive, unavoidable, and thus to be expected.
- Depending on how one copes with stressful events, the experience of stress can be positive (healthy and vital) or negative (sick and exhausted).
- Since people differ in a variety of ways, each person's means of and success in coping with stressful incidents will vary.
- A mental-physiological mechanism known as the general adaptation syndrome helps one to adjust to demands for change.
- By definition, stress is the nonspecific response of the body to any demand for change. The demand can be from within or from one's surrounding environment.
- Police supervisors are subjected to megachanges. As a result, they typically experience high levels of stress.
- The supervisor is in a key position to help others cope with stressful events and, in turn, their vitality.

Structured Exercise 10–2

The way to reduce physical stress is relatively simple. The principal underlying physical stress control is that it is impossible for anyone to exist in two contradictory states simultaneously. You cannot be short and tall at the same time. You cannot be pregnant and not pregnant concurrently. Vigor and fatigue cannot coexist. Similarly, it is impossible to be stressed and physically relaxed at the same time. If you know how to find a state of physical relaxation and how to sustain it, you will be better able to prevent the occurrence of physical stress overload, and you will be able to control excessive tension once it has occurred.

A stress-control formula is useful here. You need to learn how to focus on physically relaxed states, learn how to rehearse physical relaxation responses until they can be achieved quickly and with ease, and then learn when and how to implement the physical relaxation response at a time preceding or during a stressful event.

Focusing on a physically relaxed state is achieved by three means:

First, use diaphragmatic breathing in slow, four-second "in" and four-second "out" excursions to assist the relaxation process. Lie down on a flat surface, facing up, and place your hand on your stomach. When you breathe in, your stomach should slowly rise because the diaphragm, acting like a piston, moves out of the chest cavity to suck air into your lungs. At the same time, the diaphragm descends into the abdominal cavity, pushing your intestines down and forward—the cause of your rising stomach. Exhale slowly, and your stomach falls. Your rib cage should be quite still. It is needed only during extreme exertion. Breathing to a count of four on each inhalation and exhalation is a restful breathing pattern.

Second, you must learn to relax your muscles and blood vessels. When your blood vessels are relaxed, your hands feel warm. When the blood vessels in your body are tense, your hands feel cold and clammy. You can increase the warmth of your hands by focusing on the sensations in your hand as it rests on the arm of the chair beside you. You can feel the texture of the arm of the chair upon which your hand rests. Whatever the room temperature may be, your hands can feel the sensations of airy coolness, as well as of warmth. If you wish to intensify the warmth, simply keep "warmth" in a relaxed focus in your mind. Imagine lying on a sunny beach with the sun beating down on your hand. Imagine your body filling up with warmth from the toes on up.

To relax your muscles, you can take the hand that is gently resting on the arm of the chair beside you and tense all your fingers without pressing them into the chair. Your hand will feel like it is hovering just above the arm of the chair. Tense muscles make your limbs feel light. Now relax your arm, wrist, and fingers. The limb will feel heavy as it slouches on the arm on the chair.

Third, starting from the top of your head and proceeding through every muscle and joint in your body down to your toes, contract each muscle to feel the sensation of tension—the lightness—and then the weight and heaviness associated with muscular relaxation.

You must now learn to rehearse warming your hands, relaxing your muscles and joints, and breathing slowly with your diaphragm. Take about 20 minutes to do so. Do not watch the clock—just guess at a time span of roughly twenty minutes, and rehearse the relaxation of your breathing, blood vessels, and muscles.

While relaxing your body, you may wish to simultaneously relax your mind by using a mind-focusing exercise. When I practice relaxation, I breathe in cycles of three breaths, repeating in my mind the following:

Breath 1. Give up caring
Breath 2. Heavy and warm
Breath 3. Breathe and relax

As distractions enter my consciousness, I do not let them trouble me, even if they temporarily throw me off my pattern. I simply resume my slow, three-breath cycle of

Breath 1. Give up caring
Breath 2. Heavy and warm
Breath 3. Breathe and relax

When you have rehearsed these relaxation exercises for a period of several days, you can then begin to implement them in your daily life.

Organizational Implications

A major concern for the police manager supervisor is the effects of stress on a worker's vitality to perform their job. At low stress levels, individuals maintain their current level of performance. Under these conditions, individuals are not activated, do not experience any stress-related physical strain, and probably see no reason to change their performance level. If not supervised well, these persons could become bored, lazy, and poor performers.

On the other hand, studies indicate that, under conditions of moderate stress, people are activated sufficiently to motivate them to increase performance. Stress, in modest amounts, acts as a stimulus for individual vitality. The toughness of a problem often pushes the supervisor to his or her performance limits. Similarly, mild stress can be responsible for creative activities as police personnel try to solve challenging (stressful) problems.

Finally, under conditions of excessive stress, both individual vitality and performance drops markedly. Here the severity of the stress consumes attention and vitality, causing employees to focus considerable energy on attempting to reduce the stress.

SOURCES AND FORMS OF STRESS: THE STRESSORS

We experience stress from one of three sources: personal, environmental, and organizational/social. The first source is within the individual; the latter two are external. Most often they present their demands for change in combination with one another. Let's explore the sources in more detail and then focus our attention on the four types of stress they produce for all employees in a police organization. While doing so, remember that how one handles stress determines whether it is a plus or minus to their vitality.

Three Sources of Stress

PERSONAL.   A review of all the possible personal or inner stressors would be impossible here. They can range from sexual disorders, to grief due to the loss of a loved one, to a fear of flying. We will center on those that are directly or potentially job-related. Roughly, they can be assigned to one of two categories: our emotions and our power base.

Emotions. The majority of us have received absolutely no training in how to deal with our own emotions. Responsibility One and the section on Emotional Intelligence covered this subject. At best, we have probably been given some advice on what to do during emotional periods; for example, being told that "there is nothing to fear but fear itself" when we are feeling frightened. Such advice is rarely ever truly helpful in overcoming the effects of the emotion. There are five very potent emotions that you should be able to recognize and deal with: depression, anxiety, guilt, failure, and disapproval. More will be said about these five emotions later when I discuss stress-reduction methods.

You may recall that a value is an enduring belief that a particular course of action (means or goal) is to be preferred over an alternate one, and that values cause us to behave in certain ways, to want to behave in certain ways, to think in certain ways, and to feel in certain ways. Obviously, they are extremely important to us. Hence, "we are what we value." As we learned earlier, compromising our values induces stress. When there is a conflict between our integrity (e.g., honesty) and one of our own values (e.g., trustworthiness), the alarm called anxiety may go off. Many of us do not know how to use this alarm and either fear or idealize it, instead of understanding that it is simply a signal that is calling attention to some process. When we set our values too high or exacting, we then become vulnerable to feelings of failure and guilt, and if we fail to identify or consider our values, we open ourselves to depression.

Power. The position of supervisor involves both the right to supervise and the opportunity to lead others. The right to supervise is centered in the position of police supervisor, while the opportunity to provide leadership is centered in one's personal ability to do so. Since supervision and power are closely allied, they both involve stress and responsibility. Police supervisors who feel the pangs of stress are usually responding to the use of supervisor power (by themselves or others) to cause change. For some, the term "power" suggests a negative action. I look at it as a potential force for good.

ENVIRONMENTAL. The environmental stressors can be labeled as technological, economic, or political. Frequently, an environmental stressor can be assigned to all three. For example, the computer is causing numerous and profound technological changes for the police manager (interactive terminals in the office). Economically, they require capital outlay and maintenance. And, politically, they imply power. Pollution in the work setting can be stressful (noise, air, filth, etc.). Insufficient work space often elevates tension. I could continue, but I believe you know what these stressors are because you're probably experiencing some of them right now.

ORGANIZATIONAL/SOCIAL. In this instance, I will catalog the stressors as too much, too little, uncertain conditions, and problem personalities. Although posed in a job sense, many demands for change will occur via the family and other non-departmental relationships.

Too much. There are two types of input overload, or hyperstress: quantitative and qualitative. Quantitative input overload is a result of simple demands, but too many of them for the time allotted—for example, too many phone calls to make, memos to read, or meetings to run in the time allowed. Increases in blood pressure, pulse rate, and cholesterol are associated with quantitative input overload. Qualitative input overload is a result of complexity and limited time. There are not as many tasks, but the time allotted to do these tasks is less than is needed to do them up to standard.Or,the tasks are so complex that they overwelm (intimidate) the worker.

Too little. Low levels of mental and physical activity can cause hypostress, that is, hypostress is caused by quantitative and qualitative input underloads. Naturally, certain forms of hypostress (such as recreation and self-reflection) are eustressful (desirable); but if a protracted period of nothingness is experienced, one may be confronted with hypostress, which is distressful (undesirable). Similar to hyperstress, hypostress can be either good or bad, depending on how one adjusts to its demands.

Uncertain conditions. A police supervisor is responsible for making decisions (often high-risk ones) under above-average conditions of uncertainty. Herbert A. Simon alluded to this situation when he described programmable decisions in comparison with non-programmable decisions. (The supervisor frequently experiences an arena of non-routine, non-programmable, high-risk decision making.)

Clearly, the bureaucratic, decision-making, operational turf of a police supervisor is filled with ambiguity and confusion, which may be stress-inducing.

Problem personalities. Certain types of personalities commonly act as stressors. A supervisor often simply cannot stay clear of these types of personalities; indeed, their agency may be plagued with more than its fair share of them, and the supervisor may find them in their primary social groups. However, whenever feasible, you should minimize your exposure to them.

Who are these problem personalities? (Some introspection may be helpful here, in that you ought to ask yourself if you are one of those defined.)

- The Type A person. Is aggressive, competitive for the joy of competing, in a hurry, impatient, tense, focused on self-interest.
- The worrier. Rehearses disaster scenarios; is dependent, fatalist, in frequent pain.
- The guilt-tripper. Has overdoses of conscience; exhibits rear-view-mirror thinking; is cynical, contrite at all costs, humble to a fault.
- The perfectionist. Thinks it can be done better, faster, cheaper; is drugged in optimism; ignores success and focuses on failure.
- The winner. Is addicted to winning, being number one at all costs; does nothing for fun, all for victory; creates competitive situations; belittles the loser.
- The WSM. The whining, sniveling malcontent; every organization has a few. WSMs actively seek opportunities to carp, complain, and voice displeasure. Conversely, WSMs are never available to correct any of the reasons for their constant woes.

Four Types of Stress

The four major dimensions that comprise stress or change:

1. Hyperstress. Overloaded with change
2. Hypostress. Underloaded with change
3. Eustress. Favorable or positive changes
4. Distress. Unfavorable or negative changes

The main sources of stress are implicit in each section of Figure 10–1.

Our coping mechanisms are divided into two basic categories: the subconscious and the conscious. Space does not permit adequate treatment of the subconscious mechanisms, but, essentially, the subconscious coping techniques are developed through our formative years, and we have learned to rely on one or more, much like a reflexive action. The conscious coping techniques are those that we can test and use to reduce stress and perhaps even to convert distress into eustress.

DETECTING ONE'S STRESS LEVEL

General Signs of Stress

Our mind and body report stress in many ways. For example, when stressed, we may experience the following discomforting feelings:

- Dry throat
- Nervous tic
- Stomach disorders
- Pounding heart
- Elevated blood pressure

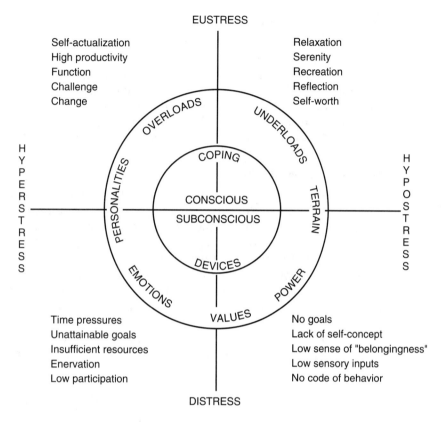

EUSTRESS

Self-actualization
High productivity
Function
Challenge
Change

Relaxation
Serenity
Recreation
Reflection
Self-worth

OVERLOADS UNDERLOADS

HYPERSTRESS HYPOSTRESS

COPING

PERSONALITIES TERRAIN

CONSCIOUS
SUBCONSCIOUS

EMOTIONS POWER

DEVICES

VALUES

Time pressures
Unattainable goals
Insufficient resources
Enervation
Low participation

No goals
Lack of self-concept
Low sense of "belongingness"
Low sensory inputs
No code of behavior

DISTRESS

Figure 10–1 Coping with Stress

- Inability to concentrate
- Muscle spasm
- Insomnia
- Sweating
- Migraine headaches

Unfortunately, many of these symptoms either are ignored or fail to alert our senses. We may be experiencing excessive stress; not coping well, if at all; and thus exposing ourselves to any number of diseases.

> Clearly, it is important for the police supervisor to develop a perceptual capability for accurately detecting signs and symptoms of distress within himself or herself and others. A supervisor's vitality depends on this capability.

Specific Signs of Stress

You now have an opportunity to assess your own and others' existing stress levels. The four questionnaires that follow should be self-administered 1) once a year, 2) at a time of frequent and/or major changes in your life, and 3) when you notice certain telltale signs of mounting tension or uneasiness in you or members of your department. The scales probe for hyperstress (eustress and distress). Hypostress cannot be effectively dealt with in the pages allotted for this subject. (The majority of police supervisors rarely experience this form of stress.)

Structured Exercise 10–3

Listed in Structured Exercise 10–3 are many episodic work-related events that have been found to stimulate stress reactions in employees. The numerical value of each event reflects the degree of disruption it causes in the average person's life. Generally, the higher the score, the greater the probability of a significant health change in the near future. (Note: Because individuals vary in their tolerance for stress, the total score should be taken as a rough guide only.)

For each of the events listed in Structured Exercise 10–3 that you have experienced during the past 12 months, place its value in the My Score column. If you have experienced an event more than once within the past 12 months, you may record its value for up to four episodes. Then add all the numbers in the My Score column to obtain your total episodic, work-related stress score.

Structured Exercise 10–3

Episodic, Work-Related Stress Evaluation

Event	Value	My Score
1. Being transferred against my will to a new assignment	81	_____
2. Being assigned to a less important job	79	_____
3. Experiencing a decrease in status	68	_____
4. Being disciplined/reprimanded by my boss	67	_____
5. Having my request to transfer to a better job rejected	65	_____
6. Sustaining an abrupt and major change in the nature of my work	60	_____
7. Learning of the cancellation of an important project in which I was involved	60	_____
8. Encountering major and/or frequent changes in policies or procedures	59	_____
9. Being promoted/advanced at a slower rate than planned	58	_____

10. Being voluntarily transferred to a new
   position or assignment (not a promotion)   52   _____

11. Facing my forthcoming retirement   47   _____

12. Experiencing a major reorganization
   in my unit   46   _____

13. Experiencing a sudden reduction in the
   number of positive strokes for my
   work accomplishments   46   _____

14. Encountering a major change
   (increase or decrease) in the technology
   affecting my job (computers, techniques)   46   _____

15. Giving a major briefing (not roll call)
   or formal presentation   46   _____

16. Encountering a significant deterioration
   in environmental conditions, such as
   lighting, noise, temperature, space, and filth   45   _____

17. Acquiring a new boss   45   _____

18. Sustaining an immediate, significant
   decrease in the pace of my work   43   _____

19. Sustaining an immediate, significant
   increase in the pace of my work   43   _____

20. Undergoing a major physical
   relocation of my workplace   31   _____

21. Acquiring an increase in status   30   _____

22. Being compelled to work more
   hours per week than usual   29   _____

23. Experiencing the transfer, resignation,
   termination, or retirement of a
   close co-worker   24   _____

24. Being promoted or advanced at
   a faster rate than expected   24   _____

25. Acquiring new subordinates   23   _____

26. Receiving a major work schedule change   23   _____

27. Acquiring new co-workers (peers)   21   _____

28. Experiencing an increase in the number
   of positive strokes for my accomplishments   20   _____

29. Encountering a significant improvement in
   environmental conditions, such as lighting,
   noise, temperature, and space   17   _____

30. Undergoing a minor physical
   relocation of my workplace   5   _____

   Total episodic, work-related stress score   _____

Listed in Structured Exercise 10–4 are many **episodic non-work events in life** that have been found to produce stress for us. The scale value of each event reflects the degree of disruption it causes in the average person's life. Generally, the higher the score, the greater the probability of a significant health change in the near future. The severity of health change also tends to increase with higher scores. (Again, since individuals vary in their tolerance of stress, the total episodic, non-work-related stress score should be taken as a rough guide only.)

The same rules apply here as in Structural Exercise 10–3. The event must have occurred within the past 12 months. If more than once, then multiply the number of times (up to four episodes) against the cited stress points.

Structured Exercise 10–4

EPISODIC, NON-WORK-RELATED STRESS EVALUATION

Event	Value	My Score
Death of spouse/partner	100	_____
Divorce/permanent separation	73	_____
Marital separation	65	_____
Jail term	63	_____
Death of close family member	63	_____
Personal injury or illness	53	_____
Marriage	50	_____
Fired from work	47	_____
Marital reconciliation	45	_____
Retirement	45	_____
Change in family member's health	44	_____
Pregnancy	40	_____
Sex difficulties	39	_____
Addition to family	39	_____
Business readjustment	39	_____
Change in financial status	38	_____
Death of close friend	37	_____
Change to different line of work	36	_____
Change in number of marital arguments	35	_____
Mortgage or loan over $10,000	31	_____
Foreclosure of mortgage or loan	30	_____
Change in work responsibilities	29	_____
Son or daughter leaving home	29	_____
Trouble with in-laws	29	_____
Outstanding personal achievement	28	_____

Spouse begins or stops work	26	_____
Starting or finishing school	26	_____
Change in living conditions	25	_____
Revision of personal habits	24	_____
Trouble with boss	23	_____
Change in work hours or conditions	20	_____
Change in residence	20	_____
Change in schools	20	_____
Change in recreational habits	19	_____
Change in church activities	19	_____
Change in social activities	18	_____
Mortgage or loan under $10,000	17	_____
Change in sleeping habits	16	_____
Change in number of family gatherings	15	_____
Change in eating habits	15	_____
Vacation	13	_____
Christmas season	12	_____
Minor violation of the law	11	_____
Total episodic, non-work-related stress score		_____

Structured Exercise 10–5

Stressful day-to-day, long-term work conditions are listed in Structured Exercise 10–5. Indicate the relative frequency with which you experience each of the following sources of stress by assigning the correct number:

Frequency Scale

1. Never

2. Infrequently

3. Occasionally

4. Frequently

5. Always

LONG-TERM WORK-RELATED STRESS EVALUATION

Frequency	Condition
_____	**1.** I am uncertain about what is expected of me.
_____	**2.** My peers appear unclear about what my role is.
_____	**3.** I have differences of opinion with my superiors.
_____	**4.** The demands of others for my time are in conflict.
_____	**5.** I lack confidence in top management.
_____	**6.** My boss expects me to interrupt my assigned work for new priorities.
_____	**7.** Conflict exists between my unit and others it must work with.
_____	**8.** I get feedback only when my work is unsatisfactory.
_____	**9.** Decisions or changes that affect me are made without my knowledge or involvement.
_____	**10.** I am expected to endorse the decisions of management without being informed of their rationale.
_____	**11.** I must attend meetings to get my work done.
_____	**12.** I am cautious about what I say in meetings.
_____	**13.** I have too much to do and too little time in which to do it.
_____	**14.** I do not have enough work to do.
_____	**15.** I feel overqualified for the job I have.
_____	**16.** I feel underqualified for the job I have.
_____	**17.** The personnel I supervise are trained in a field that is different from mine.
_____	**18.** I must go to other units (bureaus) to get my job done.
_____	**19.** I have unsettled conflicts with my peers.
_____	**20.** I get no personal support from my peers.
_____	**21.** I spend my time "fighting fires," rather than working according to a plan.
_____	**22.** I do not have the right amount of interaction (too much or too little) with others (bosses, peers, staff).
_____	**23.** I do not receive the right amount of supervision (too much or too little).
_____	**24.** I do not have the opportunity to use my knowledge and skills.
_____	**25.** I do not receive meaningful work assignments.
_____	Total

List below any ongoing sources of stress you experience at work that are not included in the evaluation form.

_____

_____

_____

_____

_____

_____

Long-term stress, even after we become accustomed to it, causes pressures that induce illness, lower our feelings of satisfaction, and inhibit growth and work effectiveness. When many episodes involving work-related change occur in an organization in which people are already working in long-term, highly stressful conditions, the use of sick leave and the seriousness of illnesses, accidents, and inattention to work can increase rapidly.

———◆·▶◀·◆———

Structured Exercise 10–6

———◆·▶◀·◆———

Listed in Structured Exercise 10–6 are several potentially stressful long-term, non-work conditions of life at home and in our society generally. Indicate how stressful each is for you personally by selecting a number from the severity scale.

Severity Scale

  1. Not stressful

  2. Somewhat stressful

  3. Moderately stressful

  4. Very stressful

  5. Extremely stressful

Long-Term Non–Work-Related Stress Evaluation

Severity	Condition
_____	1. Noise (traffic, airplanes, neighbors, etc.)
_____	2. Pollution (air, water, toxic waste, etc.)
_____	3. Personal standard of living and ability to make ends meet financially
_____	4. Crime and vandalism in immediate neighborhood
_____	5. Law and order in society
_____	6. Personal long-term ill health
_____	7. Long-term ill health of family member or close friend
_____	8. Racial tensions
_____	9. Regular drug or alcohol abuse of family member or close friend
_____	10. Concern over future of my own career
_____	11. Concern over values or behaviors of family members
_____	12. Political situation in this country
_____	13. Possibility of war
_____	14. Concern over financing my own retirement, my children's education, and so on
_____	15. Economic situation in this country
_____	16. Changing morals in our society (regarding family life, sexuality, and so on)
_____	Total

List here any ongoing non-work-related sources of stress you experience that are not included in the evaluation form.

_____

_____

_____

_____

Reliable Data

The four instruments that you've completed are awareness scales. Many people have discovered that they accurately forecast degrees of our human vitality (or lack of same). The first scale, in particular, is exceptionally well known and accepted; it has over 60 years of hard data to demonstrate its ability to detect distress.

The first step in any stress management and vitality program is to secure reliable data. The bottom-line scores are indicants (not guarantees) of vitality. From our professional perspective and human experience, the following scores or higher should cause you reflective concern:

- Episodic, work-related   300 points
- Episodic, non-work-related   150 points
- Long-term, work-related   64 points
- Long-term, non-work-related   33 points

My observations plus scientific validation of the four scales give me cause to alert you to their predictiveness. If I self-administer the scales (and I do annually) and discover my score on one (and especially more) of the scales to be above that cited above (mine have been so on a few occasions), then I immediately check for signs of distress and simultaneously implement a program of wellness and enhanced vitality. (I've done this, too.)

Prevention

If practical, compare the scores you've posted with other people who have completed the scales. Focus on common and dissimilar results and particular stressors. Also, share your thoughts and feelings about the levels and types of stress you are now experiencing.

Here are some additional ways that you can use the four evaluation sheets to maintain your health and prevent illness:

- See if you can find a pattern to the four sets of results.
- Determine if one type or source of stress is more prevalent than the others.
- Discuss your scores with a friend or police colleague to provide additional insights.
- Remind yourself of the amount of change that has happened to you by posting the four evaluation sheets where you and your family can easily see them.
- Think about the meaning of each change for you, and try to identify some of the feelings you experience.
- Think about ways that you can best adjust to each change.
- Be compassionate and patient with yourself. It is not uncommon for people to become overwhelmed by all the stresses in their lives. It takes a while to put into effect coping strategies to increase your vitality.
- Acknowledge what you can control and what you cannot control, and, when possible, choose which changes you take on.
- Try out the wellness management and relaxation techniques presented in this chapter, and incorporate the ones that work best for you into your own personalized vitality program.

CONVERTING STRESS INTO VITALITY

Now that we have learned about the sources and effects of stress and our own stress levels, we can consider wellness management and our need for vitality. Keep in mind that a healthy police supervisor is in much better shape to be an effective one. Obviously, this holds true for all police employees.

> Although many people associate vitality only with fitness, nutrition, or stress reduction, vitality is really much more. Vitality brings us into a testing ground of self-responsibility and self-empowerment.

VITALITY MANAGEMENT

The goal of vitality management is not merely stress reduction. Life would be boring without stress. While you usually think of stressful events or stressors as being negative, such as the injury or death of a loved one as we saw earlier, they can also be positive. For instance, getting a new home or a promotion at work brings with it the stress of change of status and new responsibilities. The physical exertion of a good workout, the excitement of coming up with a solution to a difficult problem, and the pleasure of watching a beautiful sunset are all examples of eustress. Distress, or negative stress, occurs when you perceive that the challenge facing you is dangerous, difficult, painful, or "unfair," and you are concerned that you may lack the resources to cope with it. You can actually increase your ability to deal with distress by integrating into your everyday life positive activities, such as viewing a colorful garden or landscape, regular exercise and relaxation, enjoyable social contacts, sensible dietary practices, optimistic and rational thinking, and humor and play.

Research shows that performance and efficiency actually improve with increased stress, until performance peaks as the stress level becomes too great. Vitality management involves finding the right types and amounts of stress, given your individual personality, priorities, and life situation, so that you can maximize your performance and satisfaction. By using the tools presented here, you can learn how to cope more effectively with distress, as well as add more eustress or stimulating challenges, pleasure, and vitality to your life.

TAKING FOUR STEPS

With your goals in mind, you are now positioned to take the following steps:

Step 1: Affixing Responsibility

Twenty-four centuries ago in Greece, Hippocrates, the Father of Medicine, told his disciples that disease is not only suffering (pathos), but also work (ponos); that is, disease is the fight of the body to restore itself to normal. This is an important point, and one that, although constantly reinforced in the intervening centuries, is not yet generally acknowledged even today. Disease is not a mere surrender to attack; it is also a fight for health. Unless there is fight, there is no disease. Or, to state this another way, our vitality is our responsibility. And we must work at it!

Step 2: Personal Mastery

The central practice of personal mastery involves learning to keep both a personal vision and a clear picture of current reality before us. Doing this will generate "creative stress." Stress, by its nature, seeks resolution, and the most natural resolution of this stress is for our reality to move closer to what we want.

People who are convinced that a vision or result is important, who can see clearly that they must change their life in order to pursue wellness, and who commit themselves to that result do indeed feel compelled. They have assimilated the vision not just consciously, but also unconsciously, at a level where it increases their vitality.

We may not be able to command ourselves to snap instantly into this frame of mind, but the discipline of personal mastery suggests that we can, as individuals, cultivate a way of "vitality" thinking that leads us gradually to it. The more we practice vitality thinking, the more we will feel competent and confident, and the more we will allow ourselves to be aware of the creative stress that can pull us forward if we cultivate it.

Personal mastery teaches us not to lower our vision, even if it seems as if the vision is impossible. It teaches us that the content of the vision is not important in itself. It's not what the vision is; it's what the vision does.

Personal mastery also teaches us not to shrink back from seeing the world as it is, even if it makes us uncomfortable. Looking closely and clearly at current reality is one of the most difficult tasks of this discipline. It requires the ability to ask yourself, not just at quiet times, but during times of stress, "What is going on right now? Why is my reality so difficult?"

Finally, personal mastery teaches us to choose. Choosing is a courageous act: picking the results and actions that will make you more vital.

Step 3: Reliable Data

While medical science continues to develop new means to keep us alive, we nullify such efforts by refusing to slow down, relax, and consume less. Our American way of life is killing people at an early age. The United States is 16th among countries in the world for male longevity and eighth for female longevity. (The greatest life expectancy in the industrialized world is in Sweden.) It appears that it is our lifestyle, as well as fear of old age, that is killing us off before we reach our longevity potential. An undisciplined, random, fast-paced existence is dangerous to our wellness. It is essential that we know our varying levels of change. The two sections on general and specific stress signs afford us the opportunity to reliably measure our life-change units.

In knowing ourselves, we can, if we choose, know our stress. And in knowing our stress factors, we are in a position to take accurate and positive action. In other words, by assuming the responsibility for your health, you automatically create the need for reliable data about it.

Step 4: An Action Plan for Wellness

It seems that everyone has a particular vitality enhancement program that he or she wants others to use. What works for one person may not work for the other. Jogging, for example, may be helpful stress therapy for one public employee, while another may find it harmful to his or her knees. Hence, a vitality program must be custom-designed to meet the specific requirements of the individual.

I propose five fundamental vitality strategies. The astute police supervisor will select components from one or more of these strategies and *act on them* in order to maintain one's vitality while combating the harmful consequences of distress, discouragement, and depression.

STRATEGY A—SUPPORTIVE RELATIONSHIPS

Supportive Structures

- Build supportive structures in one's home, which will include secluded times for family rituals and protected settings for recuperation. Build supportive structures within oneself, which are associated with one's own attitude toward discomfort, work, personal needs, and the like.

Helpful People

- "No person is an island." This statement has proven helpful in terms of mental health and coping with stressors. Each person needs people, especially helpful people, who will give support when one is depressed, anxious, unhappy, angry, or simply distressed. (To whom do you turn when you are experiencing a strong sense of impending confusion or failure?)

Give and Take

- In establishing a supportive relationship, one should remember two things: 1) A supportive relationship requires cultivation; if it is unattended, it may dissolve; and 2) be certain that the relationship is reciprocal—that is, that there is both giving and taking.

Positive Strokes

- It takes positive strokes to develop emotionally healthy persons with a sense of "OKness." Without supportive relationships, this would be impossible.

Stay-Away-from Folks

- Avoid negative, pessimistic doomsayers. Hang out with the "got-to people" and avoid "stay-away-from folks."

STRATEGY B—MENTAL DISCIPLINE

Keep It Simple

- Learning to reduce the complexity and the number of tasks that confront you will help to reduce stress. You will cope more effectively when problems are handled one by one, on a priority system, and in manageable installments.

Time Management

- Learning to reduce the time pressures on yourself will help to reduce stress. Nature has been good enough to give us a natural reflex for reducing time pressures when faced by overwhelming stress, but many of us fight nature's automatic mental stress-control mechanism. The old adage "Who's going to know the difference in 100 years?" seems proper here.

Mind Focusing

- Mind-focusing exercises are very helpful ways of reducing mental stress. Various meditative methods have been developed and promoted to help people unload tensions by focusing their minds on neutral thoughts, such as a mantra, a number, or deep breathing. In effect, meditation allows you to put down your mental burdens several times a day, to rest your mind for 20 minutes, and then to pick up your burdens once again with more mental energy. It has been found that people who practice mind-focusing or spiritual meditation respond better to stress and seem to recover much more rapidly from the effects of stress than do non-meditators.

Comfort Zone

- All of us need a comfort zone, which causes us to feel good, to feel secure; indeed, a comfort zone allows us to feel our feelings. A "safe and happy place" (SHP) should be one of your own choosing, but you must find one if you have not already done so. Your SHP may be a particular room, a camper van, a fishing stream, an athletic club, a mountain trail, a book—anything, anyplace. Moments of self-renewal, relaxation, introspection, and serenity can and frequently do occur there.

Avoid the 90-10 Trap

- Most of us tend to focus our attention, thinking, and conversations on the worst 10 percent of our lives. The 90 stands for the 90 percent that happens during our day that is usually pretty good. We seem to dwell on what's wrong with life instead of what's right or OK with it. I'm not suggesting that we bury the bad stuff. I'm suggesting that the 90 percent is also worthy of attention—that is, accentuating the positive. Problems steal too much of our time. It's easier to deal with the stress and hassles of life when you're also aware of what's right with your life. Consider for a moment the people you know who evidence a lot of vitality. I bet you they frequently point out what is great, good, right, and positive. **Avoid the 90-10 trap; your vitality depends on it.**

Strategy C—Helping Others

While it is hard to know what to say to a person who has been struck by a distressful event, it is easier to know what not to say. Anything critical of the distressed person ("don't take it so hard"; "try to hold back your tears, you're upsetting people") is wrong. Anything that tries to minimize the person's pain ("it's probably for the best"; "it could be a lot worse"; "she's better off now") is likely to be misguided and unappreciated. Anything that asks the individual to disguise or reject their feelings ("we have no right to question God"; "God must love you to have selected you for this burden") is wrong as well.

People under enormous adverse conditions need sympathy more than advice, even good and correct advice. There will be a time and place for that later. They need compassion, the sense that others feel their pain with them. They need physical comforting, people sharing their strength with them, holding them rather than scolding them.

The phrase "Job's comforters" has come to describe people who want to help but who are more concerned with their own needs and feelings than they are with those of the distressed person, and this makes things worse. As a supervisor-as-leader there are things that you should anticipate and address in a person suffering from a distressful circumstance:

- Anger
- Guilt
- Jealousy

Be There

Seeking out the unfortunate person is the first and most important step you can take in your responsibility to help a co-worker through a bad situation. It is not pleasant to see a grieving co-worker, and most of us would rather avoid the experience. Your mere presence will be significantly comforting and encouraging to them.

Listen Carefully

Empathetic listening is best. Do not, do not lose your self-control by, for example, injecting, "I understand what you're experiencing." Listen! Once you're certain that the person has finished speaking, then you are in a position to say (if you really mean it), "I'm sorry about what has happened to you; how can I help?" Remember, by **being there** and **listening**, you have already helped a lot.

Being Angry Is OK

Typically, the injured person is angry about their misfortune. They need to know that it's OK to be angry. "Cheer up, my friend, it's not that bad" only adds to the person's misery. If angry, hopefully the person is able to focus on the issue and not turn it on himself. Anger turned inward instead of discharged outward causes depression. Distress is bad enough without depression casting its intensifying gloom on the situation.

Who's Responsible for All This Mess

The distressed person will usually engage in the blame game; "Who caused this horrible situation?" The answers can be: 1) I did it to myself; 2) You did it to me; 3) God caused this; and 4) Stuff happens. Like anger, the blame game is OK if you're willing to work your way through it.The first response is "I'm sorry; forgive me." The second response is "I forgive you." The third is a response that, if not appropriately addressed, can erect a barrier between us and all the sustaining, comforting resources of religion. The fourth answer is in reality at response—distress is not distributed very widely; everyone gets his share. "It's unfair, rotten, totally undeserved, but it's my turn, and I'm going to work my way through it."

Jealousy: Why Not You?

For us to suffer distress is bad enough. But for us to suffer it while those around us don't is even worse. "Everyone except me on the police lieutenant's list will be promoted." "Everyone except me who asked for a transfer got one." "Everyone except me has a happy marriage." We know that we hurt ourselves more than anyone else by feeling jealous. But we still feel it.

Perhaps the only cure for jealousy is to realize that the people we resent for not being in our miserable condition probably have emotional wounds and physical scars of their own. They may even be envying us. "You think you've got problems? Let me tell you my problems, and you'll realize how well off you are." This won't help the affected person. As mentioned above, the "Why me?" is best answered by "Why not you?" Apparently, it is your turn.

Chronic Distress Syndrome

If the above remedies do not lessen the burden, the frustration, and the depression associated with the problem, then the supervisor should recommend that the person seek professional counseling. Remember, this recommendation applies equally to you, the supervisor-as-leader.

STRATEGY D—THE THREE Rs

- Reading for fun and enjoyment
- Relaxation as a voluntary control of stress
- Recreation as a release and as a revitalization

STRATEGY E—ALTRUISTIC EGOISM

Altruistic Egoism

- Hans Selye coined the expression and advanced the practice of "altruistic egoism," which basically is looking out for yourself, but in an altogether different frame of reference than you might initially suspect. Selye went on to reveal that this self-ism is to be developed in and around being necessary to others. Eliciting the support and goodwill of others is a key ingredient in the practice of altruistic egoism.

Earning Benevolence

- "Earn thy neighbor's love." This motto, unlike love on command, is an enduring part of our human nature. Who would blame anyone who wants to assure his or her own self-worth and happiness by accumulating the treasure of other people's benevolence? Avoid remaining alone in the midst of the overcrowded society that surrounds you. Trust people, despite their apparent untrustworthiness, or you will have no friends, no support. If you have earned your neighbor's love, you will never be alone.

Structured Exercise 10–7

There are some tabloids that report on events such as "Mother Gives Birth to Eighty-Year-Old Twins." You'll find them at newsstands and markets. Recently, I spotted a front-page headline, "The Ultimate Secret to Stress Reduction." For $0.50, how could I go wrong? Here is what I learned.

A fellow in Canton, Ohio, buys an enormous amount of Jell-O. When distressed, he puts it into his bathtub, gets in, and lies there until it congeals. He assured me, the reader, that it works. His worries were removed, no more troubles, aches and pains gone.

Well, I didn't try it. It made for amusing reading, though. You know, it probably helped him. The reason for this scenario is simple: What works for one person may not work for another.

Now, here is what I learned. Wellness programs must be custom-designed. What works for me may not help you. Nonetheless, you must identify and apply those techniques that avoid the barriers of distress and provide the carriers of success. At this point, proceed directly to item five under Discussion.

KEY POINTS

- Stress is a natural and unavoidable phenomenon.
- Stress is a demand for change.
- Too much or too little stress lessens our vitality.
- When stress is mismanaged, it can be harmful.

- There are three sources of stress: 1) personal, 2) environmental, and 3) organizational/social.
- There are four types of stress: 1) hyperstress, 2) hypostress, 3) eustress, and 4) distress.
- Due to the very nature of the job, a police supervisor is assured of experiencing all four types of stress—especially hyperstress.
- Distress can seriously reduce the vitality of a police supervisor.
- The police supervisor should be alert for the general and specific symptoms of distress.
- The police supervisor-as-leader should maintain a program of vitality by 1) recognizing that he or she is responsible for his or her health, 2) developing personal mastery, 3) collecting reliable data on his or her stress level, and 4) designing and using a customized plan for wellness.

DISCUSSION

1. How are one's vitality and integrity connected?
2. An earlier section dealt with the reality of "turbulent changes." As a group, identify the five major changes affecting you or your work group.
3. Of the four stressors listed as organizational/social, which one seems to dominate in your organization?
4. In terms of episodic, work-related stress events, cite three events you personally feel are the most stressful. Discuss them as a group. Be alert for similarities and uniqueness.
5. Drawing from the five strategies for wellness, custom-design a wellness action plan for yourself.

TEAMWORK

RESPONSIBILITIES

ORGANIZING

The police supervisor is responsible for designing a work structure that facilitates all employees' making a maximum contribution to accomplishing the mission of the department.

And Moses chose able men out of Israel, and made them heads over the people, rulers of thousands, rulers of hundreds, rulers of fifties, and rulers of tens.

And they judged the people at all seasons: The hard causes they brought unto Moses, but every small matter they judged themselves.

—Exodus 18:25–26

With all prior responsibilities attended to, the supervisor is now faced with organizing the staff into a cohesive, focused, and dynamic work unit that is capable of implementing a community-oriented policing program.

As with everything else in our lives, organizations are changing. When speaking about change today, we often hear the word "radically"—for example, the radical changes in information technology. Additionally, the type or frequency of change is usually referred to as "chaotic" (or some other synonym).

Organizational change is certainly not radical. At best, it has been evolutionary for some organizations. Many organizations have resisted even evolutionary or minor changes. Regardless of whether an organization welcomes or stonewalls change, chaos plagues organizations in their endeavors to adapt to new ways or hold fast to the old.

223

A lot of police organizations are making a full commitment to the implementation of community-oriented policing (COP). Some of them realize that in doing so they must change their "culture" or attitudes and skills. I agree that beliefs, attitudes, and skills need to be modified in order to support a COP effort. But unless there is also a shift in governance (how we distribute power, purpose, and rewards), the efforts will be more cosmetic than foundational.

Many of us live two lives. One life is personal, with choices, freedom, interdependency, caring, loyalty, and trust. The other life is organizational, with directions, control, dependency, indifference, and self-serving behavior.

This chapter covers aspects of the police organization that have been most resistant to change, namely, the distribution of power, purpose, and rewards. It seeks to reintegrate parts of ourselves with the mission of our police agencies. We'll start by examining the concept of **governance.**

GOVERNANCE

Thus far we have concentrated on supervision and the supervisor-as-leader. The concept of governance recognizes the political nature of our lives and workplace, and serves as an umbrella for both. A leader must cope with decisions on how to govern an organization. Again, governance encompasses questions about **service, community, power, commitment, purpose, and achievement.**

If those who govern answer the above questions based on a **top-down, bureaucratic, hierarchical point of view,** you'll get one set of answers. Those who answer with a **bottom-up, agile, form of governance** in mind give us a totally opposite approach. Top-down or bottom-up—which is best? Let us explore both types of governance, recognizing that they exist in various combinations in all organizational settings.

Top-Down Governance

The top-down organization on paper looks like a rigid pyramid. It consists of many layers of managers and supervisors; it thrives on written policies and rules; it emphasizes complexity. The manager and supervisor are the boss, and authority is top-down. This is a **bureaucratic organization.**

- *Service.* The managers and supervisors decide on what types and quality of services are best for the community.
- *Community.* The people served are seen and served as one, as if they share a sameness.
- *Power.* Power is viewed as having clearly defined boundaries. It is centralized at the top of the department.
- *Commitment.* There is bottom-up commitment to the bosses and elite work groups.
- *Purpose.* The purpose of the department and its divisions is defined by top management.

- *Achievements/Advancements.* Opportunities to achieve and be rewarded for it (e.g., promotion, a better job) are limited to those that daily demonstrate a commitment to the top managers.

> Top-down governance relies on a bureaucratic organization to get the mission accomplished. Also, management is primary and leadership secondary when using this type of governance.

Bottom-Up Governance

The bottom-up organization looks like a fluid Frisbee. It consists of a few layers of leader-managers with little attention to official emblems of rank; it thrives on flexibility and action; it emphasizes simplicity. The leader is the senior partner, and authority is bottom-up. We refer to this as the agile organization.

- *Service.* The leader, in concert with his or her work team, communicates with the community to decide what is best for the customers.
- *Community.* The people served are seen and served as individuals, as being unique.
- *Power.* Power is understood as being infinite. It is dispersed throughout the agency. Every employee is empowered.
- *Commitment.* Similar to power, there is an equal commitment by the department to the welfare of all employees.
- *Purpose.* The purpose of the department and its divisions is determined by people representing all levels and job assignments within the agency.
- *Achievements/Advancements.* The chances for career growth and job accomplishments are unlimited and not tied to a particular manager or preferred supervisory style.

> Bottom-up governance depends on an agile organization for mission fulfillment. Further, leadership is primary and management/supervision secondary in this governance system.

Structured Exercise 11–1

Visualize an organization—one that you currently work for or one that you worked for in the past. Next, respond to the following questions about the various dimensions by circling the most appropriate number.

1. Service mix is   Service mix is decided
     decided at the top.   by everyone.

     1   2   3   4   5   6   7

2. Community is   Community is seen as
     seen as a whole.   made up of individuals.

     1   2   3   4   5   6   7

3. Power is centralized.   Power is dispersed.

     1   2   3   4   5   6   7

4. Commitment is to   Commitment is to
     top management.   all employees.

     1   2   3   4   5   6   7

5. Purpose is defined   Purpose is defined by all
     by top management.   levels in the department.

     1   2   3   4   5   6   7

6. Achievement is judged   Achievement is judged by
     by management standards.   individual contributions.

     1   2   3   4   5   6   7

Add up the numbers. The higher the sum is (36 or more), the more likely it is that you are working for a governance system that is agile and in need of leader-managers. The lower the score is (24 or less), the more likely it is that the governance system is highly structured and in need of manager-leaders.

———— ●+✕+● ————

Which One Is Best?

All things considered, and all things being equal, the bottom-up, or agile, organization is the most beneficial of the two for the delivery of high-quality police services. However, in the real world of police work, not all things are considered, and all things are not equal. Thus, before a decision is made on what form of a governance system is best for an agency, the following questions or issues must be explored:

- How much tolerance is there for making mistakes—for taking risks?
- What is the nature of the community, and what do its residents expect from their police?
- What is the skill level of the personnel?
- Do the employees support the mission of the department?
- How motivated is the staff?
- How ethical is the staff?
- How much trust is there among the personnel and among the work units?

Once the above questions have been answered and evaluated, those in power can decide on either a supervisor or a supervisor-as-leader governance system.

The type of governance system selected determines which organizational design should be used. If "supervisor and manager," then the bureaucratic, or top-down, organization is required. If "leader," then the agile, or bottom-up, organization is called for. A revolt will occur if the wrong organizational system is applied. Managers and supervisors will struggle, if not fail, within an agile organizational setting. And managers and supervisors-as-leaders will flop in a bureaucratic environment.

Structured Exercise 11–2 is a keystone for the final part of this section. Review it carefully.

Structured Exercise 11–2

Several years ago I was a police officer, and, as such, I remember a particular patrol roll call. A newly appointed sergeant appeared and introduced himself to the 12 of us. He went on to say, "This isn't a democracy. I believe in participative supervision. I'm going to supervise, and you're going to participate. I run a benign dictatorship."

Later on that evening while on patrol, my partner remarked, "It appears that this sergeant is the same as the last. Clearly, he is not interested in our ideas or opinions. He's big into control. And if we want to get along okay with him, then we best comply with his orders."

Several years afterward I recalled this episode. I saw a gross paradox in our daily lives as compared with our organizational lives. First of all, we live with political institutions that celebrate the rights of individuals to express themselves, to assemble, to pursue happiness and individual purposes, to pick their own political leaders. We pay enormous attention to the rights and procedures of due process. At times, we seem to be on the edge of anarchy, and yet we tenaciously cling to our political beliefs. Conversely, when we shift into our occupational life, those beliefs are best ignored. Consistency, control, and compliance become the dominant values.

For many years, I faced the frustrating dilemma of how to most effectively govern an organization. I was convinced that democracy would not work. Can you imagine voting on whether we should wear uniforms, who works what assignments, ethical standards, whether to evaluate employee performance or not? I was equally convinced that while a top-down autocracy could work, it was filled with such pitfalls as transparent loyalty, weak commitment, low trust, poor communications, and zero risk-taking.

If neither one of the above governance systems is relevant, then come the questions: What might prove successful? What is the most reliable alternative? Before reading further, think about these questions. What are your answers? Discuss them with your co-workers. The alternative follows.

The Alternative

When you empower employees, you are automatically creating a series of partner-ships within an agency. (Responsibility Eight, Empowerment, covered this in detail.) Community-oriented policing (COP) hinges on a police department's empowering its personnel. When this occurs, you have an organization comprised of interlocking teamwork.

ORGANIZATIONS

Organizations are social units (human groupings) deliberately constructed and reconstructed to seek specific goals. Business corporations, military units, schools, churches, and police departments are included; ethnic groups, friend-ship groups, and family groups are excluded. An organization is characterized by 1) goals; 2) a division of labor, authority, power, and communication responsibilities in a rationally planned—rather than a random or traditionally patterned—manner; 3) a set of rules and norms; and 4) the presence of one or more authority centers that control the efforts of the organization and direct them toward its goals.

The Bureaucratic Organization

It is only through enforced standardization of methods, enforced cooperation that this faster work can be assured. And the duty of enforcing the adaptation of standards and of enforcing this cooperation rests with the management alone. . . .

—*Frederick W. Taylor*

Most police organizations are bureaucratic in nature and foster top-down governance systems. Nonetheless, one normally will find a few pockets of agile thinking, where supervisors-as-leaders are in charge.

Bureaucracies are organizations that have numerous formalized rules and regulations. They are among the most important institutions in the world because they not only provide employment for a very significant fraction of the world's 6.3 billion people, but they also make critical decisions that shape the economic, educational, political, social, moral, and even religious lives of nearly everyone on earth. Figure 11–1 depicts a bureaucratic system.

THE FOUR CORNERSTONES OF BUREAUCRACY.   The bureaucratic organization developed over a number of centuries and finally matured in the 1930s. It is exemplified in Luther Gulick's essay "Notes on the Theory of Organization,"[1] in James Mooney and Alan Reiley's Principles of Organization,[2] and in Max

---

[1] Luther Gulick, "Notes on the Theory of Organization," in *Papers on the Science of Administration*, ed. Luther Gulick and Lyndall Urwick (New York: Institute of Public Administration, 1937), pp. 1–45.

[2] James D. Mooney and Alan C. Reiley, *Principles of Organization* (New York: Harper & Row, 1939).

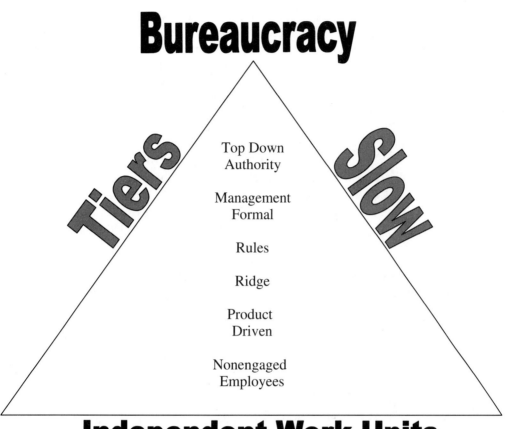

Figure 11–1 Bureaucracy, the Science of Hierarchy

Weber's writing on bureaucracy.[3] All these theorists were strongly oriented toward economy, efficiency, and executive control. These values, when combined, create a bureaucratic organization that has four cornerstones—**division of labor, hierarchy of authority, structure, and span of control.**

Of the four, division of labor is the most important; in fact, the other three are dependent on it for their very existence. The hierarchy of authority is the legitimate vertical network for gaining compliance. Essentially, it includes the chain of command, the sharing of authority and responsibility, the unity of command, and the obligation to report. Structure is the logical relationship of positions and functions in an organization, arranged to accomplish the objectives of the organization. Classical organization theory usually works with

---

[3] The best-known translation of Max Weber's writing on bureaucracy is H. H. Gerth and C. Wright Mills, trans., from *Max Weber: Essays in Sociology* (New York: Oxford University Press, 1946).

two basic structures, the line and the staff. Both structures can be arranged four ways: purpose, process, people (clientele), and place where services are rendered. The span of control concept deals with the number of subordinates a superior can effectively supervise. It has significance, in part, for the shape of the organization. A wide span yields a flat structure; a narrow span results in a tall structure.

The contemporary bureaucratic organization evolved from the thinking and practice of:

- Max Weber, who emphasized the need for rationality
- Frederick W. Taylor, who concentrated on its scientific aspects
- Luther Gulick and Lyndall Urwick, who formulated principles

WEBER: RATIONALITY.   Max Weber was a founder of modern sociology, as well as a pioneer in administrative thought. Weber probed bureaucracy, here essentially synonymous with "large organization," to uncover the rational relationship of bureaucratic structure to its goals. His analysis led him to conclude that there are three types of organizational power centers: 1) traditional—subjects accept the orders of a supervisor as justified on the grounds that it is the way things have always been done; 2) charismatic—subjects accept a superior's orders as justified because of the influence of his or her personality; and 3) rational-legal—subjects accept a superior's orders as justified because these orders agree with more abstract rules that are considered legitimate.

Power and authority. The type of power employed determines the degree of alienation on the part of the subject. If the subject perceives the power as legitimate, they are more willing to comply. And if power is considered legitimate, then, according to Weber, it becomes authority. Hence, Weber's three power centers can be translated into authority centers. Of the three types of authority, Weber recommended that rational structural relationships be obtained through the rational-legal form. He felt that the other two forms lacked systematic division of labor, specialization, and stability, and that they had no irrelevant political and administrative relationships.

Six safeguards. In each principle of bureaucracy described below, Weber's constant concern about the frailness of a rational-legal bureaucracy is apparent. His primary motive, therefore, was to build into the bureaucratic structure safeguards against external and internal pressures so that the bureaucracy could at all times sustain its autonomy. According to Weber, a bureaucratic system, to be rational, must contain these elements:

1. *Rulification and routinization.* A bureaucracy is a continuous organization of official functions bound by rules. Rational organization is the opposite of temporary, unstable relations; thus the stress on continuity. Rules save effort by eliminating the need for deriving a new solution for every situation. They also facilitate standard and equal treatment of similar situations.
2. *Division of labor.* Each person has a specific sphere of competence. This involves a sphere of obligation to perform functions that have been

marked off as part of a systematic division of labor. It provides the incumbent with the necessary means of compulsion clearly defined, and their use is subject to definite conditions.

3. *Hierarchy of authority.* The organization of offices follows the principle of hierarchy; that is, each lower office is under the control and supervision of a higher one.

4. *Expertise.* The rules that regulate the conduct of an office may be technical rules or norms. In both cases, if their application is to be fully rational, special training is necessary. It is thus normally true that only a person who has demonstrated an adequate technical training is qualified to be a member of the administrative staff.

5. *Written rules.* Administrative acts, decisions, and rules are formulated and recorded in writing.

6. *Separation of ownership.* It is a matter of principle that the members of the administrative staff should be completely separated from ownership of the means of production or administration. There exists, furthermore, in principle, complete separation of the property belonging to the organization, which is controlled within the spheres of the office, and the personal property of the official.

Weber did not expect any bureaucracy to have all the safeguards he listed. The greater the number and intensity of those an organization possessed, however, the more rational and, therefore, the more efficient the organization would be.

TAYLOR: SCIENTIFIC MANAGEMENT.   Frederick W. Taylor, production specialist, business executive, and consultant, applied the scientific method to the solution of factory problems, and from these analyses established principles that could be substituted for the trial-and-error methods then in use. The advent of Taylor's thinking in the early 1900s opened a new era: that of scientific management.

Contributions. Taylor's enormous contributions lay, first, in his large-scale application of the analytical, scientific approach to improving production methods. Second, while he did not feel that management could ever become an exact science in the same sense as physics and chemistry, he believed strongly that management could be an organized body of knowledge and that it could be taught and learned. Third, he originated the term and concept of functional supervision. Taylor felt that the job of supervision was too complicated to be handled effectively by one supervisor and should, therefore, be delegated to as many as eight specialized foremen. Finally, Taylor believed that his major contribution lay in a new philosophy of motivating workers and management.

Enforced cooperation. Taylor consistently maintained—and successfully demonstrated—that through the use of his techniques it would be possible to obtain appreciable increases in a worker's efficiency. Furthermore, he firmly believed that management, and management alone, should be responsible for putting these techniques into effect. Although it is important to obtain the cooperation of the workers, it must be "enforced cooperation."

Five methods. Taylor prescribed five methods for "scientifically" managing an organization. First, management must carefully study the worker's body movements to discover the one best method for accomplishing work in the shortest possible time. Second, management must standardize its tools based on the requirements of specific jobs. Third, management must select and train each worker for the job for which they are best suited. Fourth, management must abandon the traditional unity-of-command principle and substitute functional supervision. As already mentioned, Taylor advocated that a worker receive his or her orders from as many as eight supervisors. Four of these supervisors were to serve on the shop floor (inspector, repair foreman, speed boss, and gang boss) and the other four in the planning room (routing, instruction, time and costs, and discipline). Fifth, management must pay the worker in accordance with their individual output.

Impact. Taylor's general approach to management is widely accepted today in production-oriented business organizations. Scientific management became a movement, and it still has a tremendous influence on industrial practice. More specifically, it had a major effect on the reform and economy movements in public administration, and thus also influenced police administration. Its impact on public organizations is readily apparent at the present time; one can find numerous managers and supervisors (private and public alike) who firmly believe that if material rewards are directly related to work efforts, the worker consistently responds with maximum performance.

GULICK AND URWICK: PRINCIPLES. While the followers of Taylor developed more scientific techniques of management and work, others were conceptualizing broad principles for the most effective design of organizational structure. Luther Gulick and Lyndall Urwick were leaders in formulating principles of formal organization.

The first and main principle. Gulick and Urwick proposed eight principles, the first of which underlies and influences the seven others—division of labor. Their approach rests firmly on the assumption that the more a specific function can be divided into its simplest parts, the more specialized (e.g., homicide investigation) and, therefore, the more skilled a worker can become in carrying out his or her part of the job. They emphasized that any division of labor must be in strict accordance with one of the following four rationales:

- The major *purpose* the worker is serving, such as designing microprocessors, controlling crime, or teaching
- The *process* the worker is using, such as engineering, medicine, carpentry, programming, or accounting
- The *person* or *things* dealt with or served, such as immigrants, victims, minorities, mines, parks, farmers, automobiles, or the poor
- The *place* where the worker renders his service, such as Hawaii, Washington, Rocky Mountains, beach resorts, college campuses, or sports arenas

Structured Exercise 11–3

Small police agencies (10 or fewer employees) have little specialization. The majority of the employees are generalists, with one or two being assigned the job of chief supervisor and clerk/dispatcher. In the medium-to-large-scale departments, we find a lot of specializations (e.g., motorcycles, K-9 units, SWAT teams, field evidence technicians, field training officers, and more). Now the question—which one of the four above rationales is most appropriate for determining how to divide the work (division of labor) in a police agency? Think about it; discuss it. Once you have reached a conclusion, proceed with your reading. The answer follows.

No single rationale is better than the others! In practice, the rationales often overlap, are sometimes incompatible with one another, and are quite vague. For example, when looking at a police organization, it would be difficult not to conclude that the four rationales fail to provide a satisfactory guide to division of labor in that organization. Furthermore, it can be seen that the four rationales are prescriptive, rather than descriptive; that they state how work should be divided, rather than how work is actually divided. The planning of the division of labor in a given organization is affected by many considerations not covered by the four principles. The division may be determined by the culture in which the organization is situated, by the environment of the organization, by the availability and type of personnel, and by political factors. Organizations are made up of a combination of various layers that differ in their type of division. The lower layers tend to be organized according to area or clientele and the higher ones by purpose or process. Even this statement, however, should be viewed only as a probability. In a police organization, all four rationales operate at the same time.

Seven additional principles. Gulick and Urwick went on to underscore seven more principles for organizing:

1. *Unity of command.* A man cannot serve two masters. This principle is offered as a balance to the division of labor and conflicts with Taylor's "functional supervision."

2. *Fitting people to the structure.* People should be assigned to their organizational positions "in a cold-blooded, detached spirit," like the preparation of an engineering design, regardless of the needs of that particular individual or of those individuals who may now be in the organization.

3. *One top executive (manager).* Gulick and Urwick both strongly supported the principle of one-person administrative responsibility in an organization. Hence, they warned against the use of committees and would have choked on the words "teamwork" and "partners."

4. *Staff: general and special.* The classical writers' concern about staff assistance to top management deserves special attention. When management expressed a need for help from larger and larger numbers of experts and specialists, this need immediately raised the question of the relation of these specialists to the regular line supervisors and employees. In this instance, Gulick recommended that the staff specialist obtain results from the line through influence and persuasion, and that the staff not be given authority over the line. The next question to be answered was that of coordination. Top management would have more people to supervise, since they would be responsible for not only the line, but also the special staff. The Gulick-Urwick answer to this problem was to provide help through "general staff" as distinguished from "special staff" assistance. Significantly, general staff are not limited to the proffering of advice. They may draw up and transmit orders, check on operations, and iron out difficulties. In doing so, they act not on their own, but as representatives of their superior and within the confines of decisions made by them. Thus they allow their superior to exercise a broader span of control.

5. *Delegation.* They emphasized that "lack of the courage to delegate properly and of knowledge how to do it is one of the most general causes of failure in organization." In larger organizations, we must even delegate the right to delegate.

6. *Matching authority and responsibility.* They dealt with both sides of the authority–responsibility relationship. It is wrong to hold people accountable for certain activities if the necessary authority to discharge that responsibility is not granted. On the other side, the responsibilities of all persons exercising authority should be absolute within the defined terms of that authority. Managers should be personally accountable for all actions taken by subordinates. They set forth the widely quoted axiom that "at all levels authority and responsibility should be continuous and coequal."

7. *Span of control.* Gulick and Urwick asserted that no supervisor can supervise directly the work of more than five or, at the most, six subordinates whose work interlocks. When the number of subordinates increases arithmetically, there is a geometrical increase in all the possible combinations of relationships that may demand the attention of the supervisor.

POSDCORB.   Gulick took the concept of "management" and defined it as consisting of seven activities—which spelled out POSDCORB.

- *Planning:* the working out in broad outline of what needs to be done and the methods for doing it to accomplish the purpose set for the enterprise
- *Organizing:* the establishment of a formal structure of authority through which work subdivisions are arranged, defined, and coordinated for the defined objective

- *Staffing:* the whole personnel function of bringing in and training the staff and maintaining favorable conditions of work
- *Directing:* the continuous task of making decisions, embodying them in specific and general orders and instructions, and serving as the leader of the enterprise
- *Coordinating:* the all-important duty of interrelating the various parts of the organization
- *Reporting:* keeping those to whom the executive is responsible informed as to what is going on, which includes keeping themselves and subordinates informed through records, research, and inspection
- *Budgeting:* all that goes with budgeting in the form of fiscal planning, accounting, and control

BUREAUCRACY IN REVIEW. The words "bureaucracy" and "bureaucrat" have negative connotations. If we do not like an organization, we can label it a "bureaucracy." If we do not like a government worker, we can call him or her "bureaucratic." This is an injustice to both the organization and the person. To use these terms belies the fact that all organizations of a few or more people are bureaucracies and all workers are to some degree bureaucrats—even the agile ones and leader-managers/partnerships. While at times inefficient and frustrating, we need them to convert disorder into order.

The underpinnings of bureaucracy are three interlocking cornerstones: rationality of structure, scientific management, and principles of organization. One way of classifying these three concepts is as follows: First, Weber's writing was primarily descriptive; however, it did indicate that a particular form of organizational structure was preferable. Second, the theories of both Taylor and the Gulick-Urwick team were prescriptive; that is, they expressed the one right way to manage and organize a body of people. It is the "one right way" thinking that gets bureaucracies into trouble. The agile organization rejects such thinking with its motto "there are many right ways."

The Agile Organization

An organizational structure, once created, should be flexible and responsive to the developing needs of the organization and changes.

—David Packard

Success today and in the future depends on police organizations that can **create new knowledge** that results in **value-added services**. Success now and in the future will depend on police employees who have a passion for the profession, who generate new ideas—ways of doing things that result in new knowledge, which in turn results in innovative and unique services. With these current and future demands, do we want to place our bet on consistency, control, and compliance?

> The agile organization and its teamwork style of governance are not an idle, idealistic dream. They exist. Most of them are in the private sector. They are beginning to emerge in government—see police agencies evolving as agile organizations.

CONTINUITY AND CHANGE.   The governance system of an agile organization is constantly reconfiguring in order to balance continuity (its core values) and change (internal and external cultural and technological demands). The agile organization and its primary components are shown in Figure 11–2. The subsections that follow briefly describe each of the seven components.

Speed

- Today's environment, with its virtually real-time information exchanges, demands that an institution embrace speed.

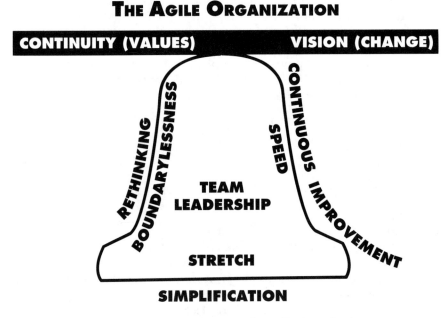

Figure 11–2   The Agile Organization

- Faster, in almost every case, is better! From decision-making to performance-making to communications to services, speed, more often than not, ends up being the success differentiator.
- If it's worth doing, it's worth doing poorly.

Boundarylessness

- Those in a boundaryless organization have an obsession for finding a better way—a better idea—be it a source, a colleague, another organizational unit, or a neighboring organization or one on the other side of the globe that will share its ideas and practices.
- Aligned with not boundaryless behavior is a rewards system that recognizes the adaptor or implementer of an idea as much as the originator.
- Creating this open, sharing element magnifies the enormous and unique strength of an organization—an endless stream of new ideas and best practices.
- Deploy "seam teams." These are work teams that link up and integrate two or more operations, for example, traffic units that work as a common unit to combat a drug-infested area.
- Bureaucracy-bashing is ensuring that written rules, memorandums, and the like do not hamper operational efficiency. The larger the operations manual, the more it will burden an agency.
- Tier-trashing is keeping the number of horizontal levels to a minimum. The more tiers, the more inefficiency. Remember: keep it simple, keep it lean.

Stretch

- In an organization where boundarylessness, openness, informality, and the use of ideas from anywhere—and speed, with its bias for action—are increasingly a way of life, an overarching operating principle—stretch—is a natural outgrowth.
- Stretch, in its simplest form, says "nothing is impossible," and the setting of stretch targets inspires people and captures their imaginations.
- Stretch does not mean "commitments are out." Stretch can occur only in an environment where everyone is totally committed to maintaining a rigid set of core values—integrity, trust, quality, boundaryless behavior—and to outperforming every one of their global competitors in every market environment.
- Stretch does mean we are not fixated on a meaningless, internally derived, annual budget number that does nothing but make bureaucrats comfortable.
- A stretch atmosphere replaces a grim, heads-down determination to be as good as you have to be and asks, instead, "How good can you be?"

Simplification

- The overlay for speed, boundarylessness, stretch, and everything else you do is simplification!
- Simplify everything you do.

- Use straightforward communication with one another and even simpler communication with your customers.
- The efficacy of statistics, budget data, and the like will be measured by their simplicity, and that simplicity will improve their quality, their cost, and their speed in reaching the intended consumer.

Rethinking

- At least annually, compare the performance of an operation or an agency with the performance of all others (benchmarking), with the best becoming the standard to be met by all the following year.
- Conventional policy-making ranks programs and activities according to their good intentions; rethinking ranks them according to their results.
- On a routine basis, reinventions should be expected and not celebrated as unique.
- Downsizing per se is not rethinking—it may cause "amputation before diagnosis." It can be a casualty, rather than a cure.
- Rethinking is identifying the activities that are productive, those that should be strengthened, promoted, and expanded.
- Rethinking does not give us answers, but forces us to ask the right questions.
- Place particular focus on:
  - Performance objectives
  - Quality objectives
  - Cost objectives
- See "Continuous Improvement."

Continuous Improvement

- Continually evaluate everything that you do.
- Place particular focus on:
  - Performance objectives
  - Quality objectives
  - Cost objectives
- Link the improvements to some form of an incentive or recognition.
- Make incremental improvements before the service reaches a peak or goal.

Team Leadership

- Team leadership = a swarm of people acting as one; folks that have left behind their self-interest; they supervise things and lead people. With people, fast is slow and slow is fast—it takes time.
- There is no place for halfhearted interest or halfhearted effort.
- Even the most capable supervisors have trouble transitioning from an emphasis of command-and-control supervising (micromanaging) to team leadership. Causes: Simple human nature—reclaiming the sandbox for themselves—reverting to old habits. "Corecracking of a team is like having

a baby tiger given to you; it does a wonderful job of keeping the mice away for about 12 months, and then it starts to eat the kids."

- Transitional tips: 1) Don't be afraid to admit ignorance; 2) think about what you take on, not what you give up; 3) learn when and where to intervene; 4) get used to learning on the job; and 5) learn to really share (let go of) power.

AGILITY IN REVIEW.   Some of the elements of agile organizations are often in place. We frequently see innovative personnel rating systems, self-managing teams, total quality efforts, teamwork, customer attentiveness, and flattened pyramids. They are rarely, however, put together in a pervasive governance strategy. As a result, we end up too often working against ourselves. We share control with the left hand and take it back with the right. One moment we are on the fast track toward agility, and the next moment we are instituting more bureaucratic controls.

Figure 11–2 depicts the pivotal role that the team supervisor-as-leader has in striking a balance between continuity (core values) and vision (change). The demand for change is constant. Those managers and supervisors who are overly comfortable in their jobs prefer a rigid and stable organization, as compared with a flexible and agile one.

Structured Exercise 11–4

It was at our team-building sessions that it became clear that some of the rhetoric heard at the top level—about involvement and excitement and turning people loose—did not match the reality of life at the line level. The problem was that some of our managers and supervisors were unwilling, or unable, to abandon big-department, big-shot autocracy and embrace the values we were trying to grow. So we defined our leader-manager styles, or "types," and how they furthered or blocked our values. And then we acted.

Type I not only delivers on performance commitments, but also believes in and furthers our values. The trajectory of this group is "onward and upward," and men and women who comprise it will represent the core of our senior leadership into the next century.

Type II does not meet commitments or share our values—it will not last long here.

Type III believes in the values, but sometimes misses commitments. We encourage taking swings, and Type III is typically given another chance.

The "calls" on the first two types are easy. Type III takes some judgment; but Type IV is the most difficult. One is always tempted to avoid taking action because Type IVs deliver short-term results. But Type IVs do so without regard to values and, in fact, often diminish them by grinding people down, squeezing them, stifling them. Some of these learned to change; most couldn't. The decision to begin removing Type IVs was a watershed decision—the ultimate test of our ability to "walk the talk"—but it had to be done if we wanted our employees to be open, to speak up, to share, and to act boldly outside traditional "lines of authority" and "functional boxes" in this new learning, sharing environment.

A Case for Agile Organizations

The way a police department is organized affects employee motivation and performance. There are bureaucratic organizations in which the person at the top issues an order and it is passed on down the line until the person at the bottom does as he or she is told without question or reason. This is precisely the type of police organization I am arguing against. I am convinced that the objectives of COP can best be achieved by people who understand and support them and who are allowed flexibility in working toward common goals in ways that they help determine are best for their operation and their department.

It Isn't Working

Some of the basic ideas we hold about how to run police agencies and organize work aren't working. We have been burdened with a belief that control, consistency, and predictability are essential. **Even our efforts to implement empowerment and team leadership are curtailed by our innate need for control, consistency, and predictability.**

Changing the Structure Isn't Enough

A common management paradigm is that changing the organization structure will change the values and behavior of personnel. Changing structure alone is never enough. If you make structural changes (e.g., move the internal affairs unit from investigations to the chief's office), but the value of maintaining central consistency and predictability remains untouched, nothing really changes.

We have been swinging between centralization and decentralization for decades in police work. Decentralization usually means that instead of one chief at the top, we now have several deputy chiefs running decentralized divisions. Yes, decentralization presents a change in structure. But it does not automatically foster a different pattern or style of supervising and leading.

Boss Is Out, Coach Is In

The notion of the supervisor as "boss" in a professionally led police organization is nonsense. Supervisors no longer plan, organize, delegate, and control; they act as coaches, trainers, resources, and advisors. But they are not distinct and separate from their teams. They are player/coaches. **They're in the game and not observing from the bench.**

Organization = Interdependence

"Organization" is literally another word for interdependence. We need each other for a thousand reasons, both emotional and practical. That is why most of us live in communities. When you fly across our nation, any nation, note the open space with people huddled in small villages, medium-sized cities, and large metropolises. The problem we face is that the organizational forms that we have inherited and use do not fulfill our need for security, freedom, and service. Police supervisors-as-leaders are attempting to meet these needs by answering these questions:

- What will it take for me to claim my leadership and create a work unit of my choosing? (In turn, they are resisting the yoke of bureaucratic control.)
- What is it I uniquely have to offer? What do I wish to leave behind here? (Clearly, they are wanting to make a difference.)
- When will I finally choose adventure and accept the reality that there is no safe path? (These supervisors accept that their security comes from within themselves.)

Democracy has as its essence a widely distributed sense of ownership and responsibility. Creating interdependence or "teamwork in police work" is a way of affirming the democratic experience. This experience inside police organizations assures broader forms of participation in the community. And this broader participation translates into community-oriented policing.

We have swallowed the belief that police organizations, and even communities, can survive only with the strict enforcement of consistency and control. If we believe this is true, a police-community partnership will never happen. So what we do within the police workplace makes an enormous difference. *The supervisor's work unit must become the crucible from which the partnership is forged and community policing rediscovered.*

KEY POINTS

- Governance includes leadership and supervision plus the political nature of our organizational lives.
- Top-down governance is found in bureaucratic organizations.
- Bottom-up governance is found in agile organizations.
- A bottom-up or supervisor-as-leader style of governance is not a democracy.
- It is imperative that there be a fit between the type of governance and the type of organizational structure.
- Organizations are social units deliberately constructed to attain goals.
- Of all the cornerstones and principles of bureaucracy, division of labor is the most important.
- The agile organization maintains a balance between consistency (value) and change (vision).

- Organizations and the interdependence of work units and police employees are synonymous.
- Community-oriented policing either starts or stops in the supervisors' work unit.

DISCUSSION

1. What does "governance" mean in an organizational context?
2. What are the differences between top-down and bottom-up governances?
3. What are the main features of a bureaucracy?
4. What are the key aspects of an agile organization?
5. Thinking about your organization, how bureaucratic is it? How agile is it?
6. I intentionally did not pose any questions about Structured Exercise 11–4. Reread the exercise and discuss the merits and downsides of this department's approach for achieving value compliance.
7. Why isn't the agile organization more prevalent among police departments?
8. Why is one reason that COP fails a lack of internal teamwork?

PERFORMANCE

The supervisor's responsibility for an employee's job performance encompasses planning for it, setting specific objectives, and measuring their attainment.

I am a great believer in luck, and I find the harder I work, the more I have of it.

—Thomas Jefferson

> Team leadership (Responsibilities One through Five), team-building (Responsibilities Six through Ten), and organizing (Responsibility Eleven) have set the stage for developing a system for measuring change in performance over time.

There were two fellows hard at work next to a road. One carefully dug holes while the other waited a moment and then filled them up. It all appeared rather foolish, and finally a supervisor who demanded an explanation confronted the workers. The fellow who dug the holes said he had been doing the same job for more than 10 years; his cohort quickly chimed in that he had been filling the holes for the same period.

Upon further questioning they confessed it made more sense in the past when a third person worked with them. His job had been to put a new tree into the hole. But when he retired, he was never replaced, so the two just kept on working as before. "Why didn't you tell somebody?" the supervisor sputtered. "Hey," they said, "you signed Jim's retirement letter. We figured you knew."

The kinds of unproductive, inefficient, and even counterproductive job performance that go on in most workplaces defy logic and reveal a great deal about the work ethic. After all, the ethical principle of responsibility includes a moral duty to improve things, to pursue excellence, and to produce and

243

demand quality performance. Yet basically good employees in virtually every workplace regularly engage in or witness some process or practice that is unhelpful, wasteful, or even harmful to the ultimate goals of the organization.

While top management is ultimately to blame, people of character shouldn't passively demean the value of their work by becoming part of anything second-rate or stupid. It may take tact and timing, maybe even some courage, but it's the supervisor's duty to be a force for excellence. The bottom line benefit is that the quality of our lives improves dramatically when we take pride in our job performance.

A SPIRIT OF PERFORMANCE

The bottom line test of a police organization is the **spirit of performance.** All 15 of the responsibilities covered in this book are intended to resonate a spirit of excellence. This spirit cannot be evoked by mere exhortations, lofty sermons, or well-meaning intentions. It *must be* evidenced in five prerequisite conditions.

Prerequisite One—Non-Negotiable High Standards

The focus of a police agency must always be on performance. The first practice is setting **non-negotiable high performance standards** for the group as well as for each officer. The department must establish a habit of achievement. However, performance does not mean "success every time." Rather, performance is a "batting average." It will—indeed, it must—have room for mistakes and even for failures. What performance has no room for is complacency and low standards.

Prerequisite Two—Opportunities

Everyone must have the **opportunity** to grow career-wise, experience rewards for good work, enjoy their job, and sense being a valued part of their work team. Here the viewpoint is converting obstacles into opportunities and problems into solutions. The work force seizes on opportunities to get the best results for its community.

Prerequisite Three—Character

It is here that the quest for high performance turns to the **character** of the organization. In doing so, we again reflect on the first three responsibilities—values, ethics, and vision. Together they formulate and articulate a supervisor's character. Moreover, if enthusiastically pursued and clearly demonstrated, they enlarge the supervisor's character to include leadership as well.

Prerequisite Four—Emotional Intelligence

The supervisor, the leader, sets the emotional standard. (Emotional intelligence was examined more profoundly in Responsibility Nine.) No matter what you set out to do, your success depends on **how** you do it. Understanding the powerful role of emotions in the workplace distinguishes the leaders as compared with the supervisors. In any human group, the leader knows that he has maximal power to sway everyone's emotions. The leader knows that when people feel good, they work at their best. The leader knows that, more than anyone else, he creates the conditions that directly determine a police officer's ability to work well—high performance! The leader possesses, in essence, above-average **emotional intelligence.** Without a healthy dose of the heart, a supervisor may supervise, but he **does not lead.**

Prerequisite Five—Teamwork

High performance depends on teamwork. Groups of people working together are both smarter and achieve much more than they could individually. It is the leader who balances a team's focus on the task at hand with attention to the relationships among the team members. The glue that holds people together in a team and that commits people to an organization is the emotions they feel. Officers take their emotional cues from their boss. Hence, **the leader sets the emotional standard.** Optimistic, enthusiastic leaders get the best out of their staff.

With the five prerequisites in place, we can proceed on the path of attaining high job performance. The path actually commenced in **Responsibility Three—Vision** and its coverage of strategic thinking. We pick up on our journey now by taking three significant steps by:

- Planning for performance
- Setting performance objectives
- Performance evaluation

PLANNING FOR PERFORMANCE

Planning is the process of implementing objectives. It concentrates on the **means** (how it is to be done), as well as the **ends** (what is to be done). Planning can be further defined in terms of whether it is **informal** or **formal.** All police supervisors engage in planning, but it may be only the informal variety. Nothing is written down, and there is little or no sharing of objectives with others in the organization.

When I use the term "planning," I am implying formal planning. There exist specific objectives. These objectives are typically committed to writing and available to organization members. They cover a period of months or years. Finally, specific action programs exist for the achievement of these objectives; that is, supervision and management have clearly defined the path they want to take in getting from where they are to where they want to be.

Why Planning?

Why should police supervisors engage in planning? Because it 1) gives direction; 2) reduces the impact of change; 3) minimizes waste and redundancy; 4) sets the standards to facilitate control; and thus increases performance.

Direction. Planning establishes coordinated effort; it gives direction to supervisors and officers alike. When everyone knows where the agency is going and what they are expected to contribute toward achieving the objectives, there should be increased coordination, cooperation, and teamwork.

Change. Planning is a way to reduce uncertainty through anticipated change. Planning forces supervisors to look ahead, anticipate changes, consider the impact of these changes, and develop appropriate responses.

Waste. Planning can reduce overlapping and wasteful activities. Coordination before the fact is likely to uncover waste and redundancy.

Standards. Planning reinforces the objectives or standards that are to be used to facilitate control. In the controlling function, we evaluate actual performance against the objectives, identify any significant deviations, and take the necessary corrective action. Without planning, there can be no control.

Performance. The above planning leads to increased performance.

> Do not assume that all efforts require planning. After all, planning can be time-consuming and costly. The key question is this: Does the planning effort appear to be justified in view of the expected gains or outcomes?

Two Types of Planning

Plans that are organization-wide, that establish the organization's overall objectives, and that seek to position the police organization in terms of its environment are called strategic plans. Plans that specify the details on how the overall objectives are to be achieved are called operational plans.

STRATEGIC PLANS. Strategic planning typically encompasses a long-term time frame (three to five years or more), has an open-ended perspective, and attempts to predict emerging "driving forces." This form of planning is now being used by police organizations.

OPERATIONAL PLANS. There are two categories of operational plans: 1) **single use,** and 2) **standing.** The first is nonrecurring, such as multi-agency police planning for the 2008 Olympic Games. In other words, any plan that identifies how the organization's primary objectives are to be achieved, is developed for a specific purpose, and dissolves after this purpose is accomplished is a single-use plan.

A standing plan is likewise comprised of objectives. In this case, the objectives are long-term with slight modifications, as needed, over time.

Both types of operational plans depend on clear and measurable objectives. When these are in place, the stage is set for supervising by objectives (SBO).

SUPERVISING BY OBJECTIVES

Supervising by objectives is essentially a threefold process that:

1. Sets a course of desired direction—the objective
2. Motivates the person to proceed in that direction—the result
3. Ensures self-control via feedback—the managing/supervising

SBO necessitates setting goals that are **tangible, verifiable,** and **measurable.** Rather than using goals to control, SBO seeks to use them to motivate. The remainder of this section concentrates on the development and use of SBO in police organizations. The practice of SBO by police supervisors has yielded enormous positive payoffs for the overall organization.

SBO operationalizes the concept of objectives by devising a process by which objectives cascade down through the organization. As depicted in Figure 12–1, the organization's overall goals are translated into specific objectives for each succeeding level (i.e., division, bureau) in the police department. This linking ensures that the objectives for each unit are compatible with and supportive of those of the unit just above it. At the individual level, SBO provides specific personal performance objectives. All police personnel, therefore, have an identified specific contribution to make to their unit's performance. If all the individuals achieve their objectives, then their unit's objectives will be attained, and the organization's basic goals are pursued:

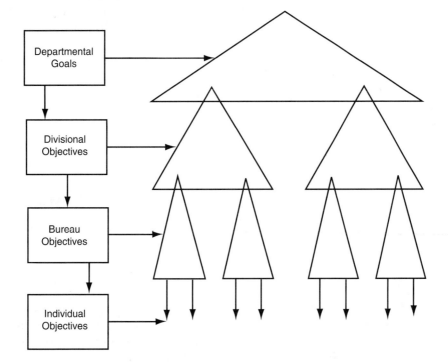

Figure 12–1   From Goals to Objectives

- Crime control
- Crime prevention
- Order maintenance
- Human services

Goals and Objectives

Once the overarching goals and the more specific objectives have been decided, the supervisor can "supervise" by them. While the literature on SBO is extensive and covers both public and private organizations, the term still remains subject to varying definitions. Peter Drucker first coined the term in 1954 and describes SBO as a mutual understanding between the manager and his or her subordinates of what their contribution will be for the organization over a given period of time. It thus establishes parameters of self-control and common direction. Moreover, it establishes parameters that target the individual and the agency, both in the direction of accomplishing the much-to-be-desired goals. (Drucker used Managing by Objectives.)

Who Sets Objectives?

Objectives should be established by the supervisor in light of 1) his expected contribution to the agency, 2) the expectation of his subordinates, and 3) the expectation of their manager. The supervisor's manager has, as the supervisor should have, the ultimate purview for approval or rejection.

To accomplish all three, a sizable amount of information exchange must occur. Thus, managing supervisors, or supervising police employees, requires special efforts not only to establish common direction. Mutual understanding can never be attained by "communications down." It can result only from "communications down, up, and across." It requires the superior's willingness to **listen** to his staff.

SETTING OBJECTIVES

The objective-setting process consists of seven interrelated steps:

1. Identification of the issue
2. Definition of the issue in specific, operational terms
3. Development of alternative strategies to deal with the issue
4. Selection of the appropriate alternative
5. Implementation
6. Evaluation
7. Feedback

Step 1: Identification of the Problem

At first glance, this might appear to be an oversimplification, but experience has shown that this step is often the most difficult part of the entire process.

For example, let us assume that a sergeant in a medium-sized police department has the responsibility for supervising a team of 14 police officers. In addition to this overall responsibility, he is responsible for the division's in-service training program and supply requisitioning. He is actively pursuing his own formal education and will soon be awarded his associate of arts degree from the local college. The chief of police is interested in converting the traditional patrol patterns and assignments to a community-oriented policing (COP) program. The agency has never experienced such an ambitious undertaking and, in fact, is understrength by approximately four persons. Because the department uses a formal hierarchy, the sergeant's immediate supervisor is a lieutenant (of which the agency has four). The chief has selected the sergeant to research, develop, and present to him a position paper exploring the team-policing concept for their agency.

Various techniques can help here. These include thinking reflectively, analyzing available data, generating new data about the problem, brainstorming, using paper slip techniques (index cards), making personal observation, and asking someone internal or external to the agency who may have had more experience with such issues. The critical part, however, remains thinking clearly about the issue and then writing it down in the most specific terms possible. This might require several attempts; it is important to keep at the task until satisfied that what has been written is an accurate statement about the issue—and that it is the *real* issue.

Step 2: Specific Statement

This step of the process is somewhat similar to the identification step; however, it is separated due to its importance. In addition to the advice and cautions offered previously, the supervisor should probe on the "objective statement." It is often productive to use colleagues and a work group as a sounding board to modify, correct, or reinforce the objective statement and to assure the supervisor that what has been written is, in fact, a specific issue statement amenable to solution and measurement.

Step 3: Alternative Strategies

Here the supervisor is to develop as many alternatives as possible to solve the issue. In the first phase of the exercise, the supervisor should not disregard any possible alternative. The same techniques indicated before can be utilized to do this—ranging from individual thinking to group thinking. After all the possible alternatives have been identified, the supervisor can then proceed to reduce the list to the handful that hold the most promise.

Factors that affect the decision to leave an alternative on the list or remove it are almost limitless. A few of the more outstanding include:

- Time
- Money
- Personnel
- Political ramifications
- Tradition and custom
- Attitudes
- Skill of the participants

Step 4: Selection of an Alternative

This step is what the supervisor has been aiming toward from the start of the process. After following the preceding steps, the supervisor is finally ready to select the paramount one and implement it. One caution deserves to be reinforced here; that is, the best alternative is not always the most feasible one. The supervisor should be aware of this and should not become disillusioned if the "number one" alternative cannot be implemented. This is caused by a variety of reasons, ranging from money to politics to personal bias.

Step 5: Implementation

In preparing to implement the selected alternative, the supervisor should have thought through the alternative to the point where he or she knows which individuals are going to be impacted, how they will be affected, and where the alternative will be exercised. In effect, the supervisor has a "battle plan" for following through with the selected alternative.

Step 6: Evaluation

Performance evaluation is highlighted in the final section of this chapter.

Step 7: Feedback

I am using the term "feedback" to mean communicating the results of the objective-setting process back to those above and below us in the hierarchy. Whether the results are favorable or unfavorable, it is imperative that we communicate the results back into our system. This is done for the following reasons:

- It keeps people informed of results.
- It leads to refined objectives, one building on the results of the last.
- It continues the process of constantly refining our ability to affect issues in our work group.
- It builds a database on which to build future objectives and decisions.

In reviewing the theme of this section, that the objective-setting process is critical in the supervisor's role of problem-solving, the following series of questions should be asked of each objective:

- Is the objective a guide to action?
- Is it explicit enough to suggest certain types of action (alternatives)?
- Does it suggest tools to measure and control effectiveness?
- Is it challenging?
- Does it reflect the reality of internal and external constraints?

Structured Exercise 12–1

This exercise is intended to build your skill as a supervisor in the use of SBO. Based on the agency for which you work, select one of the following subjects, or generate one of your own. Write a goal (objective) statement related to the subject, using no more than 250 words. Be certain that the goal statement is clear, specific, and attainable. A few subjects of concern might be:

- Residential burglary rate
- Commercial burglary rate
- Commercial robbery rate
- Officer-involved traffic accidents
- Citizen complaints
- Response times
- Care and maintenance of equipment
- In-service training

If in a group setting, divide into teams of five to seven individuals. Each person should read aloud his or her goal statement. Then collaborate to refine the statement into a highly practical objective worthy of implementation in a police department. This process should be repeated at least once or twice. Practice ensures your successful use of this powerful supervisor's tool.

Roadblocks

Much like the "I've got good news and bad news for you; which do you want first?" jokes, I have revealed but one side of SBO—the good news. Now for some bad news. SBO is not without roadblocks. As expressed thus far, the advantages are that police managers and supervisors are encouraged to think seriously about their objectives, and to try to get them into meaningful and also measurable terms; also, it encourages forecasting, planning, and dialogues between all administrative levels. The disadvantage is that the system is basically foreign to those systems that have developed in both industry and government.

PERFORMANCE EVALUATION

Performance evaluation encompasses three key purposes: 1) behavioral motivation, 2) control, and 3) feedback. To a large extent your success as a supervisor is directly related to your ability to appraise the performance of your assigned personnel.

Performance evaluation (or performance appraisal or rating) accurately is both a process and a method by which a police agency obtains feedback on and provides guidelines for the effectiveness of its personnel—feedback, in the sense that past work effort is **evaluated,** and **guidelines,** to the extent that performance objectives are specified for the immediate future. Traditionally, the evaluation process and methods were designed with feedback as an end in mind; having guidelines as part of the evaluation system is more recent. An evaluation system that uses both feedback and guidelines is commonly referred to as SBO.

Performance evaluation is very challenging for several reasons. **First,** it must serve many purposes, from evaluating the success of selection decisions, to assessing the effectiveness of a leader, to evaluating training efforts, to determining the quantity and quality of individual work effort. **Second,** the assessment of performance itself is a difficult measurement task because so many factors influence performance, including environmental, organizational, and individual factors. **Finally,** a great number of ethical and emotionally charged issues arise when performance is evaluated. The results of the process can have profound influences on the job, career, attitude, personal self-concept, and general sense of well-being of a police employee.

> Personnel decisions can be made without performance evaluation systems. They can be made by drawing random numbers, by choosing whomever you like best, by choosing the person you owe a favor to, by choosing someone who wears the best-smelling aftershave lotion or perfume, and so on. Clearly, an effective organization requires a proficient process and method for assessing the past performance and the future potential of its most valuable asset: human resources.

Performance evaluation serves at least the following purposes:

1. Promotion, separation, and transfer decisions
2. Feedback for each employee regarding how the organization views his or her performance
3. Evaluations of relative contributions made by individuals and entire departments in achieving higher-level organizational goals
4. Reward decisions, including merit increases, promotions, and other rewards
5. Criteria for evaluating the effectiveness of selection and placement decisions, including the relevance of the information used in those decisions
6. Ascertaining and diagnosing training and developmental needs for individual employees and entire divisions within the organization
7. Criteria for evaluating the success of training and development decisions
8. Information upon which work-scheduling plans, budgeting, and human resources planning can be based
9. Specification of new performance objectives (SBO) for the ensuing time period

Performance Evaluation Must Be Job-Related

All the frustrations to which police supervisors and employees point when performance is reviewed can be summarized by two terms: *reliability* and *validity*. Both terms are qualities of the evaluation process and refer to the adequacy of the information that is generated and employed in subsequent decisions about employees.

Job Analysis Leads to Reliability and Validity

The prime means for a police agency to ensure the job relatedness (reliability and validity) of a performance evaluation system is job analysis. A job is a relatively homogeneous cluster of work tasks carried out to achieve some essential and enduring purpose in an organization; job analysis consists of defining the job and discovering what the job calls for in employee behaviors. Job analysis, then, is a procedure for gathering the judgments of people who are knowledgeable about the organization, the positions within it, and the specific content of a job. Furthermore, the content of the job is defined to be specific work activities or tasks. In effect, job analysis is a broad term describing an entire series of judgments that are made in the design of an organization.

Selecting a Performance Appraisal System

There are several critical factors to assess when designing or selecting a performance appraisal system:

1. Specific **organizational and environmental properties,** such as technology and the design of the agency
2. Unique **individual characteristics** that influence police performance, including specific skills and abilities and motivation levels
3. The mix of specific **work behaviors** that are appropriate, given departmental and individual officer considerations
4. The mix of **relevant performance** dimensions, given the agency and personnel involved
5. The specific set of **goals** to be achieved at divisional and unit levels

Rater and Rating Errors

Errors in the performance appraisal process mainly occur in the rater or in the process itself. There are four common types of errors to guard against: halo errors, strictness errors, leniency errors, and central tendency errors.

HALO ERRORS.   These occur when an evaluator incorrectly treats two or more dimensions of performance as if they were identical or highly correlated. For example, if a police employee's work performance in report writing is observed as "superior," the evaluator accidentally assigns the same high mark to "personal appearance."

STRICTNESS ERRORS.   This type of error occurs when an evaluator rates all employees as very poor performers. Ratings given by this type of evaluator tend to cluster closely toward the low end of the rating scale.

LENIENCY ERRORS.   These are the opposite of strictness errors; with leniency errors, the evaluator mistakenly gives all employees uniformly high ratings. Ratings given by this type of evaluator cluster at the high end of the scale.

CENTRAL TENDENCY ERRORS.   These errors are similar to leniency and strictness errors, except that in this case the ratings made by the evaluator cluster artificially at the middle of the scale.

Structured Exercise 12–2

As a new police supervisor, you take your job most seriously, especially performance rating. During your recent two-week Supervisor's Training Course, eight hours (10 percent) were devoted to the do's and don'ts of rating.

Your agency uses a rating scale, which it applies once a year, in the month of March. Your lieutenant instructed you and the other field sergeant to administer the scales. He went on to add, "In the next few months, a number of critical personnel decisions will be made. Your ratings are likely to determine the outcome of some of these pending decisions."

You have a fairly good feel for the police personnel in your unit as compared with the other sergeant's. If anything, your group is a slight cut above the other crew. Nonetheless, you recognize that your staff is not perfect. The results of your first rating are 1) two "improvement needed," 2) four "competent," and 3) one "outstanding." All seven officers read, discussed with you, and signed the form. No problem!

Three days later it was revealed that your colleague sergeant rated all seven of his personnel "outstanding." Rumors and complaints quickly surfaced among your team of officers. The lieutenant has asked to see you and the other sergeant about this situation. What is on your mind? What are you planning to say? What is your position(s) on this matter? How might it be resolved?

THE PERFORMANCE DOMAIN RATING SCALE

Police agencies have recognized the urgent need for making their evaluation method more relevant to the performance of a police officer. To this end, they have often succeeded in designing highly valid and reliable rating scales. These scales are produced in conjunction with the performance domain; that is, what the officer should be doing in his or her work assignment is what is appraised.

This can be referred to as a performance domain rating scale (PDRS). A PDRS is job-related and thus does not fall prey to the inadequacies of a global rating scale (GRS). Figure 12–2 presents a PDRS that (with necessary modifications) may improve the effectiveness of your overall rating system. (Keep in mind that this particular PDRS does not apply to other performance domains, such as non-sworn, supervisory, and so on.) Depending on the unique characteristics of each agency, three to six PDRS's may be required to ensure and maintain job-related personnel evaluations. One final comment: A key feature of a PDRS that is often overlooked is that it depends on narrative comments.

Of the many available examples of a PDRS, I chose to include here the Arvada (Colorado) Police Department's. On behalf of Chief Ahlstrom, Commander Scott wrote a letter of explanation as follows. (His letter is one of the reasons that I decided to present their PDRS.)

In order for you to better understand these evaluations, I would like to provide you with some background information on the process used to arrive at the content and format of these evaluations. Since time immemorial, supervisors and officers within the department have complained about a variety of concerns with the previous evaluation formats. Supervisors expressed the desire to have a check-off type of evaluation form. At the same time, officers and supervisors were concerned with the fact that a generic evaluation for a given rank did not address the specifics found within particular job assignments, i.e., the difference between detective, patrol officer, traffic officer, narcotics officer, etc.

In the interim, the city Personnel Department and the City Manager's Office came down with a mandate that the various city departments would develop evaluations which would have weighted values for various performance categories and would also be utilized, based upon overall score, to determine salary increases or decreases. When the original mandate came down from the City Manager and Personnel Department, performance categories were examined for content and revised to a greater or lesser degree to more accurately reflect the expectations of various assignments within the department. Nevertheless, the final forms were still somewhat generic and really did not address the specific expectations of particular assignments.

. . . I began the revision process for the performance evaluations within the Operations Bureau. I took the previous evaluation format which, in essence, consisted of a series of performance categories which were then explained by a paragraph of narrative detail. These performance categories were then broken down by myself into particular elements within a category with a point rating of 1 to 5 for the level of performance for each of those particular elements within a category. The category was then weighted based upon input from supervisors and the personnel to be evaluated. This weight value was then multiplied times the raw score to give an overall score for that performance category. At the end of the evaluation, the supervisors are to tabulate all of the calculated scores (raw score times weight value) to calculate a final raw score. This raw score is then divided by the total possible points for that particular evaluation to determine a percentage score, which is then used to determine the overall quality of performance and which can then be correlated with the City's breakdowns for salary increase or decrease.

I have instructed each of the elements and units within the Operations Bureau to critically evaluate and review the performance evaluation for each of their units. They are then authorized as a unit to revise the performance evaluation . . . based upon what they perceive as those elements which specifically address the performance and expectations in

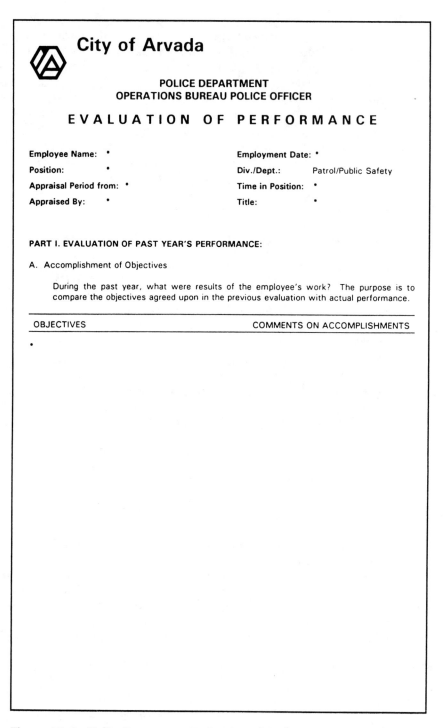

Figure 12–2 Police Department Evaluation of Performance (Courtesy Arvada Police Department, Arvada, Colorado)

PART II. PERFORMANCE STANDARDS

Evaluators are to review each and every item of performance under each of the Standards. The degree to which an employee is <u>capable</u> of engaging in a specific item may vary with the shift or assignment.

When evaluating the employee, the evaluator is to check off the appropriate rating for each element of an evaluation category. Each rating is given a value as follows:

Unsatisfactory	= 1
Below Expectations	= 2
Meets Expectations	= 3
Exceeds Expectations	= 4
Distinguished Performance	= 5

After completing the evaluation of each element of a category (i.e., Customer Service - Community Problem Solving), the evaluator is to total the rating scores in that category and multiply by the <u>Weight</u> for that category. This provides a score for that category. At the conclusion of the evaluation, all category scores are totalled to yield a final evaluation <u>total</u> which is divided by the possible total score of 935 to give the percentage score which can be used (as can the point score) to determine the overall performance rating of the employee.

The supervisor must be able to articulate, in detail, the justification for a specific performance category (element) score. "Description of Performance Guidelines" as found in the <u>Supervisor's Guide to Performance Evaluations</u> is to be used when assigning one of the 5 performance levels to a given Standard of performance. A narrative explanation <u>must</u> accompany any score which is either a "Distinguished" or below the "Meets Expectations" level. This narrative must detail the reasons for the score and, in the case of "Below Expectations" and "Unsatisfactory", there must be a plan explaining what is necessary to improve performance to a "Meets Expectations" level. These comments are to be done by listing the letter (a, b, c, etc.) of the corresponding element in the "Comments" section of the page, followed by the brief explanation.

When a general category (i.e., Customer Service) contains a series of "4" (Exceeds Expectations) ratings, the evaluator must justify that rating, but may provide that justification in the "Comments" area with detailing each sub-section (i.e., a, b, f, i).

Figure 12–2   *(Continued)*

1. CUSTOMER SERVICE/COMMUNITY PROBLEM SOLVING - WEIGHT 3	1	2	3	4	5
a. Responsive to service requests	•				
b. Displays helpful, cooperative attitude					
c. Sensitive to citizen needs					
d. Participates in community programs including Neighborhood Watch Meetings, D.A.R.E. classes/graduations, community meetings					
e. Actively identifies and recognizes the origins of community problems, evaluates issues and develops possible solutions to problems					
f. Awareness of and use of community/citizen/city government resources					
g. Appropriate use of citizen contacts					
h. Achieves a positive community image					
i. Effective initiation of and follow-up on Police Service Requests					
TOTAL (Element Score)					

Weight 3 x Total of All Element Scores ____•____ = Performance Standard Score ___•___

COMMENTS:

•

2. TEAMWORK/INTERPERSONAL ACTIONS - WEIGHT 2	1	2	3	4	5
a. Takes steps to eliminate bias in the department when observed	•				
b. Cooperates with others in establishing reasonable objectives and achieving desired results					
c. Displays behavior which builds trust and mutual respect and cooperation among fellow workers					
d. Has a positive approach when participating in routine activities, assignments, and problem solving					
e. Avoids unnecessary confrontation and adequately resolves conflicts when necessary					
f. Shares information with other members of the organization					
g. Respectful when interacting with co-workers and supervisors					
h. Actively seeks the opportunity to assist peers with their work performance					
i. Displays an awareness of shift/department workload and makes himself/herself available to assist fellow workers					
j. Makes comments and takes action to constructively enhance a team environment					
TOTAL (Element Score)					

Weight 2 x Total of All Element Scores ____•____ = Performance Standard Score ___•___

COMMENTS:

Figure 12-2   *(Continued)*

3. COMMUNICATIONS - WEIGHT 3	1	2	3	4	5
a. Radio transmissions are clear, concise and follow procedures	•				
b. Expresses thoughts in writing and orally in a clear, concise, and well organized manner					
c. Displays good penmanship, grammar, and spelling in written reports					
d. Courtroom testimony is clear, accurate, and prepared					
e. Demonstrates ability and willingness to listen					
f. Understands and properly carries out instructions and orders					
g. Able to give and receive constructive feedback					
h. Ability to adjust communicative style for differing groups and situations					
i. Follows chain of command					
j. Comments, suggestions, and criticisms are presented in a constructive manner					
k. Written reports are grammatically correct and clearly understandable					
TOTAL (Element Score)					

Weight 3 x Total of All Element Scores ____•____ = Performance Standard Score ___•___

COMMENTS:

•

4. INITIATIVE - WEIGHT 3	1	2	3	4	5
a. Accepts direct responsibility for District/assignment	•				
b. Shows initiative in everyday work activity - identifies and addresses community problems - initiates PSR's based upon knowledge of problems					
c. Ability to adapt to change					
d. Strives to improve the work product					
e. Serves as a role model for peers					
f. Ability to work constructively with a minimum of supervision					
g. Volunteers to direct or manage tough assignments					
h. Demonstrates ability to organize and coordinate various activities/operations					
i. Generates ideas and approaches to improve Police Department/City performance and the operation of the organization					
j. Maintains activity and productivity levels consistent with shift averages and expectations of supervisors and the community					
k. Looks for, and engages in, non-assigned productive activities which try to fulfill the community's needs.					
l. Looks for opportunities to conduct follow-up investigation on own initiative					
TOTAL (Element Score)					

Weight 3 x Total of All Element Scores ____•____ = Performance Standard Score ___•___

COMMENTS:

Figure 12–2 *(Continued)*

5. PROFESSIONAL JUDGEMENT - WEIGHT 3	1	2	3	4	5
a. Demonstrated awareness of impacts of decisions	•				
b. Ability and willingness to make sound decisions based on available information without the assistance of supervisors					
c. Willing to take acceptable risks, but not recklessly					
d. Accepts responsibility for decisions and the subsequent results					
e. Proper use of police discretion					
f. Sensitive to needs of community or individuals					
g. Alert to surroundings and able to understand and react quickly and appropriately					
h. Has full understanding and application of the laws, rules and procedures governing the use of force, pursuit policy, search and seizure, arrest, and domestic violence					
i. Exercises proper degree of assertiveness when needed					
TOTAL (Element Score)					

Weight 3 x Total of All Element Scores ____•____ = Performance Standard Score ___•___

COMMENTS:

•

6. WORK PERFORMANCE/QUALITY - WEIGHT 3	1	2	3	4	5
a. Keeps current with legal changes and changes in Rules and Procedures Manual	•				
b. Proper recognition, collection and preservation of evidence					
c. Demonstrated understanding and application of State/Federal Laws, Municipal Ordinances, Departmental Rules and Procedures, Rules of Criminal Procedure, legal decisions, and directives					
d. Knowledge of and proper use of equipment and investigative techniques: Radar, Intoxilyzer, camera equipment, crime scene equipment (fingerprinting), computers Nystagmus, firearms, to include follow-up activities when appropriate					
e. Assignments/investigative reports are properly carried out and completed in a timely manner					
f. Knowledge of police patrol districts					
g. Continuous adherence to the RPM and other procedural guidelines					
h. Work product is consistently completed in a professional, thorough manner					
i. Documentation is an accurate reflection of a thorough investigation to include the elements of the crime, proper classification, correct report formatting, complete witness information, MO, and suspect information					
TOTAL (Element Score)					

Weight 3 x Total of All Element Scores ____•____ = Performance Standard Score ___•___

COMMENTS:

Figure 12–2   *(Continued)*

7. PERSONAL APPEARANCE, GENERAL SAFETY PRACTICES AND PRIDE IN WORKING ENVIRONMENT - WEIGHT 1	1	2	3	4	5
a. Cares for uniform, equipment, police facility, vehicle, and weapons as required	•				
b. Cognizant of personal health and keeps physically fit					
c. Maintains positive image in appearance and demeanor at all times among peers and members of the public					
d. Exercises proper field survival practices					
e. Operates motor vehicles in a safe and prudent manner - obeys traffic laws					
TOTAL (Element Score)					

Weight 1 x Total of All Element Scores _____•_____ = Performance Standard Score ___•___

COMMENTS:

•

8. PROFESSIONAL AND ORGANIZATIONAL COMMITMENT - WEIGHT 2	1	2	3	4	5
a. Is a positive role model for others to emulate	•				
b. Demonstrates loyalty and commitment to department and profession					
c. Continually strives to improve the image of the Arvada Police Department in the eyes of the public					
d. Demonstrates pride in the performance of others as well as self					
e. Demonstrates understanding of and commitment to Accreditation Standards					
f. Takes overt steps to overcome and combat bias in the community					
TOTAL (Element Score)					

Weight 2 x Total of All Element Scores ___•___ = Performance Standard Score ___•___

COMMENTS:

•

Figure 12–2   *(Continued)*

PART III. Overall Rating

1. Customer Service/Community Problem Solving   _____

2. Teamwork/Interpersonal Actions   _____

3. Communications   _____

4. Initiative   _____

5. Professional Judgement   _____

6. Work Performance/Quality   _____

7. Personal Appearance, General Safety Practices, and Pride in Work Environment   _____

8. Professional and Organizational Commitment   _____

TOTAL POINT SCORE   _____

Total $\dfrac{\text{Point Score}}{\text{935 Points}}$ = __*__ %

OVERALL RATING SCORE = __*__

	Below	Meets	Exceeds	Distinguished
Unsatisfactory [_]	Expectations [_]	Expectations [_]	Expectations [_]	Performance [_]
(20-34)	(35-54)	(55-71)	(72-91)	(92-100)

Relative to this employee's overall work record during this evaluation period, I recommend: (Include status and salary recommendations within the parameters listed in the "City of Arvada Supervisor's Guide to Performance Evaluations")

•

PART IV. EMPLOYEE ASSESSMENT

Based upon current performance, what are the <u>current</u> employee strengths and development needs?

A. Employee Strengths:

•

B. Development Needs:

•

Figure 12–2 *(Continued)*

C. Enter other comments relevant to the employee's performance.

•

PART V. ESTABLISHMENT OF OBJECTIVES FROM •   TO •

This section establishes the objectives to be accomplished during the next evaluation period. Objectives should be as specific as possible, including where appropriate, completion date. The supervisor's objectives for the employee <u>and</u> the employee's objectives for her/himself are to be included.

OBJECTIVES	PLANS TO MEET THE OBJECTIVE	PROPOSED COMPLETION DATE
•		

Figure 12–2 *(Continued)*

PART VI.

Comments:

_____   _____   _____
Supervisor's Signature   Title   Date

Comments:

_____   _____   _____
Lieutenant's Signature   Title   Date

Comments:

_____   _____   _____
Bureau Commander's Signature   Title   Date

Comments:

_____   _____   _____
Chief of Police's Signature   Title   Date

Comments:

_____   _____   _____
Admin. Ass't. Signature   Title   Date

Comments:

_____   _____   _____
Personnel Signature   Title   Date

Figure 12–2   *(Continued)*

PART VII.

Any comments which the employee would like to make, or modifications of performance evaluation by the Supervisor due to the discussion of this evaluation, should be noted here.

My Supervisor reviewed and discussed the contents of the Performance Evaluation with me. My signature below does not indicate whether I agree or disagree with this evaluation.

_____   _____
Employee's Signature   Date

Employee Comments Reviewed By:

_____   _____   _____   _____   _____
Supv. Init.   Div.Hd. (Lt.) Bur.Cmdr.   C.O.P.   Admin.
              Init.   Init.   Init.   Asst. Init.

_____
Personnel
Init.

Figure 12–2   *(Continued)*

Police Officer Performance

935 Possible Points

	Percentage Spread	Point Spread	Salary Adj.-*Scale
Distinguished	97-100	906-935	10%
	92-96	860-905	9%
Exceeds	87-91	813-859	8.5%
	82-86	766-812	8%
	77-81	720-765	7.5%
	72-76	673-719	7%
Meets	67-71	626-672	6%
	60-66	561-625	5%
	55-59	514-560	4%
Below	50-54	467-513	2%
	40-49	374-466	0
	35-39	327-373	-2%
Unsatisfactory	30-34	280-326	-3%
	25-29	233-279	-4%
	20-24	187-232	-5%

*Non-top step employees - Increases are only possible up to the maximum top step.

Figure 12-2   *(Continued)*

their particular unit. For example, the undercover officers, while they are still police officers, have very specific performance criteria that are much different than the detectives (police officers) and street officers (police officers). In this way, each unit can develop a customized evaluation for the members of that unit. They are free to add, delete, and revise the elements within the performance criteria for that unit, based upon their specific expectations and job duties. This will allow for the customization of evaluation forms for specific ranks and assignments within the Operations Bureau. This allows the evaluation process to be dynamic and changeable through the years as programs and priorities change with time. In the end, the total possible points will vary, depending upon the degree of customization for that particular form, but the percentage utilized by personnel for determination of salary increase or decrease will still be available by dividing the total possible points into the performance points totaled at the end of the form.

While this all may seem fairly complex and confusing, it is being done in a systematic manner in an attempt to reduce the amount of confusion felt by the supervisors and employees. I would like to call your attention to page 2 of each of the performance evaluations, making special note of the areas which state that documentation must be provided to varying degrees depending upon the evaluation score for each of the elements within an evaluation category. This is to insure that supervisors are, in fact, able to justify the scores given to their personnel and . . . to provide feedback, and in the case of the low expectations performance, a program for improvement, to both the employee being evaluated and the individuals reviewing all performance evaluations.

Recommendations for the Design and Implementation of a Personnel Evaluation System

Time to summarize. Remember the common precept of this entire book: that there is no one best way to do anything, organizationally speaking. However, there are better ways of doing things. The 13 steps described here are a better (not perfect) way to assess police personnel.

1. *Job analysis: What is to be evaluated?* The first step to be taken in building a reliable and valid evaluation process is to conduct a comprehensive, in-depth job analysis.

2. *Multiple raters.* It is recommended that multiple raters be used in completing the form—for example, the current supervisor, the most recent past supervisor, and a supervisor who is on the same work shift. The present supervisor would be responsible for coordinating efforts and conducting the one-on-one interview with the officer. There are many advantages to the use of more than one rater, such as enhanced objectivity, improved clarity, more information, and greater acceptance on the part of the ratee.

3. *The raters.* There are five possible sources of performance appraisal: a) supervisors, b) peers, c) the person being evaluated, d) subordinates of the person to be appraised, and e) people outside the immediate organization, such as citizens. Who the best person is to make the appraisal depends on the purpose of the appraisal and the level of the criteria being evaluated (immediate behavior versus intermediate and ultimate outcomes). Most performance appraisals are made by an officer's

immediate superior. This is particularly true when the major purpose of the appraisal is evaluation, rather than employee development.

A few police agencies have tried to introduce evaluation by peers, and self-evaluation, pointing out that these two methods work best under conditions of high interpersonal trust, highly specialized skills, and high visibility among peers, and when development rather than evaluation is the major purpose to be served by the appraisal.

4. *Trained raters.* I have frequently asked police supervisors and managers if they are required to assess the performance of their subordinates' work activities, and the majority say yes. However, when I ask the same group of people if they received any training on rating, the most common answer is no! *Those responsible for rating should be trained as raters.*

5. *Rating the raters.* We have also perceived that, although rating is acknowledged to be a highly fundamental and critical task of a police supervisor, in many cases the raters are not rated on their own willingness or ability to rate. In other words, a paramount dimension is being missed in terms of assessing a supervisor or manager's performance, which would be analogous to expecting patrol officers to behave with proper attitudes toward the public, but not rating them on their citizen contacts. Raters should be evaluated on their rating skills.

6. *A rating manual.* All performance evaluation systems need a guide or a manual. Without a set of common definitions (such as the meaning of "community and human relations"), instructions, and procedures, the entire process is apt to suffer severe problems of ambiguity and integrity. A pertinent rating manual should address the obligations and concerns of the police agency, the police rater, and those to be assessed. A manual is a must.

7. *Significant (critical) incidents: a database.* We are prone to have a better recall of the immediate past, which is human nature. Thus, when rating, a rater normally has a clearer remembrance of those events that occurred over the preceding few weeks than of those that occurred months ago. Indeed, by being "officer perfect" shortly before evaluation, one can probably receive a fairly high evaluation.

This phenomenon cannot be totally eliminated, but fortunately it can be guarded against through the use of the significant (critical) incident technique (SIT). The critical incident technique (CIT) was first introduced in a business setting as a single method for evaluating a person's performance. (I prefer to substitute the term "significant" for "critical" to avoid the negative connotations of the latter term.)

The SIT involves the recording of what can be termed significant or highly important behavior on the part of a police officer, which can be of either a positive or a negative nature. Over the course of the evaluation period, the rater documents the significant behavior of his or her ratees (typically, two to three are generated per week). At the time of rating, the supervisor should utilize this database for purposes of completing the rating form and the interpersonal interview. The SIT is most useful in fulfilling the activity that follows next.

8. *Feedback:* Event and time-triggered. Police employee-supervisor feedback is a clear-cut must. It can be event feedback, time-triggered feedback, or preferably both. In event feedback, as favorable conduct is observed it should be positively reinforced (such as "Good job, officer. Let's discuss it for a few minutes."), and as misconduct is witnessed, it should be corrected ("Hey, officer, you really fouled up! Let's discuss it for a few minutes."). Most of us want to know when we are doing right or wrong—not once every six to 12 months, but at that moment in time, so that we can continue or abandon a particular behavior. Such events are best made a part of a SIT. Feedback is the breakfast of champions!

9. *Supervision by objectives.* While you as a supervisor should initiate the SBO process, it is best structured as a two-way channel. As a type of a contract, both parties ought to be included in drafting and approving the agreement. Because an SBO statement acts as a basis for both past and future performance ratings, it should encompass the thinking of both the rater and the ratee. All police supervisors should separately produce tentative SBO contracts for employees. Concurrently, employees should be requested to independently generate their own contracts. Once both contracts have been finished, the two should confer and negotiate a final form.

    Both event feedback and time-triggered feedback are necessary. Monitoring an employee's performance assists in determining when each type should be applied. Time-triggered feedback is especially relevant for SBO in that set time periods or milestones should be reviewed according to schedule on a one-to-one basis (supervisor-subordinate). This is where SITs and counseling merge to act as a reinforcer or corrective motivator for getting the needed performance. (Figure 12–2 has SBO built in.)

10. *Making mission statements happen.* In Responsibility Three, I underscored the importance of a leader's projecting a vision of where the department is headed and why. Some agencies have put muscle into their mission statements by expanding them into performance rating systems. In other words, the values and standards comprising the department's mission are being looked for in an employee's daily work effort. Connecting performance appraisal to a mission statement increases the likelihood that it will be practiced and not just preached.

11. *Avoiding failure.* Here are some reasons why a performance evaluation flops:
    - There is no face-to-face discussion.
    - There is no preparation by either party.
    - There is little identification of actual performance problems.
    - There has been little communication about performance during the period being appraised.
    - Supervisors have been concerned only with bad performance.
    - There has been no follow-up effort afterwards.
    - Appraisal has just been a once-a-year event, not an ongoing process.

12. *Employee preparation.* An employee should be prepared to answer the following questions:
  - What do you feel was your biggest accomplishment or major contribution to the department?
  - In what areas do you feel you didn't perform well?
  - What prevented you from performing well in these areas?
  - What can be done to make your performance better?
  - What area would you like to develop over the next appraisal period?
  - As your supervisor, how can I help?

13. *Self-appraisal.* As a supervisor, you should ask at least the following questions about your performance as a rater:
  - How did I do overall?
  - Did I set up good two-way communication?
  - Did the employee truly understand the deficient areas?
  - Was the employee really receptive to my suggestions for making changes?
  - Did I concentrate on behaviors and avoid personality factors?
  - Has the interview opened up new lines of communication?
  - What must I do to follow up in the next week, month, and year?
  - What will I do to motivate the employee to improve performance?

360-Degree Performance Appraisal

Most performance rating systems make a mistake from the viewpoint of accountability. Police supervisors should be appraised by those to whom they are accountable. Leadership means accountability to those over whom we have power.

The following questionnaire should be administered to your staff. Besides affording you an opportunity to learn about your supervisory practices, it will elevate trust, teamwork, empowerment, and a host of other positive workplace values.

Structured Exercise 12–3

How Does My Performance Rate?

Ask the people who work with and for you—as well as your boss—to answer these questions about you. Ratings are on a scale of 1 to 5. A 5 means you exhibit a behavior "to a very great extent"; a 1 means "not at all."

The police supervisor . . .

( ) 5 To a very great extent   ( ) 2 To a little extent
( ) 4 To a great extent   ( ) 1 Not at all
( ) 3 To some extent   ( ) NA Does not apply

1. Recognizes broad implications of policies
( )5   ( )4   ( )3   ( )2   ( )1   ( )NA

2. Understands complex concepts and relationships

( )5   ( )4   ( )3   ( )2   ( )1   ( )NA

3. Analyzes problems from different points of view

( )5   ( )4   ( )3   ( )2   ( )1   ( )NA

4. Makes decisions in the face of ambiguity

( )5   ( )4   ( )3   ( )2   ( )1   ( )NA

5. Makes sound decisions based on adequate information

( )5   ( )4   ( )3   ( )2   ( )1   ( )NA

6. Is quick to adapt to new situations

( )5   ( )4   ( )3   ( )2   ( )1   ( )NA

7. Translates departmental strategies into clear objectives and tactics

( )5   ( )4   ( )3   ( )2   ( )1   ( )NA

8. Provides clear direction and defines priorities for the team

( )5   ( )4   ( )3   ( )2   ( )1   ( )NA

9. Fosters the development of a common vision

( )5   ( )4   ( )3   ( )2   ( )1   ( )NA

10. Acts decisively

( )5   ( )4   ( )3   ( )2   ( )1   ( )NA

11. Is open and candid with others

( )5   ( )4   ( )3   ( )2   ( )1   ( )NA

12. Genuinely cares about the welfare of others

( )5   ( )4   ( )3   ( )2   ( )1   ( )NA

13. Empowers others to do their work

( )5   ( )4   ( )3   ( )2   ( )1   ( )NA

14. Champions new initiatives within and beyond the scope of the job

( )5   ( )4   ( )3   ( )2   ( )1   ( )NA

15. Involves others in the change process

( )5   ( )4   ( )3   ( )2   ( )1   ( )NA

16. Has the confidence and trust of others

( )5   ( )4   ( )3   ( )2   ( )1   ( )NA

17. Shows consistency between words and actions

( )5   ( )4   ( )3   ( )2   ( )1   ( )NA

18. Persists in the face of obstacles

( )5   ( )4   ( )3   ( )2   ( )1   ( )NA

19. Puts a top priority on getting results

( )5   ( )4   ( )3   ( )2   ( )1   ( )NA

How You Rate.   If you score all 4s and 5s, you are viewed as competent. Focus on fine-tuning and making the most of those strengths.

If you score 3 on any item, determine how important the skill or behavior is to your job. If it's important, try to improve.

If you score below 3, it's fix-it time. Target those areas for development.

> Organizational performance is derived from individual performance; individual performance is heavily dependent on an accurate and valid personnel evaluation process. Also, a well-designed evaluation process is only as effective as the boss who is responsible for administering it.

KEY POINTS

- High performance includes five prerequisites: 1) non-negotiable high standards; 2) workplace opportunities; 3) one's character; 4) emotion intelligence; and 5) teamwork.
- Planning is a process for implementing goals and objectives.
- Police supervisors who plan their work typically outperform others who do not.
- In SBO, the objectives must be specific, set in collaboration with the employee, and used to measure performance.
- SBO is comprised of seven sequential steps:
  1. Identify the problems.
  2. Create a specific statement.
  3. Develop alternative strategies.
  4. Select a strategy.
  5. Design an implementation plan.
  6. Evaluate the results.
  7. Provide feedback to the police employee.
- The three main obstacles to SBO are:
  - A resistive working culture
  - Lack of top management backing
  - Departmental constraints

- The three key reasons for assessing a person's performance are behavioral. They are control, motivation, and feedback.
- Performance evaluation serves a large number of purposes, ranging from making decisions about promotions through dealing with SBO contracts.
- For a performance evaluation system to be reliable and valid, it must be job-related.
- Job-related performance appraisal systems are based on a job analysis.
- An internally and externally sound performance rating system must include:
  - A job analysis
  - A rating method
  - More than one rater
  - Trained raters
  - Raters who are rated for their rating skills
  - A rating manual
  - The recording of significant incidents
  - Feedback
  - SBO
  - Making mission statements happen

DISCUSSION

1. Is the phrase "to protect and serve" a goal or an objective? Why?
2. Convert the statement "We had best reduce our burglary rate" into an objective.
3. Besides the budget, can you identify one or more plans in your agency (if not your department, then someone else's)?
4. What do reliability and validity mean? How do they differ? What is the best tool for ensuring that they exist in a rating process?
5. It is underscored in this chapter that the raters must be trained to ensure the integrity of a performance appraisal process. What are some of the ways to train police supervisors as raters?
6. How might individual feedback on performance enhance teamwork? How might it hinder it?

CONFLICT

The police supervisor is responsible for anticipating, defining, and solving personal, interpersonal, and group conflicts with precision and compassion.

The day soldiers stop bringing you their problems is the day you have stopped leading them. They have either lost confidence that you can help them or concluded that you do not care. Either case is a failure of leadership.

—Colin Powell

We live and work in an imperfect world. Mistakes are made—most involve those of the mind, while some deal with the heart. Most often it is the supervisor who has the primary responsibility for resolving them.

Most police officers are honest, hardworking, and helpful human beings. They project a positive mental attitude (PMA) and will make your job as a supervisor a rewarding one. Regretfully, the majority of police organizations possess a few individuals who are seemingly dedicated to making things miserable. As their supervisor, however, you can master their fate.

Supervision is a people process. A select few people will command more of your thinking and attention than others. People problems can come at you on an individual or on a group basis (the whole crew is malingering). Solving people problems—singular or plural—is a major job responsibility for you.

Problem police employees come in a variety of symptomatic packages. Basically, they can be categorized as either honest (making mistakes of the mind) or dishonest (making mistakes of the heart). Oddly, the honest problem employee—for example, the "whining, sniveling malcontent" (WSM)—is frequently more difficult to handle. The dishonest officer is detected, apprehended, discharged, and probably prosecuted. The WSM requires considerably different treatment.

As a leader you are destined to expend a large portion of your energy on the handling of problem employees. They will tax your patience, at times push your anger control, and test your ability to develop a creative response. However, you must not lose sight and contact with the PMA's, the productive and team-spirited employees. Concentrate on, reinforce, and reward the productive officers. The strength of your work team is **centered here.** Remember what I said in the Overview Chapter . . .

> Nobody said supervising was easy. If it were easy, everyone would be doing it.

The remainder of this chapter examines conflict as potentially both a positive and a negative human force.

CONFLICT

Human conflict is to be expected; indeed, **a certain amount of internal conflict is healthy.** An analogy would be the necessity for tension on the mainspring of a watch. At the same time, however, too much tension will cause it to break. In an organizational setting, too much conflict is counterproductive to goal attainment. The police supervisor is in a unique position to control the degree of conflict in an agency.

When I use the term "conflict," I am referring to perceived incompatible differences resulting in some form of interference or opposition. Whether the differences are real or not is irrelevant. If people perceive that the differences exist, then a conflict state exists. Additionally, this definition covers a range that includes the extremes, from subtle, indirect, and highly controlled forms of differences to overt acts, such as physical altercations, job terminations, and criminal acts.

Competition is different from conflict. Conflict is directed against another party, whereas competition is aimed at obtaining a goal without interference from another party. If misdirected, competition can lead to conflict.

Conflict: A Plus or a Minus?

The response to the question of conflict being either a plus or a minus in a work group is, "It all depends."

Some conflicts support the goals of the organization; these are functional conflicts of a constructive form. Additionally, there are conflicts that hinder an organization in achieving its goals; these are dysfunctional conflicts and are destructive forms.

Of course, it is one thing to argue that conflict can be valuable, but how do you tell if a conflict is functional or dysfunctional? Unfortunately, the demarcation is neither clear nor precise. No one level of conflict can be adopted as acceptable or unacceptable under all conditions. The type and level of conflict that create healthy and positive involvement in achieving one department's goals may, in another department—or in the same department at another time—be highly dysfunctional. Functionality or dysfunctionality, therefore, is a judgment call on your part. Hence, it remains for you to make intelligent judgments concerning whether conflict levels in your unit are appropriate, too high, or too low.

Value of Conflict

If harnessed and channeled, conflict does the following for you and your team members:

- Acts as a major stimulant for change
- Fosters creativity and innovation
- Clarifies issues and goals
- Encourages individuality
- Enhances communication
- Increases energy within a unit
- Promotes cohesiveness
- Is psychologically healthy

As a supervisor it is imperative that you respect an officer's individuality and preferences as long as they do not detract from getting police work done in a professional and legally accepted manner. If you, as a supervisor, push for uniformity and ignore individual strengths and styles, you are promoting the negative aspects of conflict.

Sources of Conflict

Conflict can emanate from one of four sources: 1) existing conditions (especially novel ones), 2) our attitudes, 3) our thoughts, and 4) our behavior. Typically, all four combine to produce the conflict.

Fortunately, most conflicts are of minor importance. Few police officers are likely to be psychologically crippled by trying to decide between two patrol routes. Few of us encounter daily conflicts that we cannot respond to in a routine or "programmed" manner. The police officer, however, generally experiences the unusual. He or she is more often than not faced with highly diverse, non-programmable choices. Briefly stated, the police officer typically deals with novelty, rather than familiar and routine problems.

> Today there is a hidden conflict in our lives between the pressures of acceleration and those of novelty. One forces us to make faster decisions, while the other compels us to make the hardest, most time-consuming type of decision.

Structured Exercise 13–1

Name_____

Organizational Unit Assessed _____

INSTRUCTIONS.   The purpose of this index is to permit you to assess your organization with regard to its conflict-management climate. On each of the following rating scales, indicate how you see your organization as it actually is right now, not how you think it should be or how you believe others would see it. Circle the number that indicates your sense of where the organization is on each dimension of the Conflict-Management Climate Index.

1. Balance of Power

| 1 | 2 | 3 | 4 | 5 | 6 |

Power is massed either at the top or at the bottom of the organization.

Power is distributed evenly and appropriately throughout the organization.

2. Expression of Feelings

| 1 | 2 | 3 | 4 | 5 | 6 |

Expressing strong feelings is costly and not accepted.

Expressing strong feelings is valued and easy to do.

3. Conflict-Management Procedures

| 1 | 2 | 3 | 4 | 5 | 6 |

There are no clear conflict-resolution procedures that many people use.

Everyone knows about, and many people use, a conflict-resolution procedure.

4. Attitudes toward Open Disagreement

| 1 | 2 | 3 | 4 | 5 | 6 |

People here do not openly disagree very much. "Go along to get along" is the motto.

People feel free to disagree openly on important issues without fear of consequences.

5. Use of Third Parties

| 1 | 2 | 3 | 4 | 5 | 6 |

No one here uses third parties to help resolve conflicts.

Third parties are used frequently to help resolve conflicts.

6. Power of Third Parties

| 1 | 2 | 3 | 4 | 5 | 6 |

Third parties are usually superiors in the organization.

Third parties are always people of equal or lower rank.

7. Neutrality of Third Parties

| 1 | 2 | 3 | 4 | 5 | 6 |

Third parties are never neutral but serve as advocates for a certain outcome.

Third parties are always neutral as to substantive issues and and conflict-resolution methods used.

8. Your Leader's Conflict-Resolution Style

| 1 | 2 | 3 | 4 | 5 | 6 |

The leader does not deal openly with conflict, but works behind the scenes to resolve it.

The leader confronts conflicts directly and works openly with those involved to resolve it.

9. How Your Leader Receives Negative Feedback

| 1 | 2 | 3 | 4 | 5 | 6 |

The leader is defensive and/or closed and seeks vengeance on those who criticize him or her.

The leader receives criticism easily and even seeks it as an opportunity to grow and learn.

10. Follow-Up

| 1 | 2 | 3 | 4 | 5 | 6 |

Agreements always fall through the cracks; the same problems must be solved again and again.

Accountability is built into every conflict-resolution agreement.

11. Feedback Procedures

| 1 | 2 | 3 | 4 | 5 | 6 |

No effort is made to solicit and understand reactions to decisions.

Feedback channels for soliciting reactions to all major decisions are known and used.

12. Communication Skills

| 1 | 2 | 3 | 4 | 5 | 6 |

Few if any people possess basic communication skills, or at least practice them.

Everyone in the organization possesses and uses good communication skills.

13. Track Record

| 1 | 2 | 3 | 4 | 5 | 6 |

Very few if any successful conflict-resolution experiences have occurred in the recent past.

Many stories are available of successful conflict-resolution experiences in the recent past.

Conflict-Management Climate Index Scoring and Interpretation Sheet

INSTRUCTIONS: To arrive at your overall Conflict-Management Climate Index score, total the ratings that you assigned to the 13 separate scales. The highest possible score is 78 and the lowest is 13. Then compare your score with the following conflict-resolution-readiness index ranges:

Index Range	Indication
60–78	Ready to work on conflict with little or no work on climate
31–59	Possible with some commitment to work on climate
13–30	Very risky without unanimous commitment to work on climate issues

Assess your overall score. If in a group setting, compare your bottom-line results to those of others in your group. Attempt to explain your lowest and highest scores per item. Use case examples when possible.

CONFLICT MANAGEMENT

Leaders who manage conflicts best are able to draw out all parties, understand the differing perspectives, and then find a common ideal that everyone can endorse. They surface the conflict, acknowledge the feelings and views of all sides, and then redirect the energy toward a shared ideal.

Handling relationships, however, is not as simple as it sounds. It's not just a matter of friendliness. Rather, conflict management is friendliness with a purpose: moving people in the right direction, whether that's agreement on a patrol strategy or enthusiasm about a new piece of technology.

Socially skilled leaders tend to have resonance with a wide circle of people—and have a knack for finding common ground and building rapport. That doesn't mean they socialize continually; it means they work under the assumption that nothing important gets done alone. Such leaders have a network in place when the time for action comes. And in an era when more and more work is done long-distance—by e-mail or by phone—face-to-face communication, paradoxically, becomes more crucial than ever.

> Being an adept negotiator is important to your success as a supervisor because 1) you are destined to experience conflicting situations and groups, and 2) you are in a front-line position to convert potentially negative conflict into positive problem-solving.

SIX STEPS YOU CAN TAKE FOR GETTING TO YES

Whether in police work, a personal business transaction, or our own family, we reach most decisions through negotiation. Even if we go to court, we almost always negotiate a settlement before trial. Although negotiation takes place every day, it is not easy to do successfully. Our natural approaches for negotiation often leave us and others dissatisfied, fatigued, or withdrawn—and frequently all three.

We find ourselves in a "Catch-22." We envision two ways to negotiate, easy or tough. The easy negotiator wants to avoid personal conflict and so makes concessions readily in order to reach agreement. This person wants an amicable resolution; yet they often end up exploited and feeling bitter. The tough negotiator perceives any situation as a highly competitive contest of wills in which the side that takes the more extreme positions and perseveres wins. Such people need to win; yet they often end up creating an equally tough response, which exhausts them and their resources and harms their relationship with the other side. Other typical negotiating strategies fall between tough and easy, but each includes an attempted trade-off between getting what you want and getting along with people.

A Better Way

There is a third and better way for you, as a leader, to negotiate. It is neither tough nor easy, but oddly both! It can be referred to as principled negotiations. This approach strives to decide the issues on their merit, rather than who wins. It urges that you look for mutual gains wherever possible and that, where your interests conflict, you should agree that the result will be based on fair standards, independent of your will and that of your adversary. The method of principled negotiations is tough on the merits, easy on the people. It employs no tricks and no posturing.

> Principled negotiation shows you and your opponent how to obtain what you are entitled to and still be civil. It enables you to be equitable while protecting both of you against being taken advantage of. What follows is an all-purpose strategy. Unlike almost all other conflict-resolution strategies, if your adversaries learn this one, it does not become more difficult to use; it becomes easier. If they read this chapter, all the better for the two of you.

First: Don't Bargain over Positions

When we bargain over our positions, we tend to lock ourselves into those positions. The more we clarify our position and defend it against attack, the more committed we become to it. As more attention is paid to positions, less attention is devoted to meeting our underlying concerns. Agreement becomes less likely. Any agreement reached may reflect a mechanical balance of the difference between final positions, rather than a solution carefully forged to meet our legitimate interests.

1. Arguing over positions creates, at best, unsatisfactory agreements.

2. Arguing over positions is inefficient because the conflicting parties usually start at an extreme position and stubbornly hold to it, while at times making small concessions. This is highly time-consuming and thus inefficient.

3. Arguing over positions endangers an ongoing relationship because each side tries to force the other to change its position.

4. When there are many parties involved, all of the above are compounded because coalitions are formed.

Second: Being Nice Is Not the Answer

Many people understand the high costs of hard positional bargaining, particularly for the parties and their relationship. They hope to avoid them by following a more pleasant style of negotiation. Instead of seeing the other side as adversaries, they prefer to see them as "friends." Rather than emphasizing a goal of victory, they emphasize the necessity of reaching agreement. In a soft negotiation game, the standard moves are to make offers and concessions, to trust the other side, to be totally affable, and to yield as necessary to avoid confrontation. However, any negotiation focused on the relationship runs the risk of producing a weak agreement. More seriously, pursuing a soft and friendly form of positional bargaining makes you vulnerable to someone who plays a hard game of positional bargaining. In positional bargaining, a hard game dominates a soft one. The remedy for playing hardball is not pitching marshmallows.

The answer to the question of whether to use soft positional bargaining or hard is "neither." Change the game! The new game proposed to you is referred to as principled negotiation, or negotiation on the merits. It consists of four basic points. Each point deals with a basic element of negotiation and suggests what you should do about it:

1. People: Separate the people from the conflict.

2. Interests: Concentrate on interests, not positions.

3. Options: Generate a variety of options before deciding what to do.

4. Criteria: Insist that the solution be based on some objective standard.

Each point is examined further in the sections that follow.

Third: Separate the People from the Conflict

This point acknowledges that you and I are creatures of strong emotions who often have radically different perceptions and have difficulty communicating clearly. Emotions typically become entangled with the objective merits of the problem. Taking positions just makes this worse because people's egos become identified with their positions. Hence, before working on the substantive problem, the "people problem" should be disentangled from it and dealt with separately. We should see ourselves as working side by side, attacking the problem, not each other. Hence, the first proposition: Separate the people from the conflict.

Fourth: Concentrate on Interests, Not Positions

The second step was not intended to overcome the drawback of concentrating on people's stated positions when the object of a negotiation is to satisfy their underlying interests. A negotiating position often obscures what you really want in a conflicting set of situations. Compromising between positions is not likely to produce an agreement that will effectively take care of the human needs that led people to adopt these positions. This step **concentrates on interests, not positions.**

Fifth: Generate a Number of Options

The third step responded to the difficulty of designing solutions while under pressure. Trying to decide in the presence of an adversary narrows your vision. Having a lot at stake inhibits creativity. So does searching for the right answers. Keep in mind that usually there is more than a single right solution or answer to the conflict.

Set aside a designated time to think up a wide range of possible solutions that advance shared interests and creatively reconcile differing interests. Hence, *before trying to reach agreement, invent numerous options for mutual gain.*

Sixth: Adopt Objective Criteria

Where interests are directly opposed, an employee may be able to obtain a favorable result simply by being stubborn. That method tends to reward intransigence and produce arbitrary results. However, as a supervisor you can counter such an employee by insisting that his or her single say-so is not enough and that the agreement must reflect some fair standard independent of the naked will of either side. This does not mean insisting that the terms be based on the standard you select, but only that some fair standard—such as custom, expert opinion, prior decisions, or law—determine the outcome.

By discussing a fair criterion, rather than what the parties are willing or unwilling to do, neither party need give in to the other; both can defer to a fair solution. Hence, *adopt objective criteria.*

Structured Exercise 13–2

Tackle the following cases using the "six steps for getting to yes." Have one member of your group serve as an observer and recorder of the deliberations. When finished with each case, critique your problem-solving process in respect to the seven steps.

PROBLEM 1. Ten workers, all over 50 years of age, from the department's Communications and Data Processing Unit have submitted a letter of complaint to the chief about the status of the older workers in their unit. As they explain it, the nature of the communications and data processing systems operation is such that college-trained, younger people are constantly being brought into the unit to work on a part-time basis. These youngsters, in their view, are more interested in short-term benefits and working procedures than are the older workers. When initially receiving the complaint, the Chief told them that considerable savings are achieved by the employment of the younger workers. The older employees have hinted they may seek redress through the Fair Employment Practices Commission. What should the chief say and do at this point?

PROBLEM 2.   The captain in command of the Uniform Field Operations Bureau (patrol and traffic) has complained bitterly to the chief on two occasions that the department's Special Operations Bureau (SOB) has significantly reduced the quality of police–citizen relationships. He has asserted that the personnel in his unit are making every effort to provide just and effective law enforcement. The captain finds that the SOB, however, disrupts the development of a mutually supportive police–community relationship by its heavy-handed tactics. When questioned, the lieutenant in charge of the SOB indicated that his special enforcement staff was clearly successful in reducing major felonies. Furthermore, he implied that perhaps the captain was getting "soft" and could best be assigned elsewhere. The sheriff is convinced that both individuals are dedicated and professional individuals. Also, both have highly commendable performance records with the department. How should the chief resolve this situation?

PROBLEM 3.   Sixty percent of the detectives in the Investigations Unit filed a grievance regarding their performance evaluations. The percentage of grievances has been going steadily upward. The chief is beginning to think that the reason for this occurrence is that a grieving employee almost always gets some portion of his rating raised. Increasingly, it appears that the feeling among the detectives seems to be "Why not?" or "If the other guy does it, I had better also." How should the immediate situation be handled? What should be done in the long run?

PROBLEM EMPLOYEES

At times I've been a problem employee. I confess to being overly critical, incessantly complaining, and being miserably cantankerous. What about you?

Problem employees frequently are unaware of their misbehavior, usually lack social skills, and often do not have self-discipline. Basically, they have low emotional intelligence. These people push and on occasion violate ethical standards of conduct. While fewer in number, others flagrantly violate ethical and professional norms and even the law.

Earlier I argued that there is no such thing as "business ethics" or "police ethics." Ethics are plainly and irrefutably ethics. Ditto for "work ethics." Your personal responsibility for being fair, truthful, courteous, helpful, loyal and so on does not change from your home to your work. It does not change from playing sports to financial investing. Ethics are ethics; they are not situational.

Problem employees are relatively few in number; a reasonable estimate is up to five percent of a police agency. But, they demand a lot of a supervisor's time and energy. There are many supervisors who expend more effort on conflicts created by problem employees than on supervising police work. Prado's law relates that 80% of your time will be directed toward 20% of your staff.

For purposes of simplicity, I've categorized problem employees as: 1) malcontented; 2) immoral; 3) unprofessional; and 4) criminal. Obviously, an unhappy or unethical employee may belong in more than one category.

Problem Employee 1—The Malcontent

The malcontent is the most common type of all the problem employees. In any instance, they are the most difficult to correct. They cause minor conflicts, then disappear, only to surface again to create more conflict. They're always happy to be a part of the problem, but they shun any responsibility for helping solve it. This employee is capable of being a daily doomsayer, a chronic malingerer, or a producer of low-quality police services. They grate on the supervisor, their co-workers, and most unfortunately the people they're paid to serve. They are internally miserable, depressed, and sour. Worse still, they want others to feel the same.

> Their bad attitudes and sloppy behavior are contagious. If unchecked, the malcontented employee will lower team morale, as well as the quality of services.

Helping the Malcontent

You can help the problem police employee toward better behavior only after you have reassured him that you are trying to help him—not looking for an excuse to get rid of him. No approach does more harm with a person of this nature than the "better get yourself straightened out or you will lose your job" attitude on a supervisor's part. You have to believe, and make the employee believe, that your intentions are good, that you want to help. Then you must give the person every opportunity to help themselves. This approach is called counseling, and there are 15 rules for you to follow:

1. **Listen** patiently to what the employee has to say before making any comment of your own. This act on your part may be sufficient to resolve the difficulties.
2. **Refrain from criticizing** or offering hasty advice on the employee's problem.

3. **Never argue** with a police employee while you are in the process of counseling.

4. Give your **undivided attention** to the employee.

5. **Probe beyond the mere words** of what the employee says; listen to see if the officer is trying to tell you something deeper than what appears on the surface.

6. Recognize what you are counseling an employee for. And **don't look for immediate results.** Never mix up the counseling interview with some other action you may want to take, such as discipline.

7. Find a **quiet place** where you won't be interrupted and won't be overheard. Try to put the employee at ease. Don't jump into a cross-examination.

8. Depending on the nature of the situation, **multiple sessions** may be necessary. They should last from 15 to 30 minutes per session.

9. If after **two counseling sessions** you are not making progress, you should consult with your manager about other options.

10. This is a major job responsibility and you must not avoid it.

11. Look at your task as a **fact-finding one,** just as in handling grievances.

12. **Control** your own emotions and opinions while dealing with the employee.

13. Be absolutely sold on the **value of listening,** rather than preaching.

14. Recognize your own limits in handling these situations. **You're not a clinical psychologist.** You're a person responsible for getting results out of your assigned officers.

15. If all else fails, then you still have your prerogative to **use discipline.**

Make no mistake: handling a police employee who has become a malcontent can be frustrating. Sometimes it can become downright unpleasant. But the sooner you confront the person, the sooner the problems get solved.

> The belief that employees are basically good and therefore can be corrected is one of the most widely held beliefs in formal organizations. Yet it is both untrue and harmful. Those who believe in innate human goodness view the battle for a better employee as primarily a struggle between the individual and the department. The battle is within the individual and centers on one's character.

Earlier I stressed that problem employees represent a very small percentage of the department. I believe that many of them can and will correct their wrongful behavior. I also believe that, unfortunately, a few are losers. And there is nothing that you can do about it—no matter how hard you try. What you can and must do is assist them in exiting the department.

Problem Bosses

Similar to problem employees, problem bosses are fortunately few in number. But, because they direct the work of other people, their impact on the organization can be more drastic. They can make the workday of several people meaningless and miserable. They are avoided and rarely listen with any give-and-take.

Anyone who has ever worked in an organization for very long knows the type. Often they deservedly acquired the label of "chickenshit." They generate maximum anxiety over issues of minimum significance. This term refers to behavior that makes police work worse than it need be: petty harassment; open abuse of power and prestige; meanness disguised as discipline; and insistence of the letter rather than the spirit of regulations. This type of supervisor is clearly no leader. This person is small-minded and ignoble and takes the trivial seriously. This type can be recognized immediately because it never has anything to do with providing police services.

Drawing the Lines: Morally, Professionally and Legally

It is impossible to construct an effective system of accountability (see Figure 13–1) without a strong and functional mechanism for maintaining behavioral control over police personnel. While the exclusionary rule, criminal and civil actions against police officers, and other external remedies serve as important constraints, you must accept primary responsibility for controlling the vast discretionary power of police officers.

Unfortunately, some police supervisors have not yet accepted this challenge, and this is the basic reason why there has been constant pressure for civilian review boards, ombudsmen, and other such external review agencies.

Your agency may be efficient and large enough to afford an "internal investigations" or "professional responsibilities" unit.

> The creation of an internal investigation unit does not relieve you of the need to maintain discipline. On the contrary, it strengthens it by providing assistance to supervisors on request in the investigation of alleged misconduct of their team members.

While the community may disagree with or be uncertain about what constitutes police misconduct, the police cannot. Granted, without community consensus on this subject, the problem is a highly perplexing one for our police. Nonetheless, wrongdoing must be defined and policies must be set by the agency. Lines must be clearly drawn. Essentially these lines should encompass three forms of misconduct: 1) legalistic, 2) professional, and 3) moralistic. The first involves criminal considerations; the second may or may not be

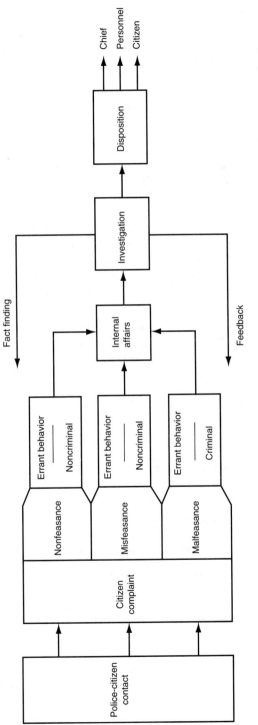

Figure 13–1 Internal Discipline: A System of Accountability (Paul Whisenand and Fred Ferguson, *The Managing of Police Organizations*, 2nd ed., © 1978, p.349. Reprinted by permission of Prentice Hall, Inc., Englewood Cliffs, N.J.)

criminal in nature, but does entail professional considerations; and the third may or may not include professional canons, but does embody personal ethics. Each form of errant behavior is examined further in the following paragraphs. It will be noted that there is a descending degree of clarity or precision with each type of wrongdoing. Conversely, there is an ascending degree of administrative ambiguity on police and procedural violations. We start with the more vague type of misconduct—moralistic.

Problem Employee 2—Moral Misconduct

If an officer thinks certain citizens are deserving of aggressive police practices, the likelihood of his or her behaving aggressively is enhanced, perhaps to the point of overreaction or even physical abuse. Or, if the officer thinks certain citizens are deserving of no police attention, the likelihood of his or her behaving passively is increased, perhaps to the extent of no reaction, and thus the possibility of corruption occurs. Nonetheless, it is at the very crux of other forms of misconduct. The **"Use of Force"** is one example of moralistic misconduct.

The United States Constitution entrusts police officers with special powers not given to ordinary citizens. Police, while engaged in their lawful duties, have a legitimate right to use force to overcome resistance.

In situations involving use of force or injury sustained while in police custody, the agency should anticipate that the injured person will file a claim alleging negligence or excessive force. In order to reduce or eliminate liability arising from false or frivolous claims against a department or individual officers, it is critical that all uses of force and in-custody injuries be thoroughly investigated and documented.

An unbiased police investigation and accurate documentation immediately following a use of force or in-custody injury will help to protect a department and officers against liability and will identify unacceptable behavior, procedural concerns, and training needs. Additionally, the law enforcement services provided by the department will be viewed by the public as fair, impartial, and sensitive to the dignity and worth of each individual. See Figure 13–2, which displays excerpts of a use-of-force policy.

Problem Employee 3—Professional Misconduct

This form of misconduct can range from physical to verbal abuse of a citizen. On the one hand, a criminal or civil violation may have occurred, while on the other, agency standards of professional conduct may be at issue. The possibilities for wrongdoing in this instance can fall within two rubrics: the law, and professional conduct "unbecoming an officer." The distinction, again, between this type of wrongdoing and corruption is that no personal gain for the officer or others is involved. The key question is this: What conduct is permissible? Hence, there is a need for established policies, procedures, rules, and sanctions that explicitly encompass the conduct of police employees. **Sexual harassment** is one example of professional misconduct (and moralistic as well).

POLICY

Officers shall use the lowest level of force necessary under the circumstances to properly perform their lawful duties. Officers should regard it as a matter of professional pride to be able to quietly, skillfully, and with a minimum of force arrest a suspect or bring order to a disorderly situation.

Definitions

Deadly Force.   That force which when used might cause death or serious bodily injury or in the manner of its use or intended use is capable of causing a substantial risk or death or serious bodily injury.

Serious Physical Injury.   Physical injury which creates a reasonable risk or death or which results in admission to a medical facility.

Deadly Weapon.   Any instrument used for lethal purposes including a firearm or other instrumentality which in the manner of its use could cause death or serious bodily injury. This includes impact weapons.

Injury.   Refers to any physical harm inflicted by police or sustained while in police custody and includes any wound, bruise, abrasion, or complaint of pain.

Force.   Any action taken to control, restrain, overcome or stop a suspect's unlawful resistance. Police presence alone is a form of control; this control is frequently enough to bring about order to volatile situations. The following are the Levels of Force:

- **Level 1.** Verbal control techniques that rely on voice, tone, and voice inflection to gain a subject's compliance.
- **Level 2.** Hand-applied force to gain compliance, and includes defensive techniques, e.g., come-along holds, pressure point control, take-downs, and control techniques and chemical agents.
- **Level 3.** The use of personal weapon techniques (fist-, elbow-, knee- and kick-strikes), taser, K-9 and impact weapons (batons) that could temporarily incapacitate a subject (flashlights and radio pac-sets are not designed as weapons, and their use as an impact weapon is not authorized unless clearly necessitated by circumstances).
- **Level 4.** The highest level of force which includes the use of firearms or deadly weapons to stop a subject.

Supervisory Responsibilities

- The assigned sergeant will assume command of the scene. The sergeant will identify all officers who have been involved in the use of force and who are witnesses to the incident. Statements will be obtained from all officers involved or identified as witnesses.
- The sergeant will also identify all civilian witnesses to the incident, obtain their statements and record their full name, address, and telephone numbers.
- The sergeant will thoroughly investigate the incident and take necessary action when required (provide medical care, approve arrests, make notifications, etc.).

Figure 13–2   Use-of-Force Police Excerpts (Courtesy of Santa Ana Police Department, California)

Since 1977, police managers have had to deal with increased employee rights, civil litigation, and recruiting problems. But no issue is more complex than sexual harassment in the police environment. Currently, it is estimated that 15 percent of the sworn personnel are female, and this percentage will continue to increase. I predict that by the year 2010, one in five officers will be female. (The Equal Employment Opportunity Commission [EEOC] has targeted police agencies to have staff of which 50 percent will be women after the year 2000.)

Legal Definition

Let us review how the legal definition of the term has evolved:

1964: The Civil Rights Act of 1964 is enacted. It contains a provocatively novel amendment banning job discrimination on the basis of sex, which foes of the law had hoped would derail it.

1975: In the first reported sexual harassment decision under the new law, involving two women who claimed they suffered repeated verbal abuse and physical advances from a supervisor, an Arizona federal district court rules the act does not cover such a claim.

1977: A Washington federal appeals court rules that sexual harassment is discrimination under the act, in a case in which a woman alleged that her job was abolished in retaliation for refusing a supervisor's sexual advances.

1980: The EEOC issues landmark sexual harassment guidelines prohibiting unwelcome sexual advances or requests that are made a condition of employment, as well as conduct that creates a hostile work environment.

1986: The U.S. Supreme Court upholds the validity of the EEOC guidelines and rules that sexual harassment that creates a hostile or abusive work environment is a violation of the act.

1991: A Florida federal district court rules that nude pinups in the workplace can create an atmosphere that constitutes sexual harassment; a California federal appeals court rules that a hostile environment should be evaluated from the standpoint not of a "reasonable person," but of a "reasonable woman."

1993: The U.S. Supreme Court rules that a hostile work environment need not be psychologically injurious, but only reasonably perceived as abusive.

Compliance

The U.S. Supreme Court (*Meritor Savings Bank* v. *Vinson,* 447 U.S. 57, 1986) decided that a policy stating that there were to be "no unwanted sexual advances between employees and that employees must report this type of unwanted conduct to management" does not comply with all the mandates cited by the Vinson ruling.

What can police agencies do to comply? Establishing preventive policies and training will lessen the likelihood of liability if a complaint is filed.

Sexual harassment is more than supervisory employees making demands for sex on the threat of adverse employment decisions. Employers may also be liable for physical and verbal conduct of a sexual nature that has the purpose or effect of creating a hostile work environment. It is behavior that is indicative of a "hostile atmosphere," such as sexually stereotyped insults and jokes, demeaning propositions and remarks, indecent or vulgar comments, staring or ogling that causes discomfort or humiliation, demands for dates that are viewed as offensive, and physical harassment.

Protection

How can a department protect itself from this liability?

- Have an explicit anti-harassment policy.
- Publicize and enforce the policy.
- Make clear that the hostile-environment type of harassment is covered.
- Regularly and repeatedly publish the policy.
- Establish a grievance system that allows employees to report all incidents of sexual harassment.
- Administratively and promptly investigate all allegations. If the allegations are sustained and warrant disciplining the offending employee, you should consider entering into a compromise with the offended employee to reduce the chance that he or she will seek further remedy outside the department.
- Communicate the facts and the resulting discipline to the employees. (Don't use names.) Reinforce that this type of behavior will not be tolerated and that discipline can result.

See Figure 13-3 for an example of a policy statement on sexual harassment.

Problem Employee 4—Criminal Conduct

Criminal misconduct is also commonly referred to as "corruption." Police corruption is an extremely complex and demoralizing crime problem, and it is not new to our generation of police personnel. Police corruption includes: 1) the misuse of police authority for the police employee's personal gain; 2) activity of the police employee that compromises, or has the potential to compromise, his or her ability to enforce the law or provide other police service impartially; 3) the protection of illicit activities from police enforcement, whether or not the police employee receives something of value in return; and 4) the police employee's involvement in promoting the business of one person, while discouraging that of another person. Police corruption means, therefore, acts involving the misuse of authority by a police officer in a manner designed to produce personal gain for the officer or for others. And this is illegal!

CITIZEN COMPLAINTS

Frequently, you will be the first to hear a citizen's complaint. "I want to see your supervisor" is a pervasive request on the part of a citizen who feels he or she has been mistreated. A complaint starts with its receipt, then proceeds to an

277.10 Policy Statement. It is the policy of the county of San Bernardino Sheriff's Department to provide a work environment free from unwelcome sexual overtures, advances, and coercion. Employees are expected to adhere to a standard of conduct that is respectful to all persons within the work environment. The Sheriff's Department will not tolerate any form of sexual harassment, nor will it tolerate any act of retaliation against any person filing a complaint of sexual harassment.

277.20 Definition. Sexual harassment is defined as unsolicited or unwelcome sexual advances, requests for sexual favors, and other verbal, physical, or visual conduct of a sexual nature when:

- Submission to such conduct is made either explicitly or implicitly as a term or condition of an individual's employment.
- Submission to or rejection of such conduct by an individual is used as the basis for employment decisions affecting such individual.
- Such conduct has the purpose or effect of unreasonably interfering with an individual's work performance or creating an intimidating, hostile, or offensive working environment.

277.30 Sheriff's Department Responsibilities and Procedures. The Sheriff's Department recognizes its obligation to take immediate and appropriate action if an incident of sexual harassment occurs and to avoid or minimize the impact of any incident of sexual harassment. The Sheriff's Department will pursue all reasonable preventive measure to ensure employees are not subjected to sexual harassment. Pursuant to these obligations, the Sheriff's Department will do the following:

- Investigate any complaint of sexual harassment. The investigation will be immediate, thorough, objective, and complete. The investigation will be conducted in as confidential a manner as is compatible with a thorough investigation of the complaint and is consistent with the rights of employees under the Personal Rules and state law.
- Fully inform any complainant of his rights and any obligations to secure those rights.
- If a complaint of sexual harassment is proven by an impartial investigation, prompt and appropriate remedial action will be taken. An employee found to have harassed another employee or applicant will be subject to disciplinary action, up to and including dismissal. In addition, appropriate steps will be taken to prevent any further harassment or retaliation, and action will be taken to remedy the loss, if any.
- The Sheriff's Department will disseminate this policy to all employees and will include this policy in all orientation packages for new employees.

Figure 13–3   Policy Statement on Sexual Harassment (Courtesy of the San Bernardino Sheriff's Department, California)

investigation, and concludes with adjudication. More specifically, the three phases are as follows.

Phase 1: Complaint Receipt

1. A viable complaint reception provides you with a useful tool for officer performance evaluation.
2. It is imperative that all complaints (letters, telephone, in person) be investigated.
3. A form should be designed and used for complaint processing (see Figure 13–4).
4. The complaining citizen should be given a completed copy of the form as a receipt.

Phase 2: Investigation

1. All supervisors assigned should be given specific training in investigating internal discipline complaints and should be provided with written investigative procedures.
2. Every police agency should establish formal procedures for investigating internal misconduct allegations.
3. Every supervisor should conduct internal investigations in a manner that best reveals the facts, while preserving the dignity of all persons and maintaining the confidential nature of the investigation.
4. Every police agency should provide all its employees at the time of employment and, again, prior to the specific investigation with a written statement of the employees' duties and rights when they are the subject of an internal discipline investigation.
5. Every police chief should have legal authority during an internal discipline investigation to relieve police employees from their duties when it is in the interests of the public and the police agency.
6. All internal discipline investigations should be concluded within 30 days of the date the complaint is made unless an extension is granted by the chief executive of the agency.
7. Results of the investigation should be submitted to the complaining party.

Phase 3: Adjudication

The role of the supervisor during Phase 3 is normally that of an advisor to the police manager. More than anyone else, the immediate supervisor should be able to evaluate the overall conduct and performance level of his or her staff and, if a penalty is indicated, to determine how severe it should be. Or, conversely, the supervisor may argue that 1) the officer should be exonerated, 2) the complaint is unfounded (the act did not occur), or 3) the complaint is not sustained (insufficient facts to make a determination). If the charge

CITY OF ANAHEIM, CALIFORNIA

Police Department

MESSAGE FROM THE CHIEF OF POLICE

The Police Officer of today works in an extremely complex society. A goal of the Anaheim Police Department is to ensure that the public is served in a most efficient and effective manner by highly trained Police Officers.

To assist us in achieving this goal, you, as an individual, can help by letting us know if you have a complaint. Rest assured that your complaint will be quickly, professionally, and objectively investigated in order to arrive at all the facts which will clear the Officer's name or substantiate the individual's complaint, whichever is appropriate.

Roger Baker

Roger Baker
Chief of Police

POLICE COMPLAINT PROCEDURE

HOW DO I FILE A COMPLAINT? If you wish to file a formal complaint, it will be necessary for you to complete a Personnel Complaint form. You may obtain this form at the front counter of the Police Department, the City Clerk's Office, any Anaheim Public Library, the Community Services Office, or by calling or writing the Anaheim Police Department and requesting that a form be sent to you. When the Personnel Complaint form is filled out, it should be delivered to the Anaheim Police Department, 425 South Harbor Boulevard, or mailed to P.O. Box 3369, Anaheim, CA 92803-3369.

WHAT WILL HAPPEN TO THE OFFICER? It will depend on what the Officer did. If the Officer's actions were criminal, he/she could be dealt with in the same way as any other citizen. If the Officer's actions were improper but not criminal, he/she may be disciplined by the Chief of Police. If the Officer is falsely accused, the complainant may face civil and/or criminal action.

WILL I BE TOLD OF THE RESULTS OF THE INVESTIGATION? Yes. You will receive a letter from the Chief of Police advising you of the disposition of your complaint.

MESCHIEF.RWG   JR:RWG:lml

P. O. Box 3369, Anaheim, California 92803-3369

Figure 13–4   (Courtesy of the Anaheim Police Department)

CITY OF ANAHEIM, CALIFORNIA

Police Department

UN MENSAJE DEL JEFE DE POLICIA

El policia de hoy en dia trabaja en una sociedad compleja. Una de las metas del Departamento de Policia de Anaheim, es la de asegurar que al publico se le sirva de manera eficiente y efectiva por un Cuerpo de Policia lo mas altamente entrenado posible.

Usted, como una persona particular, puede ayudarnos a lograr esta meta, haciendonos saber si tiene alguna queja, la cual se investigara rapidamente, profesionalmente y objectivamente, para asi poder descubrir los hechos que absolveran de toda culpa el nombre del agente de la Policia, o justificaran la queja de la persona particular, cualquiera de las dos que sea la apropiada.

Roger Baker

Roger Baker
Jefe de Policia

PROCEDIMIENTO PARA PRESENTAR UNA QUEJA

¿COMO REGISTRO UNA QUEJA? Si usted desea registrar una queja formal, sera necesario que complete una forma que usted puede obtener en la oficina de la policia de la ciudad de Anaheim, la oficina del escribano de la ciudad (office of the City Clerk), cualquier sucursal de la biblioteca, la oficina de servicios de la comunidad, o puede llamar o escribir al departamento de policia de Anaheim para solicitar una forma por correo. Cuando complete la forma, devuelva al departamento de policia de Anaheim, 425 South Harbor Boulevard, o mandela por correo al P.O. Box 3369, Anaheim, CA 92803-3369.

¿QUE LE PASARA AL AGENTE DE LA POLICIA? Esto depende en lo que haya hecho. Si cometio una accion criminal, se le tratara igualmente como cualquier otra persona que haya cometido una accion similar. Si fue una accion impropia, el Jefe de la Policia se encargara de disciplinarlo. Si por el contrario, se determina que usted hizo una queja falsa a sabiendas, se le puede someter a un proceso civil o criminal.

¿ME DIRAN EL RESULTADO DE LA INVESTIGACION? Si. Usted recibira una carta del Jefe de la Policia, donde la comunicaran la accion que tomo tocante su queja.

MESCHIEF.RWG   JR:RWG:ksl

P. O. Box 3369, Anaheim, California 92803-3369

Figure 13–4   *(Continued)*

ANAHEIM POLICE DEPARTMENT

PERSONNEL COMPLAINT/QUEJA DEL PERSONAL   File Number: _____

Print your NAME, ADDRESS and PHONE NUMBERS, BUSINESS & HOME / En Letra de Molde Escriba su Nombre, Domicilio, y Numeros de Telefono, Trabajo Y Casa

Print the DATE, TIME and LOCATION OF THE INCIDENT / Fecha, hora y Sitio del incidente

Print the NAMES, ADDRESSES and PHONE NUMBER OF any Witnesses / Nombres, Domicilios y Numeros de Telefonos de Testigos

DESCRIBE the incident in detail. Begin in the space below and if more space / Describa en detalle el incidente. Empiece en el espacio de abajo, y si necesita mas espacio, is needed, continue on a second sheet. Sign all pages.   continue en una segunda hoja. Firme todas las paginas.

YOU HAVE THE RIGHT TO MAKE A COMPLAINT AGAINST A POLICE OFFICER FOR ANY IMPROPER POLICE CONDUCT. CALIFORNIA LAW REQUIRES THIS AGENCY TO HAVE A PROCEDURE TO INVESTIGATE CITIZENS' COMPLAINTS. YOU HAVE THE RIGHT TO A WRITTEN DESCRIPTION OF THIS PROCEDURE. THIS AGENCY MAY FIND, AFTER INVESTIGATION, THAT THERE IS NOT ENOUGH EVIDENCE TO WARRANT ACTION ON YOUR COMPLAINT. EVEN IF THAT IS THE CASE, YOU HAVE THE RIGHT TO MAKE THE COMPLAINT AND HAVE IT INVESTIGATED IF YOU BELIEVE AN OFFICER BEHAVED IMPROPERLY. CITIZEN COMPLAINTS AND ANY REPORTS OR FINDINGS RELATING TO COMPLAINTS MUST BE RETAINED BY THIS AGENCY FOR AT LEAST FIVE YEARS. IT IS AGAINST THE LAW TO MAKE A COMPLAINT THAT YOU KNOW TO BE FALSE. IF YOU MAKE A COMPLAINT AGAINST AN OFFICER KNOWING THAT IT IS FALSE, YOU CAN BE PROSECUTED ON A MISDEMEANOR CHARGE.

I have read and understood the above statements, and have presented true and accurate facts. I understand that if I knowingly make a false accusation, I may be subject to criminal or civil action.

USTED TIENE EL DERECHO DE HACER UNA DEMANDA EN CONTRA DE UN OFICIAL DE POLICIA POR CUALQUIER CONDUCTO INAPROPIADO. LA LEY DE EL ESTADO DE CALIFORNIA REQUIERE QUE ESTA AGENCIA TENGA UN PROCESO PARA INVESTIGAR DEMANDAS DE CIUDADANOS. USTED TIENE EL DERECHO A UNA DESCRIPCION ESCRITA DE ESTE PROCESO. ESTA AGENCIA PUEDE ENCONTRAR, DESPUES DE INVESTIGAR, QUE NO HAY DEMASIADA EVIDENCIA PARA TOMAR ACCION EN SU DEMANDA. AUNQUE ESO SEA EL CASO, USTED TIENE EL DERECHO PARA HACER LA DEMANDA Y TENERLA INVESTIGADA, SI USTED CREE QUE UN OFICIAL DE POLICIA SE COMPORTO INAPROPIADO. DEMANDAS DE CIUDADANOS Y CULQUIER REPORTES O ENCUENTROS RELACIONADOS A DEMANDAS TIENEN QUE SER MANTENIDAS POR ESTA AGENCIA POR LO MENOS DE SINCO AÑOS. ES ENCONTRA DE LA LEY HACER UNA DEMANDA QUE USTED SEPA QUE ES FALSA. SI USTED HACE UNA DEMANDA EN CONTRA DE UN OFICIAL DE POLICIA, SABIENDO QUE ES FALSA, USTED PUEDE SER PROCESADO(A) POR UN CARGO DE LEY.

Yo e leido y entiendo los datos de harriba, y e presentado datos eficientes y verdaderos. Yo entiendo que si ago una acusacion falsa sabida, yo estoy subjeto a accion criminal o civil.

Signature/Firma _____   Date / Fecha _____

FORM ISSUED BY: _____   DATE: _____

FORM RECEIVED BY: _____   DATE: _____   TIME: _____

ASSIGNED TO: _____   DISTRIBUTION: WHITE - Special Investigations, GREEN - Chief, CANARY - Division Commander, PINK - Watch/Bureau Commander, GOLDENROD - Complainant

APD-296 Rev. 1/96

Figure 13–4 *(Continued)*

against the officer is sustained, then the supervisor can recommend one of the following penalties:

- Oral reprimand
- Written reprimand
- Remedial training
- Loss of time or of annual leave in lieu of suspension
- Suspension up to 30 days (but no longer)
- Removal from service

The third phase involves the following:

1. A complaint disposition should be classified as sustained, not sustained, exonerated, unfounded, or misconduct not based on the original complaint.
2. Adjudication and, if warranted, disciplinary action should be based partially on recommendations of the involved employee's immediate supervisor.
3. An administrative fact-finding trial board should be available to all police agencies to assist in the adjudication phase. It should be activated when necessary in the interests of the police agency, the public, or the accused employee, and should be available at the direction of the police chief or upon the request of any employee who is being penalized in any manner that exceeds verbal or written reprimand. The recommendations should be advisory to the chief.
4. The accused employee should be entitled to representation and logistical support equal to that afforded the person representing the agency in a trial board proceeding.
5. Police employees should be allowed to appeal a chief's decision. The police agency should not provide the resources or funds for appeal.
6. The chief should establish written policy on the retention of internal discipline complaint investigation reports. Only the reports of sustained and, if appealed, upheld investigations should become a part of the accused employee's personnel folder. All disciplinary investigations should be kept confidential.
7. Administrative adjudication of internal discipline complaints involving violations of law should neither depend on nor curtail criminal prosecution. Regardless of the administrative adjudication, every police agency should refer all complaints that involve violations of law to the prosecuting agency for the decision to prosecute criminally. Police employees should not be treated differently from other members of the community in cases involving violations of the law.
8. If the citizen complaint is found to be intentionally malicious, then the officer has legal redress available.

See Figure 13–3 for an example of a policy statement on sexual harassment.

MEDIA RELATIONS

During the past few years there has been tremendous change in the telecommunications industry. Expansion of television news coverage, increased professional competition, and instantaneous breaking news segments and Internet news capabilities has changed the industry. Technology has allowed the media to get the message out farther, faster, and in more ways than ever thought possible. Twenty-four-hour news stations, wireless Internet, and Internet news agencies are just some of the different ways the media now cover events. Events that were at one time highly localized have now become national news. Images and stories can be broadcast into our living rooms and homes within a matter of minutes of the event's occurring. Discussion and chat rooms buzz with activity after every major breaking news story.

> The immediacy of news coverage permits little time for police agencies to react and communicate their message.

Consequences

There are significant negative consequences associated with the poor handling of media relations. These include:

- Loss of professional reputation and community support
- Civil liability
- Poor morale
- Political oversight
- Changes in political status quo
- Change in working conditions

In many instances the negative consequences of "crisis" incidents could have been negated or significantly curtailed if department personnel were prepared to respond to the media. How a police department handles crisis media communications in the first few minutes after the event sets the tone for how the community will later perceive the department. Pre-planning media relations and training can produce favorable media relations.

Crisis Communications Strategies

The following are key considerations during a crisis and regarding with the media:

1. *Take responsibility.* People want you to accept responsibility whether you're actually to blame or not. It is important to recognize that taking responsibility is not the same as taking the blame. Later investigation may

reveal extenuating circumstances, but in the end it will still be your employees who fired the gun, made the arrest, or drove code-3. Your name will still be associated with the incident regardless of the outcome.

2. **Recognize a crisis.** A crisis is best described as an event that has potentially negative media coverage for the agency. Yet in every agency there is a tendency to respond with a knee-jerk reaction to every news story that generates bad publicity. Meetings will be called, and management will want "heads on a platter," but in truth, many of the situations we see as media crises are in fact short-lived bad publicity. In strategy sessions it is important to ask, "Who really cares?" Is there widespread outrage or is negative reaction very localized within the department itself? Police agencies are often hypersensitive to criticism and will often assume immediate defensive postures. What does the average person think about the "crisis"? Elevating bad publicity to crisis levels can lower morale and cause undue stress throughout the organization. Ironically, high-profile investigations —while media-intensive and a lot of work—do not often attain the level of a crisis.

3. *Have people trained to deal with crisis communications.* A great deal of time and effort is spent training officers to prepare for just about every conceivable scenario they will face in their career. Police supervisors must be trained to have an understanding of media relations and crisis communications strategies. Law enforcement is accountable to the public, and the media take their role as a community watchdog very seriously. Like it or not, sometimes the best and only means departments have for communicating with the public is through the media. Your organization is best served by having someone who has regular and frequent contact with the media, plus supervisors who can (if necessary) interact with the media.

4. *Recognize the value of third-party support.* In crisis situations departments should have an understanding of where support will come from in the community. The media and public will often perceive "third-party" support favorably. This support could come from citizens' groups, clergy, professional organizations, internal organizations (labor associations, fraternal organizations), or even other police agencies. Many departments will use established clergy associations for support in minority communities. If the media have questions about tactics used during an operation, they could refer to recognized scholars or teaching institutions that will support the action taken. The public wants to trust law enforcement, and if uninvolved third parties lend their support, it makes law enforcement more credible. *Third-party referrals should not be made unless the third party has been contacted and thoroughly briefed on the facts surrounding the incident.*

5. *Treat the media as a conduit.* The media are a major conduit by which your organization communicates with the public. A month's worth of community meetings will not reach as many people as one article in the

newspaper. A 90-second clip on the evening news reaches an even wider audience. These opportunities to communicate must not be overlooked or avoided. Too often organizations take the stance of pulling up the drawbridge and hiding behind the walls. This "siege mentality" does more harm than good. "Siege" mentalities are the result of personal and institutional prejudice toward the media, lack of preparedness, and often-times well-meaning but bad advice. The public will view "no comment" or lack thereof as "guilty as charged." There are creative ways to say "no comment" without digging yourself deeper. Staying within the siege walls will also allow your critics to have free reign with their own point of view. You may not like the information conveyed, but the game goes on whether you participate or not; it's better to learn the rules of the game and then play to win.

6. *Do not let attorneys dictate your public relations.* You must accept the fact that you might be sued. This is America, the most litigated society in the world. Once you accept that litigation is inevitable, positions can be developed early on to minimize exposure. Many law firms in the country now work in concert with public relations firms in formulating media strategies. Attorneys, while well intentioned, are not trained to deal with or handle the media.

7. *Monitor the media.* Once your message is delivered, it must be monitored. This is how you measure the effectiveness of your strategy. Newspapers, television, and radio are some of the primary media that should be monitored. Are those who are transmitting your message to the public understanding what you said? If there are errors (contextual or factual), or the message is not being delivered clearly, it must be dealt with proactively. If necessary your position may have to be reevaluated and modified. In most crisis situations, there will be discussion on the Internet. This is an opportunity to see what the average person on the street thinks about what is happening. Someone should monitor newsgroups and chat rooms to see how the news coverage is being received. *You may find that what you thought was a crisis has generated little public interest.*

8. *Speak from the heart, not from the head.* During a crisis the public may not think rationally. People are looking for pictures and statements that communicate on the emotional level. Trying to give people facts, figures, policy, and procedure during a crisis will have little impact. The public wants to know how you and your agency feel about the incident. If in the initial stages you throw mud, you will get dirty. Attacking detractors during the initial stages of any crisis will make you look defensive and less credible. Presenting a defensive or confrontational attitude sends its own negative messages. The public wants to see sincerity, caring, and empathy.

9. *The first 24 hours are the most critical.* The first images and impressions the public sees will set the tone for future coverage. If your agency is inaccessible for comment, the message is, "you have something to hide." If your first

comments are defensive and terse, you set the stage for confrontation. Formulate your position early and remember, you have to view the crisis from an external perspective. Establishing a departmental position should be done in concert with the highest levels of management, taking into account the wide range of consequences. The bottom line is, what is the public's perception of what is occurring? It is OK to be nonjudgmental, but acknowledge it.

10. *Plan.* You can plan and prepare for crisis communications. You can establish response plans and matrices specific to your organization that will give you a roadmap. Law enforcement agencies can run through the "what ifs" just as they do with any other significant event. Regrettably, most agencies do not recognize crisis communications as a priority. Many operate under the assumption that "we have a good organization; that kind of stuff only happens to the other guy." Every time a crisis in another agency is covered in the media, they should convene and ask themselves, "If this happened here today, how would we have dealt with it?"

See Figure 13–5, a model guide for interacting with the media about police operations.

KEY POINTS

- Human conflict is a natural and, therefore, a normal phenomenon.
- It is up to the supervisor to convert dysfunctional conflict into productive energy.
- Conflict can have both positive and negative consequences for a police agency.
- Conflicts emanate from 1) existing conditions, 2) our attitudes, 3) our thoughts, and 4) our behavior.
- In negotiating ("getting to yes"), do not bargain over positions or believe that being nice will resolve the conflict.
- Furthermore, in negotiating, separate the people from the conflict; concentrate on interests, not positions; generate a number of options; and adopt objective criteria.
- Problem employees represent a small percentage of workers.
- Problem employees can engage in one of four types of behavior: 1) malcontented; 2) immoral; 3) unprofessional; and 4) illegal.
- The creation of an internal investigations unit does not relieve the supervisor of disciplinary duties.
- A citizen complaint starts with the receipt of the complaint. Next comes an investigation and finally an adjudication.
- Poor media relations have an explosive potentiality for far-reaching negative consequences. The first step in the proper handling of the media is taking responsibility (not blame) for tackling the problem.

WHAT INFORMATION CAN BE MADE PUBLIC

Arrestee Information
1. The full name and city of residence of the arrestee. The arrestee's physical description including: age, color of eyes and hair, sex, height, and weight.
2. Date and time of arrest.
3. Date and location of booking.
4. Factual circumstances surrounding arrest.
5. Amount of bail set.
6. Time and manner of release or location where the suspect is being held.
7. All charges on which subject is being held, including outstanding warrants and probation/parole holds.

Incident Information
1. Time, substance, and location of all complaints or requests for assistance.
2. Time and nature of response including, to the extent that such information is recorded:
    a. Time, date, and location of occurrence.
    b. Time and date of the report.
    c. The factual circumstances surrounding the crime or incident.
    d. General description of:
        (1) Injuries (usually nonspecific)
        (2) Weapons involved (nonspecific)
        (3) Property involved.
3. Victim, name age, and city of residence except as prohibited or would jeopardize the victim's safety or progress of investigation.

What Cannot Be Released
Prior criminal record, reputation or character of an arrestee.
The identity of a juvenile suspect or arrestee.
The existence or contents of any confession or statement given by a suspect or his/her refusal to make a statement.
Information regarding physical evidence that corroborates or impeaches a confession, admission, or other statement.
Performance level on any examinations or tests, or a suspect's refusal to submit to an examination or test.
The identity or reliability of prospective witnesses and sex crimes victims.
Personal opinions as to a suspect's guilt or innocence or merits in the case.
The name of a specific gang involved in an incident.
Details that could create an inflamed public reaction.

Schools
The media are generally allowed access to schools as long as it is not disruptive to school activities. If action is requested, it should be at the request of school authorities.

Crime and Disaster Scenes
A supervisor should be notified immediately when media are present at a scene. The media representative should be notified of the crime scene boundaries and any areas of potential risk. Disaster scenes may be closed to the general public, but news media representatives are exempt from this restriction. This does not apply to crime scenes. Airplane crashes should be treated as crime scenes.

Crime scenes should be restricted to both public and media access. It is permissible to allow the press greater access than that afforded to the general public. Reporters and photographers shall be kept sufficiently distant from a crime scene being searched or preserved to protect it from being disturbed or evidence from being destroyed or contaminated.

In any major incident the Public Information Officer can be contacted for response or as a resource.

Figure 13–5   Model Media Resource Guide

DISCUSSION

1. Have you witnessed conflict being a plus for an organization? If so, describe how it occurred and what the results were.

2. How have you dealt with a problem employee (co-worker, boss, subordinate) of late? Were you successful or not? Why?

3. Conflict can be a positive force. Why? Give examples.

4. Why not bargain over positions? Any examples?

5. Develop an actual or a hypothetical conflict. Now apply the key steps in principled negotiations to it. Critique the results.

6. Incidents of sexual harassment and use of force were presented as key supervisory issues. What are three others?

7. Peruse the newspaper for one week. How many articles were devoted to police work? How many had positive coverage? How many were negative?

COMMUNITY-ORIENTED AND PROBLEM-ORIENTED POLICING

Community-oriented policing is a strategy for forging a partnership between the police department and its customers. Problem-oriented policing is a set of tactics for making it work.

Community partnerships and problem solving—the two core components of community policing—can be accomplished in a variety of ways.

—"Community Policing Strategies," National Institute of Justice, U.S. Department of Justice

Community-oriented policing and problem-oriented policing (Responsibility Fourteen) are both an ending and a starting point. All of the previous responsibilities (Responsibilities One through Thirteen) serve as a springboard for COP and POP. At this point, it is up to the supervisor to step forward and make them a reality.

Community-oriented policing (COP) depends on police supervisors who lead their lives and manage their relationships around values and ethics. They see and believe in a mission that is devoted to serving and helping their customers. They exercise self-discipline and are not afraid of hard work. They know how and where to allocate their time. They also know that individual effectiveness precedes organizational effectiveness.

Problem-oriented policing (POP) depends on police leaders who can translate COP into operational reality. They take the goals of a mission statement and cast them into very specific and attainable objectives and projects. POP is a logical and practical component of COP.

In summary, COP gives us a destination, while POP provides answers on how to get there.

COMMUNITY-ORIENTED POLICING

Citizen Participation and Community Values

Although the acronyms COP and POP are relatively new to many, some basic elements—such as **citizen participation,** officers knowledgeable of the **community values** of the area they serve, police officer-citizen communication, and the like—are not. They were present to one extent or another in earlier policing in the United States, whether by design or as a result of individual style, especially in the late 19th and early 20th centuries, and especially in large cities with dense populations.

Police–Community Relations

During the late 1960s and 1970s, following recommendations from the President's Commission on Law Enforcement and Administration of Justice, a proliferation of federally funded police–community relations models sprang up throughout the country. The purpose was to bring police officers closer to the community, to promote mutual support, to encourage communication, and so on.

Some programs experienced relative success; others did not. Most were relegated to test areas and specific officer assignments, as opposed to total departmental understanding, involvement, and support. Even those programs held up as positive examples were, in almost every case, gradually phased out or modified in such a way as to become isolated from the mainstream of their respective agencies. The programs did little to strengthen relationships between the community and response-oriented police officers, or even between police officers assigned to "community relations" and other officers.

Team Policing

The 1970s also gave birth to team policing. Early team policing programs were burdened by lack of documented successes and failures. Those who experimented with team policing were not aware that elements of team policing would prove to be incompatible with preventive patrol and rapid response to calls for service. In the early 1970s, the Holyoke, Mass., Police Department instituted a program considered by many to be the showcase of federally funded team policing programs. At first it was unbelievably successful. The team consisted of 15 highly motivated, people-conscious officers—one captain, two sergeants, 12 patrolmen—all volunteers to be on the team. In addition to routine police functions, the focus was on human relations, language, and traditional cultures of those residing in the ward. These officers were in for the duration (no transfers), and they got to know the people and to be known by the people. And they became effective. However, after a time with a substantial infusion of more federal dollars, the program was expanded, ward by ward, and ward by ward it began to fail—and did fail.

Officers assigned to the new teams were not all volunteers. Transfers were routine. Reportedly many were "old-timers" who simply would not or could not change, and they were not motivated or motivative. Some were said to be simply insensitive. A "we–they" attitude prevailed.

Why Community-Oriented Policing?

If conditions in the past indicated the need for such programs, social conditions of the 2000s dictate: the burgeoning immigration of different races and cultures, clustering together in crowded, often substandard housing areas, where the police and citizens do not share common beliefs, know or trust one another, or even speak a common language, and where it is not understood that the success of each in his or her personal role is predicated, at least in part, upon mutual respect and assistance from the other.

There are at least 22 solid reasons for adopting COP:

1. Continued reliance on random, preventive patrol should be minimized. Random, preventive patrol should be used as a strategy only when police visibility is an issue.
2. Citizens will accept a range of response times for different types of calls.
3. Differential police response strategies should be implemented to improve the leadership of dispatch/communication.
4. Effective leadership of the patrol function is dependent on effective dispatch/communication.
5. Effective leadership of criminal investigations is indirectly dependent on dispatch/communication and directly related to the patrol function.
6. Case management systems must be developed and implemented to fit the needs of various investigative functions.
7. Work demands and resource allocation studies are necessary to ensure equitable deployment of personnel.
8. The development of crime and operational analysis procedures is vital in managing patrol and investigative operations.
9. The use of directed and self-directed patrol activities for officers should increase when and where appropriate.
10. Officers assigned to the patrol function must be actively involved in criminal investigations (e.g., conducting follow-up investigations, recommending early case closures).
11. Patrol officers need enhanced status and enriched job responsibilities.
12. Attention must be devoted to reassessing the purpose and function of existing beat configurations.

13. Initiatives must be taken by the police to identify citizen service expectations and to work with citizens in addressing and resolving neighborhood crime and disorder problems.

14. To facilitate the development of stronger ties with the community, policies requiring frequent rotation of officers across shifts must be carefully evaluated.

15. Regular public forums should be established so frequent exchanges of information can occur between the police and the public, preferably between patrol officers and neighborhood residents.

16. Performance measurement systems should serve as a management tool that guides personnel development and facilitates organizational change.

17. More meaningful performance evaluation criteria must be developed to reflect the change in officer roles and responsibilities.

18. Training curricula must be redesigned so they are more relevant to and supportive of patrol and investigative operations.

19. Disciplinary processes must become part of a behavioral system that incorporates education, training, and counseling as strategies designed to assist officers experiencing behavioral problems.

20. Leadership styles must be more adaptive to varying situations and personalities.

21. Leaders (and especially supervisors) must begin directing their attention toward the qualitative aspects of service delivery processes and outcomes.

22. Police agencies must cultivate leaders who are comfortable and effective working in an environment characterized by constant demands for change.

CRIME CONTROL

The central mission of the police is to control crime. Crime-fighting enjoys public support as the basic strategy of policing precisely because it embodies a deep commitment to this objective. In contrast, other proposed strategies, such as problem-solving and community policing, appear to ignore this focus.

Reactive Police Work

Crime-fighting today mainly relies on three tactics: 1) motorized patrol, 2) rapid response to calls for service, and 3) follow-up investigation of crimes. The police focus on serious crime has also been sharpened by screening calls for service, targeting patrol, and developing forensic technology (e.g., automated fingerprint systems, computerized criminal record files). Although these tactics have scored their successes, they have been criticized within and outside policing for being reactive, rather than proactive.

Reactive tactics have some merits, of course. The police go where crimes have occurred and when citizens have summoned them. They keep their distance from the community and thereby retain their impartiality. They do not develop the sorts of relationships with citizens that could bias their responses to crime incidents.

Proactive Police Work

Finally, many police forces have developed proactive tactics to deal with crime problems that could not be handled through traditional reactive methods. In drug dealing, organized crime, and vice enforcement, for example, where no immediate victims exist to alert the police, the police have developed special units that rely on informants, covert surveillance, and undercover investigations, rather than responses to calls for service. In the area of juvenile offenses, the police have created athletic leagues and formed partnerships with schools to deal with drug abuse, gang activity, truancy, and so on. It is not accurate, then, to define policing as entirely reactive.

Community Police Work

The greatest potential for improved crime control does not lie in the continued enhancement of response times, patrol tactics, and investigative techniques. Rather, improved crime control can be achieved by 1) diagnosing and managing problems in the community that produce crimes, 2) fostering closer relations with the community to facilitate crime-solving, and 3) building self-defense capabilities within the community itself.

A DECISION FOR QUALITY

In the 1980s, police agencies began to explore the crime-fighting effectiveness of tactics that built on previous approaches. At the same time, they sought to extend them by looking behind offenses to the precipitating causes of crimes. They endeavored to build closer relations with the community and enhance the self-defense capacities of the communities themselves.

Their guiding theory was that the effectiveness of existing tactics can be enhanced if the police increase the quantity and quality of their contacts with citizens (both individuals and neighborhood groups) and conditionally include in their responses to crime problems thoughtful analyses of the root causes of the offenses. The expectation is that this will both improve the direct effectiveness of the police and enable them to leverage the resources of citizen groups and other public agencies to control crime.

Smarter, Not Harder

The 1980s saw, therefore, many police agencies attempting to "work smarter and not harder" and to "do more with less." What still remains unanswered is the consequence of shifting a whole department to a different style of policing. For example, if officers are taken from patrol and detective units to do problem-oriented or community-oriented policing, it is fairly certain that response times will lengthen—at least until the problem-solving efforts decrease the demands for service by removing the problem that is producing the calls for service. And even though longer response times do not necessarily indicate a loss in crime-fighting effectiveness, they will be perceived as indicating this because the public and the police consider rapid response to crime calls as crime-control effectiveness.

Tempting

What is tempting, of course, is to avoid deciding between these strategies and to adopt the strengths of these various approaches, while avoiding their weaknesses. This could be seen in decisions to create special units to do COP within existing organizations whose traditions and main forces remained committed to traditional patrol and investigation tactics. But this means more resources, which means more money, and more money is darned difficult to acquire.

Not a Question of Money

Community-oriented policing is not merely a matter of budget dollars. It is primarily a matter of philosophy, administrative style, and structure. COP requires a greater degree of decentralization than does the current policing strategy. It depends more on the initiative of the officers. And they reach out for a close rather than a distant relationship with the community. It is very different from the kind of current administrative posture that stresses centralization, control, and professional separation from the community, and it has a very different mission statement. Mission statements are revised to reflect the transition to community policing. The protection of life and of property is still important, but the emphasis is changed from the police's enforcing laws and making arrests to forming proactive partnerships with the community to solve problems (Figure 14–1).

> COP does not hinge on a need for more money but rather a need for administrative change, with organizational and community support, with the understanding and belief that crime is everyone's business—that the cops really cannot do it alone.

WHO'S REALLY RESPONSIBLE?

If we believe that the police department is the first line of defense against disorder and crime, and the source of strength for maintaining the quality of life, what should its strategy be? The traditional view is that the police are a community's professional defense against crime and disorder: Citizens should leave control of crime and maintenance of order to police. The COP strategy is for the police to promote and buttress the community's ability to create safe neighborhoods.

WORK ENVIRONMENT

	Communication	Leadership	Employee Development
Excellence	Organizational and community issues are openly discussed.	Community-policing and problem-solving implementation plan absorbed into ongoing strategic plan; leadership demonstrated by employees at all levels of the organization through accomplishing city goals and achieving vision.	Employees willingly hold themselves accountable for continuous process improvement.
Normalization	Open communication is practiced and encouraged.	Managers, supervisors, and lead personnel serve as models of leadership by constantly reinforcing quality philosopy, decision-making, and use of problem-solving techniques.	Employees consider improving processes through natural work groups and multi-departmental teams as an integral part of their daily operations.
Utilization	Improved communication increases flow of information and encourages employee and community input; morale improving community satisfaction.	Managers and employees routinely apply problem-solving techniques. Agency management sets parameters and uses appropriate level of participation in decision-making.	Employees make a conscious effort to apply tools and techniques in daily operations.
Understanding	Employees and managers learn methods of better communication among themselves and with the public.	Senior management outwardly demonstrates commitment by initiating and participating in team training and understanding organizational alignment.	Senior management demonstrates commitment to program; all employees involved in training.
Awareness	Awareness of need to improve communication present at all levels of organization.	Senior management has developed a plan to begin implementing community policing and problem-solving.	Introduction of community policing program to employees.

Figure 14–1   Stages of Community Policing Implementation

CONTINUOUS IMPROVEMENT

	Process Improvement	Community	Strategic Planning
Excellence	Process/system improvement is imbedded in operations and planning.	Partnering with community routine; community feedback used for planning.	Community participates in the planning process; strategic planning involves all levels of organization.
Normalization	Data collection and measurement applied to planning and decision-making.	Community requirements are exceeded; improvement ideas are solicited from community.	Vision, purpose, goals, and objectives drive the annual budget/planning process.
Utilization	Routine application of process improvement and monitoring in daily operations begins; data collection and measurement are widely utilized.	Requirements are continually met; service delivery is driven through quality indicators and service standards.	Senior Management implements the strategic plan, which supports vision purpose and goals; employees given feedback on attainment of objectives as part of performance evaluation.
Understanding	Critical processes and key measures are identified; process improvement begins.	Requirements are determined and feedback methods improved.	Vision, purpose, and goals are established; a process is developed to incorporate strategic planning into annual budget/plan.
Awareness	Employees and management are introduced to process and measurement and philosophy of COP/POP.	Internal and external stakeholders are identified; feedback methods primarily focus on complaints.	Linkages needed for budget planning, goals, objectives, and performance.

Figure 14–1 (*Continued*)

Oddly enough, when the police move in to attack dangerous street crime aggressively, the very neighborhoods plagued by disorder reject their approach. The citizens are not ready to surrender control of their neighborhoods to remote police who show them little respect. Are police the first line of defense in a neighborhood? No—citizens are! And if they are, law enforcement must first provide communities with sufficient information—in a manner that will be accepted—to understand and develop interest in the "new" relationship with community protection and the police. And then law enforcement must provide proper training and continuing education to ensure that communities are prepared to assume their new responsible role and to work within specified parameters.

IMPLEMENTATION

Changing from one style of policing to another takes time, and it is not easy. In terms of time, COP requires three to five years before significant results can be measured. Figure 14–1 shows the incremented stages of implementation. This figure contains an enormous amount of baseline summary information on COP. Study it carefully.

WHO BENEFITS?

COP will benefit both the community and the police:

Community Benefits

- A commitment to crime prevention. Unlike traditional policing, which focuses on the efficient means of reacting to incidents, COP strives to confirm that the basic mission of the police is to prevent crime and disorder.
- Public scrutiny of police operations. Because citizens will be involved with the police, they will be exposed to the "what," "why," and "how" of police work. This is almost certain to prompt critical discussions about the responsiveness of police operations.
- Accountability to the public. Until the advent of COP, officers were accountable for their actions only to police management. Now officers also will be accountable to the public with whom they have formed a partnership.
- Customized police service. Because police services will be localized, officers will be required to increase their responsiveness to neighborhood problems. As police–citizen partnerships are formed and nurtured, the two groups will be better equipped to work together to identify and address specific problems that affect the quality of neighborhood life.
- Community organization. The degree to which the community is involved in police efforts to evaluate neighborhood problems has a significant bearing on the effectiveness of those efforts. The success of any crime-prevention effort depends on the police and citizens working in concert—not on one or the other carrying the entire load alone.

Police Benefits

- Greater citizen support. As people spend more time working with the police, they learn more about the police function. Experience has shown that as people's knowledge of the police function increases, their respect for the police increases as well. This increased respect in turn leads to greater support for the police.
- Shared responsibility. Historically, the police have accepted the responsibility for resolving the problem of crime in the community. Under community policing, however, citizens develop a sense of shared responsibility.
- Greater job satisfaction. Because officers are able to resolve issues and problems within a reasonable amount of time, they see the results of their efforts more quickly.
- Better internal relationships. Communication problems among units and shifts have been a chronic problem in police agencies. Because COP focuses on problem-solving and accountability, it also increases cooperation among the various segments of the department.
- Support for organizational change. COP requires a vast restructuring of the department to ensure the integration of various functions, such as patrol and investigations. The needed changes are new management systems, new training curriculums and delivery mechanisms, a new performance evaluation system, a new disciplinary process, a new reward system, and new ways of managing calls for service.

Structured Exercise 14–1

Are there any additional benefits that should be added to those cited above? Conversely, what are the disadvantages of COP? Put your thoughts into writing, and then discuss them with a colleague(s).

PROBLEM-ORIENTED POLICING

One should view COP as an overall departmental strategy for improving police work. Similarly, POP should be treated as a tactical method for making COP work.

Problem-oriented policing (POP) emphasizes the value of being able to diagnose the continuing problems that lie behind the repeated incidents that are reported to police employees and to design and implement solutions to those problems. Herman Goldstein, one of the foremost thinkers in the police field, defines a police department as practicing POP when it:

- Identifies substantive community problems
- Inquires systematically into their nature
- Analyzes community interest and special interest in each problem
- Assesses current responses
- Conducts an uninhibited search for tailor-made solutions
- Takes initiative in implementing solutions
- Evaluates the effectiveness of solutions

Many police departments concentrate on one incident at a time as they respond to calls for service. They neglect to assemble into a single picture the separate symptoms they treat. A neighborhood may be experiencing a flood of troubles—street fights, insults to passersby, solicitation by prostitutes, pickpocketing, and drunken driving—but the department does not recognize their sources in a sports bar.

> When the sole police response to a community problem is to arrest the current troublemakers, that department is not engaging in POP.

INCIDENT- OR PROBLEM-DRIVEN

Incident-Driven

Most police agencies are incident-driven. That is, most police activities are aimed at resolving individual incidents, rather than groups of incidents or problems. The incident-driven police department has four characteristics.

First, it is reactive. Most of the workload of patrol officers and detectives consists of handling crimes that have been committed: disturbances in progress, traffic violations, and the like. The exceptions—crime prevention and narcotics investigations, for example—make up but a small portion of police work.

Incident-driven police work relies on limited information, gathered mostly from victims, witnesses, and suspects. Only limited information is needed because the police objectives are limited: Patrol officers and detectives are trying only to resolve the incident at hand.

The primary means of resolving incidents is to invoke the criminal justice process. Even when an officer manages to resolve an incident without arresting or citing anyone, it is often the threat of enforcing the law that is the key to resolution. Alternative means of resolution are seldom invoked.

Finally, incident-driven police departments use aggregate statistics to measure performance. The department is doing a good job when the citywide crime rate is low or the citywide arrest rate is high. The best officers are those who make many arrests or service many calls.

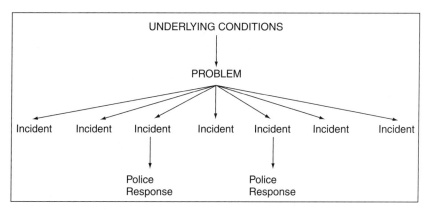

Figure 14–2 Incident-Driven Policing*

Remember, a police agency is not constrained to one strategy for accomplishing its mission. It is important, however, that if two or more strategies are adopted, they be compatible and not confrontational. See Figures 14–2 and 14–3 for a comparison of incident-driven and problem-oriented policing.

Problem-Driven

The practice of POP seeks to improve on other professional crime-fighting models by adding proactivity and thoughtfulness. It differs from COP by the emphasis on specific analysis. It assumes that the police can anticipate offenses and resolve them.

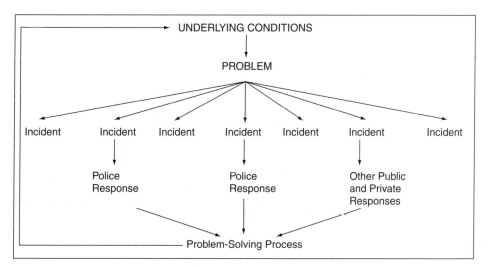

Figure 14–3 Problem-Oriented Policing*

* These two figures are used with the permission of Timothy N. Oettmeier and Mary Ann Wycoff from the article "Personnel Performance Evaluations in the Community Policing Context" that appeared in *Community Policing: Contemporary Reading*, 2nd edition by Geoffrey P. Alpert and Alex R. Piguero (Prospect Heights, IL: Waveland Press, Inc., 2000), pp. 399–400.

Problem-oriented policing takes a different paradigm about crime. In POP, it is not automatically accepted that crimes are caused by predatory offenders. True, in all crimes there will be an offender. But POP makes the assumption that crimes could be caused by particular continuing problems in a community, such as drug dealing. Hence, crimes might be controlled, or even prevented, by actions other than the arrest of particular individuals. For example, the police might be able to resolve a chronic dispute or restore order to a disorderly street. Arrest and prose-cution remain crucially important tools of policing. But ideas about the causes of crime and the methods for controlling it are expanded substantially.

> In POP, the applied imagination of police employees, sworn and civilian alike, is galvanized as a crime-fighting tool. Problem identification and problem definition are essential steps in POP. The superficial symptoms of crime are avoided, while the root causes are fervently sought. The common linkage of POP, COP, and the professional crime-fighting incident-driven model, how-ever, remains the same—crime control!

The subtle but fundamental switch in perspective requires law enforce-ment agencies to broaden their methods for responding to crime beyond patrol, investigation, and arrest. For example, the police can use negotiating and conflict-resolving skills to mediate disputes before they become crime problems. Why wait for crime to occur? Moreover, the police can take corrective action the second time they are called to the scene, rather than the sixth or seventh time, thus making timely savings in the use of police resources.

The police can use civil licensing authority and other municipal ordin-ances to enhance neighborhood security. Bars can be cautioned on excessive noise and children cautioned on curfew violations, and loitering ordinances can be expanded to reduce situations that require police involvement. The fire department can be asked to inspect "crack houses" for fire safety regulations. The public works department can be asked to inspect buildings and property for code violations. To the extent that problem-solving depends on the initiative and skills of officers and civilians in defining problems and devising solutions, the administrative style of the organization must change. Since POP depends on individual initiative, the agency must decentralize.

POP: REASONS, METHODS, PRINCIPLES, AND SARA

POP may appear to be another label for crime prevention. Or it may look like several clever tactics for "cracking down" on a specific police problem. POP is much, much more than this. It involves an organization-wide and in-depth shift in policies, practices, and thinking. POP places effectiveness first and efficiency second.

Reasons

There are eight reasons for POP:

1. *Lack of success.* There is an old adage that "Nothing succeeds so much as a successful failure." The professional crime-fighting strategy, although not a disaster, has not proven itself effective in crime control. Herman Goldstein and a few others pointed this out and in 1979 started their quest to refine an alternative policing approach.

2. *Efficiency has been inefficient.* Police management has been preoccupied with the internal operations and "doing things right": "right" statistics, "right" training, "right" procedures, and looking "right." POP addresses the highly value-laden question of "Why?" Or, rather than simply doing things right, "Are we doing the right things?"

3. *Scarce resources.* Whatever the budget, there is never enough to do the entire job. Hence, some demands for service may go begging. POP seeks to establish police priorities. If drug trafficking is the most significant problem, then the first allocation of resources goes to that, and so on. POP means priorities!

4. *Reaction.* It seems that everyone today is talking about, and doing little about, proactivity. POP requires self-initiative on the part of the police to prevent or reduce community problems.

5. *Community partnership.* POP encompasses COP or vice versa. The past has seen this partnership attempted in a random or haphazard way. POP is based on a systematic and continuing working relationship between the police and its public.

6. *Brainpower.* POP depends on the thinking of everyone in the department (sworn, civilian, part-time, whatever). Once more, we return to the need for empowerment. Unfortunately, many police agencies function as if the only "good ideas" come from the top. POP operates on the premise that good ideas can come from anyone and must be encouraged and rewarded.

7. *Culture.* POP requires that the old ways of doing things be carefully replaced with a different organizational structure and management ethic. This is difficult because most new ideas or systems are suspected of being grossly inefficient or plainly stupid. Usually, the first reaction to POP is "Big deal, we've been doing this for years." The POP culture is keyed to effectiveness and not efficiency.

8. *Expanded mission.* POP envisions an altered and much better articulated police mission. Earlier, I discussed the police mission and mission statements. It is vital to POP and to the department that everyone is "reading off the same page." In other words, the police employee, the department,

the policy-makers, and the community must understand and, it is hoped, appreciate what the police are accountable for doing.

Five Problem-Solving Methods

There are five methods by which problems can be solved, and the best one depends on the characteristics of the problem:

1. Eliminating it totally
2. Reducing . . .
3. Decreasing . . .
4. Designing . . .
5. Removing . . .

Application Principles

The five principles that serve as a guideline for the application of a successful POP program are these:

1. It must involve all department members—all ranks and units, all sworn officers and civilian volunteers, department members—in the identification, study, and resolution of problems.
2. It must foster the use of a wide variety of data sources—from internal records and officers' knowledge to other government agencies and private individuals and organizations—to understand the causes and consequences of problems.
3. It must encourage police department members to work with members of other public and private agencies to devise effective, long-lasting solutions to problems.
4. It must be capable of becoming an integral part of police decision-making, without creating special units or requiring additional resources.
5. It must be capable of being applied to other law enforcement agencies.

Problem Analysis Guide: SARA

In the late 1980s, the Police Executive Research Forum and the Newport News, Virginia, Police Department designed and tested a problem-solving process called SARA. SARA stands for:

1. *Scanning:* identifying the problem
2. *Analysis:* learning the problem's causes, scope, and effects
3. *Response:* acting to alleviate the problem
4. *Assessment:* determining whether the response worked

In addition, a Problem Analysis Guide was formulated, which suggested potential information sources (see Figure 14–4). The guide plus a Problem Analysis Report (Figure 14–5) should be helpful when completing Structured

**The Problem Analysis Guide
(List of topic headings)**

- **Actors**
  - Victims
    - Lifestyle
    - Security measures taken
    - Victimization history
  - Offenders
    - Identity and physical description
    - Lifestyle, education, employment history
    - Criminal history
  - Third parties
    - Personal data
    - Connection to victimization
- **Incidents**
  - Sequence of events
    - Events preceding criminal act
    - Event itself
    - Events following criminal act
  - Physical context
    - Time
    - Location
    - Access control and surveillance
  - Social context
    - Likelihood and probable actions of witnesses
    - Apparent attitude of residents toward neighborhood
  - Immediate results of incidents
    - Harm done to victim
    - Gain to offender
    - Legal issues
- **Responses**
  - Community
    - Neighborhood affected by problem
    - City as a whole
    - People outside the city
  - Institutional
    - Criminal justice system
    - Other public agencies
    - Mass media
    - Business sector
  - Seriousness
    - Public perceptions
    - Perception of others

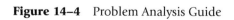

Figure 14–4   Problem Analysis Guide

OXNARD POLICE DEPARTMENT
PROBLEM ANALYSIS REPORT

1. SUBMITTED BY: B. Kelley   ID# 3399
2. Date Submitted: 07-03-02

A. PROBLEM IDENTIFICATION (SCANNING):

3. Describe the Problem: (Who, what, when, where, how, and why)
   Drug usage and dealing from a location historically known as "The Fence".
   Actual address is 232 Avenida Gaviota.

4. Problem Reported by ____ Officers on patrol ____
5. Location of Problem (circle) BEAT 1 ② 3 4 5 6 7
6. Date(s) and Time(s) Problem(s) Occurring Problem has existed in

   various degrees for 30 years.

B. PROBLEM EXAMINATION (ANALYSIS):

7. Shifts affected: (Circle)   I   II   ⓘⓘ   IV
8. Division affected: ___ Patrol ___ Investigations ___

9. Information Sources: (This list does not include all possible information sources.
   There may be other places where you can get information.) Please indicate all
   sources.

[xx] Crime Analysis Unit	[xx] Parole Office
[xx] Vice	[xx] Investigations
[xx] Crime Watch	[xx] Neighborhood Canvass
[ ] Literature Search	[xx] Citizen Complaints
[xx] Personal Observations	[ ] Surveys
[xx] Police Informants	[ ] Churches
[ ] Schools	[ ] Media
[ ] Central Records	[xx] Community Leaders
[xx] Local Businesses	[ ] DMV
[ ] Other Law Enforcement Agencies	
[ ] Government Agencies, list _____	

10. Findings: (Based on the information you have collected, describe the problem.)
    Historically a location that is a gathering point for those persons
    involved in narcotic usage, dealing and other illegal activities.
    Suspects gather on private property behind a wooden picket-type fence
    for purposes primarily to illegally use and deal controlled substances.
    These persons gather with the consent of the resident. Assaults, muggings,
    etc. have occurred to passerbys at the location. Numerous arrests and
    selective enforcement has not eliminated the problem.

Figure 14–5   Problem Analysis Report

C. STRATEGIES (Responses):

11. Goals and Objectives: (What do you expect to accomplish?)

     Eliminate the gathering of persons for illegal activities at the location.

12. Recommended strategies: (how do you expect to obtain the above result?)

     The non-resident owner of the rental property has been located and has agreed to abate the problem. Officer Kelley, the property owner, and the resident have met and the resident has agreed not to allow loiterers,

     place a lock on the gate and to

13. Date and time for implementation: __08-15-02__   (con't)

14. Expected date and time for termination: _____continual_____

15. Expected number of officers needed: _routine patrol to monitor_

16. Expected number of vehicles needed: __same__   Types: _____

D. SUPERVISORY REVIEW OF STRATEGIES:

[ ] Approved   [ ] Disapproved

Recommendations:

Date: __08-17-02__   Supervisor: _RKelly LT_

E. EVALUATION (Assessment):

17. Did you get the results you expected?

     [✓] Yes   [ ] No   [ ] Partially   [ ] Temporarily

18. Actual number of Officers Used: _Routine patrol_

19. Actual number of Vehicles Used: _____

20. Actual Number of Hours Used: _____

21. Describe the results of what happened.

22. Is any further action required? If yes, explain.

     Continued monitoring of activities at the location.

23. Additional comments:

     (12) con't.

     sign complaints against trespassers.

Figure 14–5   *(Continued)*

Exercise 14–2. The Problem Analysis Report is based on a hypothetical situation. Insert your facts as presented in the Structured Exercise.

Structured Exercise 14–2

————◆◆◆◆◆————

To: PAAC
From: Lieutenant Donald Garvey
Subject: Rugby Time Disco

DETAILS. In the last four years, the Rugby Time Disco, 1132 Hollywood Boulevard, has had a greater increase in calls for service and reported offense violations than any other liquor-serving establishment in the area.

On September 29, 2006, Officer N. Traub submitted a problem analysis report to the Problem Advisory Analysis Committee (PAAC). The majority of the complaints occurred on Wednesday nights between the hours of 2100 and 0230. On Wednesdays, the Rugby Time featured "ladies night" with $1 draft beer special. The complaints included overcrowding, disorderly persons, fights, drinking in public, drunk persons, loitering, and firearms violations.

A statistical analysis of the Rugby Time and eight other liquor establishments in the area was conducted by Officers Traub and J. Baker. During the period of January 1 through June 30, 2006, in comparison to the eight liquor establishments located in the north end of the city, the Rugby Time had 42 percent of the calls for service. From March 2005 to March 2006, the Rugby Time had 102 calls for service, with 51 calls occurring on a Wednesday night. Of the 51 calls, the majority were for fights, disorderly and intoxicated persons, and firearms violations.

The problem analysis form was approved by Sergeant R. Tiberio on September 30, 2006, after supervising the investigative work and analysis done by Officer Traub. (Officer Traub had enlisted the help of Officers Baker and S. Swanson.)

On September 21, 2006, Officer N. Traub with Officers R. Fulmer and D. Fucci observed at the establishment in plainclothes to review the inside problems. On the exterior, videotaping was conducted of violations in the area.

Using SARA

At this point, scanning and analysis have occurred. Your job is to consider the R (response) of SARA, and second the A (assessment). Each participant should list a number of possible responses, including violations, other perspectives that should be considered, who should be involved (other agencies, etc.), and strategies.

Using a chalkboard (or, preferably, a flipchart), appoint someone to list each participant's responses, one participant at a time. For each repeat, add one mark.

Your group is now the PAAC. Review all inputs, and delete those that the committee does not support. Remember, the number must be manageable, and the response must be logical—doable.

For our purpose, assessment will be PAAC's perception of the desirable and probable outcomes. At the conclusion, each participant is to score his or her responses against the final PAAC selection.

IMPLEMENTATION

Eleven interrelated steps comprise POP. The steps fall into one of three phases:

1. Identification of problems
2. Analysis of problems
3. Options

Phase 1. Problem Identification

The identification and definition of police problems encompasses Steps 1, 2, and 3. Problem identification is two-thirds of the effort in getting a solution.

WHO IDENTIFIES PROBLEMS. Police problems may be surfaced by: the community; police leadership; and line employees.

Community. Community involvement in problem identification has benefits and downsides. On the one hand, community members will express their needs and frustrations. On the other, their problems may not involve situations that the police are equipped or obligated to handle. Actually, it may be someone else's problem. For example, a needed traffic signal near a senior citizen home is not likely to be something the police can resolve. They may help—but some other agency is actually responsible for installing it. This is where candor and openness must occur.

Police leadership. Police leaders and supervisors are positioned to see the so-called big picture. I covered the importance of vision earlier.

Line employees. Of the three, the line employees are in the best position to identify problems. I spoke of empowerment earlier. Employees should be not only encouraged but also rewarded for their observations and ideas. (The term "employees" includes everyone working—paid workers and volunteers, sworn servants and civilians—for the agency.)

PROBLEMS ARE LIMITLESS. Typically, more problems will outcrop than time or resources can address. Once a list has been created, then the problems must be rank ordered. Some of the criteria for achieving this are as follows:

1. Is it really a police problem or not?
2. What is its impact (size and cost) on the community?

3. How much support can be anticipated from the community in tackling it?
4. Does it in any way threaten our civil rights?
5. How much enthusiasm do the police employees possess in combating it?
6. Is it indeed something that can be solved with existing resources?

STEP 1: GROUPING INCIDENTS AS PROBLEMS.   Police incidents are usually dealt with as stand-alone, unique events. Hence, the first component of POP is to move beyond just incident handling. It requires that incidents be looked on as symptoms of a problem. The police have to probe for relationships (how the incidents connect with one another) and conditions (the real cause of the problem).

STEP 2: FOCUS ON SUBSTANTIVE PROBLEMS.   Recurring problems are substantive problems—or what we think of as police work. Police are prone to identify substantive problems in terms of internal management (e.g., not enough staff, poor training, malingering officers, low pay). Simply, but importantly, substantive problems are those very problems that justify establishing a police agency in the first place. The "internal management" habit is tough to break. It takes time and practice. As a leader, you're responsible for making the transition.

STEP 3: EFFECTIVENESS FIRST.   Some would attempt to define effectiveness in terms of solving a problem—making something stop or go away. To conceive of doing this in police work is ridiculous and even counterproductive. After all, zero crime is impossible. Some agencies point with pride to statistics that reveal a reduced increase in crime rates over last year. *Effectiveness is defining for a specific agency, in a particular community, what ought to be tackled and in what order of priority.*

Phase 2. Problem Analysis

This phase involves Steps 4, 5, 6, and 7. The analysis of problems includes types of information, sources of information, and scientific rules.

TYPES OF INFORMATION.   Those who identified the problem in the first place are likely to be the best resource for deciding what kinds of information are needed to solve it. Brainstorming is an excellent technique for arriving at what's required.

SOURCES OF INFORMATION.   Some of the sources are:

1. Existing literature (research reports, current journals, and the like)
2. Police files
3. Knowledge of line employees
4. Victims
5. Community
6. Perpetrators
7. Other agencies (general government, criminal justice, and businesses)

SCIENTIFIC RULES. By their very nature, our police are "applied social scientists." They are constantly being challenged to think, act logically, and be objective. Long and detailed reports are turnoffs to many people. POP doesn't demand time-consuming and profound reports. A page or two is sufficient—if it adheres to the facts and is objective and logical.

STEP 4: SETTING UP A SYSTEM. Once the seemingly random incidents have been categorized into groups, a system for the collection of pertinent facts and their analysis must be designed. Crime and service statistics are helpful, but much too limited. Systematic analysis includes 1) telephone questionnaire and individual surveys of those who might know something about the problem (e.g., citizens, victims, officers, offenders, other governmental personnel), and 2) literature searches of government and private-sector repositories.

STEP 5: REDEFINING PROBLEMS. What at first blush may be a traffic problem on further analysis should be categorized as a drug problem. Problem definition can make or break a POP program. Is there any doubt that attempting to solve a traffic problem involves different methods and training than attempting to solve a drug problem? Additionally, there is an enormous difference between thinking tactically about dealing with burglars from a legal viewpoint and coping with burglary as it exists in the community. *How we perceive and label a problem ultimately determines how we go after it.*

STEP 6: WHO'S INTERESTED (OR SHOULD BE)? Simply viewing conduct as illegal is not efficient in constructing a response to a problem. To determine who is or ought to be interested in criminal activity, ask: Why is the community concerned? What are the social costs? Who is being harmed and to what degree? There are obviously many more questions of a similar bent. For the police to develop a successful plan to deal with gangs (or any other problem), they must find out who is interested in it. From this set of multiple interests will emerge a plan of attack.

STEP 7: WHAT'S WORKING NOW. I have witnessed police agencies discard successful operational practices. They tend to leap from one fad or technique to another. Frequently, the officers have the answer, but management fails to ask them. It is here that POP surfaces one of its major strengths—"If it's not broke, don't fix it." If the agency's approach to "espousal abuse" is successful, then don't fuss with it unless some other tactic can guarantee an improvement.

Phase 3. Options

The development of choices includes Steps 8, 9, 10, and 11. All right, we've found and analyzed the problem—what now are the options for hammering it? Obviously, the choices are infinite. To gain some focus here, I've placed them into nine groups:

1. *Frequent offenders.* These are the few who create many incidents. They should be targeted.

2. *Interagency cooperation.* The problem can be handed to another agency or jointly handled.

3. *Conflict management.* This means "getting to yes" via mediation and negotiation.

4. *Process of making "public" public information.* This is an underused but potentially highly potent problem-solving tool. Here are some of the uses: 1) to reduce fear, 2) to help people solve their own problems, 3) to educate people about their rights and responsibilities as citizens, 4) to warn possible victims, 5) to develop cooperation and support, and 6) to indicate what the police can and cannot do.

5. *Galvanizing of citizens.* POP depends on it! It goes beyond informing them to include organizing their support.

6. *Existing controls.* Here authority figures deploy their influence. Examples are teacher-student; apartment manager-renter; parent-child; employer-employee.

7. *Defensible space.* This denotes attempts to fortify our physical environment in some fashion, thus making crime and undesirable behavior more difficult, if not impossible. Alarm systems, anti-tampering packaging, lighting, and locking systems are a few examples.

8. *Increased or expanded regulations.* This option requires a lot of imagination and risk-taking. Some police agencies have used city building codes and land-use regulations to combat drug and prostitution problems.

9. *Legal intervention.* This also requires experimentation and a willingness to take a chance. For example, some police agencies are placing public inebriates and the mentally ill under "temporary detention." Some are using decoys and sting operations. Some may target or saturate a crime problem, such as gang violence. Some may intervene without making an arrest (traffic violations), or make an arrest without intending to prosecute (civil disturbance violations—e.g., "right to life"). More and more police agencies are aggressively confiscating property that aids in, or is the result of, a crime ("asset forfeiture").

STEP 8. CUSTOMIZED OR CANNED?   In the 1970s, the criminal justice system was filled with talk of "technology transfer." If a piece of equipment or a program functioned well in one organization, then it could be easily lifted and inserted into another. Many departments borrowed or purchased "turn-key" computers, helicopters, modified workweeks (4–10, 3–12, 5–9, and so on), and a variety of operational programs (e.g., team policing, neighborhood watch, Drug Abuse Resistance and Education). Most found that canned approaches, when incorporated into an agency, had to be retrofitted, redesigned, and restudied.

> POP relies on tailor-made responses. Problems are specific to an agency, and any method of resolving them must be specific.

POP is not implying, however, that agencies should shun the innovations of others. On the contrary, agencies should avidly seek them out and rigorously examine them for potential use.

STEP 9: TAKE THE OFFENSIVE.   Taking the offensive is accomplished in three ways. First, the initial identification of problems must be constant and systematic. Second, the police must be active in educating members of the public and placing choices before them. Third, the police should be advocates for the community (reporting if garbage is uncollected, potholes are unfilled, or vehicles are abandoned).

STEP 10: DECISION VISIBILITY.   More and more I'm seeing the officer educating the public on why certain things are or are not done. Decisions are explained. It assists members of the public in understanding that the police do not have as much authority as they think and that the police will take risks and sometimes fail—they're not infallible.

STEP 11: EVALUATION AND FEEDBACK.   Evaluation and feedback are not a concluding POP step. They are designed to support all of the other components in making incremental adjustments and improvements. For example, a reliable evaluation should be able to inform the department if its original grouping of problems was valid. **Without Step 11, POP is likely to fail.**

Structured Exercise 14–3

The exercises that follow are best handled in groups of four to eight persons.

1. *Problem analysis report.* Return to the Problem Analysis Report (Figure 14–5). Identify a problem that your agency is confronted with and complete the report. If you do not work for a police agency, then seek to secure the cooperation of a department in completing it. (You may be doing them a big favor.)
2. *Rank ordering problems.* I listed six criteria for rank ordering problems. Apply the criteria to the following problems: 1) armed robbery, 2) drug trafficking, 3) homelessness, 4) child molestation, 5) police corruption, and 6) terrorism. What does your ranking look like?
3. *Options—A.* Earlier I conceptualized at least nine avenues or options for coping with a problem. Can you add one or two more options to my list?

4. *Options—B.* Imagine that you work for a very honest, bright, and outspoken sheriff. His demeanor has irritated your major newspaper to the extent that it blasts him at every opportunity. When he gets the chance, he hits the paper back verbally. He is in charge of the highly successful regional drug-enforcement team.

   The captain that manages the unit has just informed him that three supervisory employees of the paper are trafficking in cocaine (estimated sales $7,000 per day). The users identified so far number 34, most of whom work for the paper.

   What options does he have? Which one is the best?

5. *Options—C.* Now imagine that you work for one of the leading police chiefs in your state. He reveals to you and a few others that the city manager and city council informed him that the graffiti problem had grown to the point that the city is losing revenues. In the last three years, he has used POP to decrease all major crimes. Nonetheless, they've indicated that his job hinges on his stopping the graffiti. What are his options? Which one is best?

> If POP is approached as a method for improving the police, it will fail. If, however, it is looked on as a way to solve community problems, it has a chance of working. Quality and effectiveness are being redefined, thanks to POP, from "response times" and "crime rates" to getting solutions.

KEY POINTS

- Although not identical, POP and COP are highly complementary of one another.
- A strategy encompasses the community-oriented policing programs and leadership style for achieving the department's mission.
- A police agency can adopt more than one crime-control strategy—but they must be compatible.
- POP improves on professional crime-fighting tactics by adding proactiveness and thoughtfulness.
- The common linkage among POP, COP, and the professional crime-fighting model is crime control.
- Patrol work has to be given enhanced status and rewards for POP to be successful.
- POP places effectiveness over efficiency in importance.
- POP is comprised of 11 steps that commence with the grouping of incidents together.

- Problems are best identified and defined by line employees.
- Those who identified the problem are probably in the best position to decide what kinds of information are needed to solve it.
- There are at least nine options for handling a problem.

DISCUSSION

1. What are the similarities and differences between POP and COP?
2. The professional crime-fighting strategy contains two significant flaws. What are they? How does POP avoid them?
3. How does POP differ from the professional crime-fighting model?
4. What type of structural changes must be made in an organization as it moves toward POP?
5. What can be done to make patrol work more appealing and prestigious?
6. Which one of the several ingredients of POP is the most important?
7. Eight reasons for POP were listed earlier. Rank order them in terms of their influence on causing POP to happen in police work today.
8. What are "substantive problems"? Cite some examples.
9. What are the benefits and disadvantages to having the community involved in problem identification?

ANTICIPATION

The police supervisor is responsible for sensing, clarifying, and adapting to evolving trends in his or her work environment and career field.

Only two things are infinite—the universe and human stupidity, and I'm not so sure about the universe.

—Albert Einstein

Responsibilities One through Fourteen are relatively enduring. They have a proven staying power. On occasion, the winds of change will add to or modify the steps a leader should consider taking when fulfilling a responsibility. Anticipating trends that signal the need for change is by far superior to reacting to them.

A sports commentator remarked about a highly rated team that suffered a dismal loss, "Once is an accident. Twice is a trend."

The celebrated futurist John Naisbett cautions us that we must endeavor to distinguish fads from trends. He related that fads are explosive and accompanied by a lot of hype and gimmicks. Fads are short-lived and frequently emanate from Washington, D.C. Conversely, trends emerge quietly without much fanfare. You have to concentrate on the horizon to spot them. Trends are conceptualized and take root where we live and work. The advice of the sports commentator can be relied on here. Once may be a quirk, but if you see it twice or more, then you may be looking at a trend.

WHY ANTICIPATION?

Being highly alert to developing trends and incoming demands for change and adaptation is the prerequisite for anticipation. Once you spot a trend on the move, you are able to anticipate its consequences for you as a leader and for those in your work unit. In essence, you are able to get ahead of it, perhaps harness it, and respond to it after thoughtful consideration. Trend-spotting guarantees me the time and opportunity to initiate action that is likely to succeed. Hence, one reason for enhancing your anticipatory capacity is to make early and better decisions on what to do in light of an identified trend.

Another reason for a police supervisor to be mentally anticipative is to predict trends. **Predicting trends** is different than spotting them after they have surfaced. It is also much more esoteric, and the error factor is higher. There is less risk in discovering a trend and then anticipating the consequences of your choices about how to cope with it. When you anticipate that which is unseen, you are entering the arena of future-gazing. Anticipating future trends is a blend of some luck and a lot of labor.

Community-oriented policing (COP) is not a fad; it is a trend. Thus, you can anticipate its consequences for you and your department. A more demanding anticipation for you is, What next? What type of a police services model can you anticipate eventually supplanting COP? Similarly, what might we anticipate as the next major thorn in the side of our police system? (Did you anticipate the terrorist attacks of Sept. 11, 2001 ?)

Ways to Anticipate

Many of the preceding responsibilities contain ideas or ways to enhance your ability to anticipate incoming events and trends. See in particular the section on problem-oriented policing and the SARA method.

Anticipation begins with a heightened perception of the way our lives move forward. We suspend our doubts and distractions in order to glimpse events starting to unfold. Typically, it is accompanied by a profound sense of restlessness.

Anticipation occurs when we become conscious of the coincidences in our lives. When we organize them and correctly interpret them, trends can be detected. Being acutely aware of who you are, where you are, and what you are doing is critical. Where we are today is not just the evaluation of technology; it is the evaluation of thought.

Watch for coincidences, ask why, and your capacity to anticipate will be measurably enhanced.

Trend One—Career Path Civilians

The question is not "Will we employ civilians?" but "Where and how many civilians will be employed?"

In the 1950s, some police agencies discovered that civilian employees were beneficial. Basically, civilian employees freed sworn officers to do "real" police work. Their numbers gradually grew to the point that police departments are now one civilian to every three police officers.

This trend applies not only to their number but to their power. Civilians in police agencies are paving career paths. They being promoted upward and will continue to do so. This trend will result in major divisions of a police agency being commanded by civilian employees. Civilians will supervise sworn personnel.

There is a supplemental nuance to civilization—**volunteerism.** Many agencies are growing a cadre of volunteers that complement current operations (reserves, cadets, seniors on patrol, etc.) or add new expertise (clergy, pilots, accounting, etc.). They are providing much needed services **AND** saving agencies a lot of money.

TREND TWO—TECHNOLOGY AND TOUCH

The use and influence of technology in police work will accelerate. Electronic files, laptop (palmtop) data processing, miniaturization of hardware, increased microprocessing speeds, portable digital communication devices, and more will proliferate. The information superhighway is taking shape. The majority of our mail will be e-mail or faxes. We'll be defined by our World Wide Web site. We'll be a cold fact, a set of impersonal numbers. Incidentally, those who believe data processing technology will create a "paperless" society are going to be surprised. There will be more, not less, paper.

The police supervisor will be asked to counter our loss of "self." Overriding all of the virtual reality and touchless technology will be a human being. The police leader will be expected to forge a human linkage between the officer and his or her department. The leader will be asked more than ever before to instill a feeling of appreciation and care into a cold and technology-driven working environment.

TREND THREE—WORKFORCE DIVERSITY

Workforce diversity is a well-recognized trend. The vast majority of police organizations are comprised of both genders, more than one race, two to three generations, and much more. In some parts of our country, there is no majority; everyone represents one or more minorities. One should expect that this trend will expand and accelerate. For one example, a few years ago there were a few civilians or a few female officers in our departments. Now there are many. Many police agencies report that one in three employees in supervisory and management jobs is civilian and female.

What can and should be done to understand diversity? To begin with, do not limit your thinking or approach to the notion of "cultural diversity." Workplace diversity is much more encompassing.

Being a successful supervisor in a work environment that consists of diverse employees demands that you first know yourself, and then those who work for you, very well. The majority of this text is configured to do that for you.

TREND FOUR—ETHICAL DILEMMAS

A person I know often comments, "I can resist everything except temptation." By our very nature, all of us experience temptation. Temptations can range from ordering a second piece of pie to stealing evidence from the property room. With all of the temptations bombarding us daily, our judgments are constantly being tested.

Our ability to rationalize or shift accountability exacerbates our problem in dealing with ethical dilemmas.

A police agency can and should anticipate that more employees will succumb to temptations that are unethical and/or unlawful. Fortunately, this trend can be countered, and even erased. Better recruitment and selection is one approach. Of equal importance is training! I am quick to acknowledge that integrity and ethics can't be taught. On the other hand, we know that integrity and ethics can be learned! We learn our integrity and ethics by example and constant training and retraining on doing what is right when confronted by an ethical dilemma. **As mentioned earlier, character counts, and it REALLY counts in police work.**

TREND FIVE—FEWER QUALIFIED JOB-SEEKERS MEANS MORE OLD GEEZERS

Demographics tell us that, in our nation, there will be fewer people available to work. Behind the "baby boomers" is a generation that does not contain as many folks. When you consider this in light of the large number of police employees who will retire within the next five years, there is going to be a scramble for available talent. Police agencies can and should anticipate a serious challenge in recruiting and selecting police officers and civilian employees.

Not only will there be a shortfall in the sheer numbers of employable people, but the number of those qualified to do police work is likely to diminish. Drug abuse and an absence of "life experiences" are two culprits that reduce the talent pool.

Police agencies can expect to commit an enormous amount of time and energy to attracting and then ensuring that they are hiring honest and responsible employees who can be trained to do good police work. One response to this shortfall of needed talent will be to reenlist the retirees (old geezers). Some will work part-time, others full-time. Some will telecommute, rather than work on-site. They're likely to work on a contract basis, thus preserving their retirement income. The old geezers will bring valued technical expertise and a proven work ethic.

TREND SIX—TERRORISM

International (September 11) and domestic (anthrax letters) acts of terrorism will not abate. There are a few very angry and mentally ill people in our global community who want to be heard. Their means of being heard are attempting to hurt us and scare us. A few years ago the federal government said, "Hey, we'll take care of the terrorists." That has changed to, "We need your support, cooperation, and understanding. We need you—state and local police." Our anti-terrorism strategy has forged a more open and powerful partnership among the various levels and types of criminal justice agencies.

I think I see the federal police concentrating on international terrorism while the state and local police collar domestic terrorists. I also see our local police agencies developing direct working relationships with their foreign counterparts. For example, the New York Police Department collaborating with the London Metropolitan Police, or the Los Angeles Sheriff's Department working in concert with the Cape Town Police, South Africa.

TREND SEVEN—COMMUNITY-ORIENTED POLICING: GENERATION TWO

Community-oriented policing (COP) and problem-oriented policing (POP) are not fads, but trends. Granted, some COP and/or POP programs are paper tigers. Nonetheless, many agencies are exerting enormous energy to make them operable and thus a reality. (Responsibility Fourteen covered this subject.)

The police supervisor can and should anticipate that COP and POP will change. In other words, how might they be made better? Are there any new programs or tactics that would make them more effective? Such thinking confutes the adage "If it ain't broke, don't fix it." As soon as anything proves workable, start anticipating how you can improve it.

I am having difficulty envisioning what "COP: Generation Two" will consist of. It is safe to speculate that there will be more of the same, such as volunteer programs, citizen academics, in-service training, permanent beat assignments, school resource officers, and the like. Perhaps Generation Two will emphasize physical and mental fitness programs for all employees, sabbatical leaves of three months every seven years, performance appraisal systems that are based on departmental mission and values statements, and a specialized unit of senior officers (old geezers) to handle the needs of our aging America.

TREND EIGHT—SERVICE EVALUATION

It's small, but I believe I see a trend toward service evaluation. Some police agencies, like their business counterparts, are systematically asking their customers, "How are we doing?"

A police supervisor can and should anticipate designing and implementing a method for reaching out to those that they serve and asking such questions as those that follow.

Rate the following questions from 1 through 7; 7 is high.

1. My sense of security in our community

    1   2   3   4   5   6   7

2. The quality of our police services

    1   2   3   4   5   6   7

3. My chance of being the victim of a major crime

    1   2   3   4   5   6   7

4. Overall I would rate my police agency

    1   2   3   4   5   6   7

There are three major ways to elicit feedback on a service evaluation questionnaire—telephone, mail, and a direct handout to those contacted. Those agencies that have employed such a feedback instrument have found the results reinforcing, rewarding, and helpful in anticipating evolving community needs.

TREND NINE—EARLY RETIREMENT, SHORTER CAREERS

One state recently approved for most of its police agencies "3% at 50"(3% of your salary at age 50). Those with 25 years of police work and 50 years of age can retire with 75% of their pay. At 30 years of service—90%! One agency is recruiting with a hook of "retirement after 12 years of service." Many employees are tempted, excited, and reacting to an earlier-than-expected retirement. A whole new career and second retirement program is possible.

Shorter career timelines are expensive (e.g., training new and in-service employees, funding of pension programs, loss of technical expertise). This trend fuels Trend Five—Old Geezers. One police agency (which has mastered the skill of anticipation) is asking all employees who decide to retire at 50 years of age to become paid reserves. Most have said, "OK, but you'll not see me doing any more police work." After six months, many have requested to be reemployed as a contract employee. Here are the pluses: 1) The agency secures the services and work ethic of a former and non-voluntary employee; 2) the officer more fully enjoys his work, has more leisure time, and supplements his retirement salary while building a second retirement.

It appears that police work is becoming a 25- to 30-year career commitment. Incidentally, there is no marvelous magic to retirement. It doesn't solve a lot of personal issues and dreams. For some, it actually creates them. When looking at early retirement, weigh it carefully, and weigh it again; it may have more downsides that one might first think.

TREND 10—YOUR TURN

I have identified nine trends and then briefly anticipated their impacts on you as a leader and police supervisor and your police agency. Now it's your turn to envision a trend and then anticipate its consequences for the supervisor and the department.

The 10th trend is up to you.

> So is the daily privilege and effort to fulfill all Fifteen Responsibilities up to you. I have no doubt that you and other police leaders will do so and thus make police work all the more professional, rewarding, and successful.

INDEX